"Personal/political, religion/politics, faith/power, ideology/pragmatism . . . Jim Wallis is a wrestler of values, ideas, and policies and how they interact to shape the world we live in. His deep, melodious voice is easy to listen to, but what he says takes a harder commitment to live by."

—**Bono**, lead singer of U2; cofounder of ONE.org

"Jim Wallis and I have a variety of differences on domestic and international policy, but there is no message more timely or urgent than his call to actively consider the common good."

—**Michael Gerson**, op-ed columnist, *The Washington Post*

"I love the work and books and existence of Jim Wallis. His is a profound and always-entertaining voice of reason, reconciliation, and passion for social justice and peace. Each of his books makes me wish I could get it into the hands of more politicians, right-wing Christians, left-wing Christians, secular humanists, economists, and regular people—everyone—so we could see how much we have in common and how much is at stake. Jim Wallis and I do not share many of the same political views, but we share the same heart and soul and love for God and all of God's children. Plus, he's a marvelous storyteller."

—**Anne Lamott**, author of *Help, Thanks,
Wow: The Three Essential Prayers*

"In low-key, almost seductively quiet and unpretentious prose, Wallis persuades more powerfully here than ever before. Arguing that it was 'the world' that was missing in the theology of the church in which most contemporary Americans grew up and that a long-standing emphasis on an 'atonement-only gospel' has obscured Christian allegiance to Jesus's 'gospel of the kingdom,' he lays out the theology of the latter and then issues to all Christians a rallying cry to apply that theology both in private life and in the arena of public activity."

—**Phyllis Tickle**, author of *Emergence Christianity*

"I have read all of Jim Wallis's books, books that call evangelicals to full conversion and an ecclesial faith that works. *On God's Side* is Jim's best book; it is personal, pastoral, and prophetic—a summons to a deeper conversion, to bridge-building commitments to the common good, and to a family life that grounds active faith in a common, caring community."

—**Scot McKnight**, professor of New Testament, Northern Seminary

"This is the finest of all Jim Wallis's writings. It reminded me that my actions as a citizen are a natural extension of my life as a Christian. Jim's comprehension of how Scripture and political issues relate to each other is surpassed only by the number of bridges he builds so that we can all solve problems together. Reading this book will help you be more like Jesus, especially in the public square."

—**Joel C. Hunter**, senior pastor, Northland—A Church Distributed

"Jim Wallis's new book elegantly summarizes key themes from his earlier work, but it also addresses with wisdom and clarity crucial issues that we must grapple with in the decade ahead: economics, ecology, polarization, peacemaking, the role of government, and more. And every page reflects the fact that this book was written during a sabbatical—emerging from a place of spiritual reflection and renewal, augmented by family, baseball, and fun. Arguably Jim's best book ever."

—**Brian D. McLaren**, author/speaker (brianmclaren.net)

"There are few people on the scene who can put together mature Christianity with mature politics without compromising either. Jim Wallis does it best—and does it again here."

—**Richard Rohr, OFM**, Center for Action and Contemplation, Albuquerque, New Mexico

"In this hopeful, incisive book that pulls few punches, Jim Wallis issues a passionate, stirring challenge to the church to join in God's reclamation of God's cherished world. As always, Jim gives us a way of rethinking today's pressing social issues in a vibrantly Christian way, producing fresh insights on almost every page."

—**William Willimon**, professor of the practice of Christian ministry, Duke Divinity School

"Let me be honest: I don't believe in 'must-read' books. But *On God's Side* is a very important book, especially in a time of increased polarization and lack of civility. As a pastor, I thank Jim Wallis for writing this book because it will be a vital resource for many—especially for the church, as we seek to invite, empower, and equip people for the work of the common good. In an increasingly cynical world, *On God's Side* is a fresh and hopeful word."

—**Rev. Eugene Cho**, senior pastor, Quest Church; founder and visionary, One Day's Wages

"The Christian faith requires more than mere belief. It is a faith intended to change the world because it demands that Christians work with passion for the good of their neighbors. This is the good news of the kingdom of God that Jesus first proclaimed in Luke 4, and it's a message that Jim Wallis helps us better understand today."

—**Richard Stearns**, president, World Vision US; author of *The Hole in Our Gospel*

"Without trust, no democratic society can survive. Trust is ultimately based on values. Jim Wallis's book *On God's Side* provides us valuable insight for our private and public lives."

—**Klaus Schwab**, founder and executive chairman, World Economic Forum

"If Jim Wallis and I were to sit down and discuss every word he wrote in this book, we would undoubtedly find some points of disagreement. However, Jim's challenge to followers of Jesus to grapple with what it means to live out the kingdom of God here on earth is precisely the challenge I need today. Maybe it's precisely the challenge you need, too. Read *On God's Side* and find out!"

—**Lynne Hybels**, cofounder, Willow Creek Community Church

"Vintage Wallis—a challenging call to reclaim concern for the common good, which has fallen into political, cultural, and even religious neglect. To follow Jesus Christ, the Word who created the world and the Lamb who redeemed the world, means to love near and distant neighbors and work for the common good. Read this book and roll up your sleeves!"

—**Miroslav Volf**, Henry B. Wright Professor of Theology, Yale Divinity School; founding director, Yale Center for Faith and Culture (yale.edu/faith); author of *A Public Faith: How Followers of Christ Should Serve the Common Good*

"A generation is rising that is committed to reconciling Billy Graham's message of salvation through Christ with Dr. King's march for justice. Jim Wallis in *On God's Side* presents a framework for prophetic activism, seeking a conciliatory platform for those wanting to go beyond the world of rhetoric and to reconcile covenant with community, all for the common good."

—**Rev. Samuel Rodriguez**, president, The National Hispanic Christian Leadership Conference (Hispanic Evangelical Association)

"At such a critical crossroads in our country's history, people are looking for commonsense voices on the right and left who are willing to ask difficult questions. Jim Wallis is one of those voices—winsome and reflective, yet forceful and unafraid. In *On God's Side*, Wallis again challenges Christians to think deeply about our world's greatest problems. You might not always agree with his conclusions, but every chapter of this book will stretch your mind, challenge your thinking, and push you to consider the hope summed up in its opening words: 'Our life together can be better.'"

—**Jonathan Merritt**, author of *A Faith of Our Own: Following Jesus beyond the Culture Wars*

"*On God's Side* provides an alternative to the 'me-first' ethos that has infiltrated the American consciousness. Jim Wallis weaves together Scripture, theology, and personal reflection to call us to a deeper spirituality resulting in a lived spirituality. This book is a prophetic call to the Christian community to live into the hope that our life together can be better."

—**Soong-Chan Rah**, Milton B. Engebretson Associate Professor of Church Growth and Evangelism, North Park Theological Seminary; author of *The Next Evangelicalism*

ON GOD'S SIDE

WHAT RELIGION FORGETS AND POLITICS HASN'T LEARNED
ABOUT SERVING THE COMMON GOOD

JIM WALLIS

BrazosPress
a division of Baker Publishing Group
Grand Rapids, Michigan

© 2013 by Jim Wallis

Published by Brazos Press
a division of Baker Publishing Group
P.O. Box 6287, Grand Rapids, MI 49516–6287
www.brazospress.com

Lion Hudson
Wilkinson House
Jordan Hill Road
Oxford OX2 8DR England

Printed in the United States of America

ISBN 978-0-7459-5612-1 (pbk.)

Unless noted otherwise, Scripture quotations are from the New Revised Standard Version of the Bible, copyright © 1989, by the Division of Christian Education of the National Council of the Churches of Christ in the United States of America. Used by permission. All rights reserved.

Scripture quotations marked ASV are from the American Standard Version of the Bible.

Scripture quotations marked KJV are from the King James Version of the Bible.

Scripture quotations marked Message are from *The Message* by Eugene H. Peterson, copyright © 1993, 1994, 1995, 2000, 2001, 2002. Used by permission of NavPress Publishing Group. All rights reserved.

Scripture quotations marked NASB are from the New American Standard Bible®, copyright © 1960, 1962, 1963, 1968, 1971, 1972, 1973, 1975, 1977, 1995 by The Lockman Foundation. Used by permission.

Scripture quotations marked NIV are from the Holy Bible, New International Version®. NIV®. Copyright © 1973, 1978, 1984, 2011 by Biblica, Inc.™ Used by permission of Zondervan. All rights reserved worldwide. www.zondervan.com

The internet addresses, email addresses, and phone numbers in this book are accurate at the time of publication. They are provided as a resource. Baker Publishing Group and Lion Hudson do not endorse them or vouch for their content or permanence.

Author is represented by Creative Trust, Inc., Literary Division, 5141 Virginia Way, Suite 320, Brentwood TN 37027, www.creativetrust.com.

13 14 15 16 17 18 19   7 6 5 4 3 2 1

This book is dedicated to Joy, Luke, and Jack,
who are the anchors of my life
and who teach me every day
what is important and what is not.

Contents

Preface

It's time to find a better vision for our life together. Politics is failing to solve most of the biggest problems our world now faces—and the disillusionment with elections and politicians has gone global. Politicians continue to focus on blame instead of solutions, winning instead of governing, ideology instead of civility. As the most expensive election in American history just showed, the financial checks have replaced all the balances in our public life. But cynicism cannot be our response to failed politics. Instead, we must go deeper.

Solving the world's problems requires a commitment to a very ancient idea whose time has urgently come: *the common good*. How do we work together, even with people we don't agree with? How do we treat each other, especially the poorest and most vulnerable? How do we take care of not just ourselves but also one another? How do we move beyond the interests of left and right and become accountable to a higher good? Only by inspiring a spiritual *and* practical commitment to the common good can we make our personal and public lives better.

But the public discussion we must now have about the common good concerns not just politics but also all the decisions we are making in our personal, family, vocational, financial, congregational, communal, and yes, public lives. It is those individual and communal choices that will ultimately create the cultural shifts and social movements that really do change politics in the long run.

For Christians, the idea of the common good derives from Jesus's commandment to love our neighbor—including "the least of these"—which is still the most transformational social ethic the world has ever seen. But all our faith traditions agree that loving our neighbor is required if we say we love God. Making our treatment of the most vulnerable the moral test of any society's "righteousness" or integrity is ultimately the best way to make absolutely sure that we are protecting the human life and dignity of all God's children.

A commitment to the *common good* is also the best way to find *common ground* with other people—even with those who don't agree with us or share our faith commitments. And that commitment to the common good is especially attractive to young people, who are part of the fastest-growing group in surveys about religious preference: those who check "none of the above."

The results of the US presidential election showed how dramatically a very diverse America is changing. Those changes reflect a global reality. Everywhere now, people are longing for a vision of the common good that includes us all. The common good welcomes all the "tribes" into God's beloved community, and our social behavior and public policies must demonstrate that. In places like the UK, all of Europe, and the US, governments and citizens are grappling with how to truly create a multicultural society. And as we face issues like austerity, sustainability, opportunity, and fairness in many of our countries, it is time to bring ethics, values, and moral choices into our critical decisions.

Many people feel politically homeless in the raging battles between ideological extremes. But they could find their home in a new call for the common good—a vision drawn from the heart of our religious traditions that allows us to make our faith public but not narrowly partisan and to join with others of different faiths, or even no faith, who share common moral sensibilities. We need to transcend the power of markets and the reach of governments by holding both them and all of us accountable to the common good.

To be on God's side and not merely claim that God is on ours means to live out the prayer Jesus taught us to pray: "Thy kingdom come, thy will be done *on earth* as it is in heaven." I wrote this book during a sabbatical time that drew me deeper into my own faith and into my understanding of the common good. I hope you will join the common-good conversation, which I believe could be transformative for us all.

Acknowledgments

When I teach, I always tell my students that ideas need to have "the street test"—that the lectures we have, the discussions we share, and the books we read won't really change the world or even us, in the end, unless the intellectual discourse can be tested in reality. Most of the ideas in this book have engaged "the streets" in the course of my life experience over several decades. Instead of it all just being in my head or in the clouds of academic discussion, I have tried to work and experiment with much of what is put forward here—in serious interaction and shoulder-to-shoulder struggle with many people who live very real lives in the very real world and who are trying to change it. So first I want to acknowledge and thank all those people I have met "in the streets" of many efforts to change this world. There are far too many names to mention, but I have had so many of them in mind as I wrote each chapter. For how they have shaped my mind and heart, I am so deeply grateful.

In practically getting this book conceived, done, and out, there are many people to thank. First, my agent, Kathryn Helmers. From the beginning she believed in this book and in me and gave me her best thinking and experience, which is very good, in how to frame the book. On this first book together, Kathy and I have become partners and friends. Dwight Baker, the president of Baker Publishing Group, called me himself to explain the exciting vision for Brazos Press and my book and was very convincing. Robert Hosack, executive editor, and the first person I met at Baker, showed me the depth and breadth of that vision. Bobbi Jo Heyboer ("BJ"), senior marketing director, demonstrated a great expectation and capacity to reach many people with this book; and Kelly Hughes, a seasoned publicist I've worked with before, seems always to know the best places to get the message out. My thanks to Andrew Hodder-Williams and all the folks at Lion Hudson for publishing and distributing the book in the UK and Europe.

I also want to especially thank a new generation of young people who I talk with virtually every day and who are my hope in the implementation of this book's vision for the common good. Conversations with so many of them have shaped the book at every turn. In particular, I want to thank Jack Palmer, who was an intern at Sojourners when this book was being written and who became my primary researcher and editorial dialogue partner in the final stages. Jack's research skills were stellar, his intellectual capacities very impressive, and his wisdom and judgment beyond his years. Plus, Jack was an absolute delight to work with.

Members of that new generation of leaders who have worked at Sojourners are often in conversation with me about the things this book is all about, and they sometimes offered very helpful comments. Among them are Tim King, Lisa Sharon Harper, Sondra Shepley, Cathleen Falsani, Carrie Adams, Larisa Friesen Hall, Lisa Daughtry-Weiss, Elizabeth Denlinger Reaves, Amber Hill, Sandi Villarreal, Beau Underwood, Alycia Ashburn, Ivonne Guillen, Leslie Abell, and former staffers like Aaron Graham and Chris LaTondresse.

I want to acknowledge and gratefully thank all the staff of Sojourners who faithfully and effectively kept our work going during my book-writing sabbatical. Jim Rice, the editor of *Sojourners* magazine, and his excellent veteran staff continue to put out an award-winning publication that every month is a major resource for defining the common good. Karen Lattea, our Chief Administrative Officer, has for years helped us to be the kind of organization that lives its values. And Ed Spivey Jr., our Art Director and award-winning humor columnist, has for decades made me laugh more than anyone else in the world, keeping our very big and serious ideas in human, humorous, and humble perspective. Duane Shank also assisted for this book, as he has for many others of mine.

But this book would not have been written without the support of our Chief Operating Officer, my Chief of Staff and dear friend Joan Bisset. Joan persuaded me to take a three-month sabbatical to write this book and then made it possible for me to take one—by freeing me of organizational responsibilities during that time and managing Sojourners so well all of the time. She consistently and incredibly juggled many events and appointments and cleared as much writing time for me as she could until the book was done. Joan and I go back many years, and she was part of the early days of Sojourners, as was Director of Web and Digital Technology Bob Sabath, who continues with us today, overseeing the technology of our publishing platforms. Two other members of our executive leadership team deserve a special word of thanks. Vice President and Chief Advancement Officer Rob Wilson-Black has been a primary intellectual and spiritual partner in our work, and very involved with me in the World Economic Forum. Michael Norman, our Chief Financial Officer, along with Rob, had to keep our finances going strong while I was away. Being able to trust our budget management and financial integrity to someone like Michael is a tremendous help and support, freeing me to focus on things like this book.

I want to thank the Sojourners board and its Chair, Mary Nelson, for approving and even encouraging me to take the three-month sabbatical. And I especially want to thank my longtime friend and soul mate, Wes Granberg-Michaelson, a former Chair and now Vice Chair of our board, who took a special interest in this project, found the monastery I retreated to, and all along the way gave me his best advice for what this book needed to say and do, even reading the first manuscript and giving me extraordinarily valuable feedback. Old friendships, like the ones with Wes and Joan, are often among the best and most important blessings one has in life. Ongoing conversations with some of the young leaders on our board like Adam Taylor, Peggy Flanagan, Gabriel Salguero, and Soong-Chan Rah are a regular source of encouragement.

To write a book, you need some time away to think, pray, rest, and write all day! That place has often been provided for me by my dear friend Mary Ann Richardson, a former hotel and still condo owner and Presbyterian lay leader in Daytona Beach, Florida. Both an exceptional businesswoman and biblical scholar (a rare combination), Mary Ann has talked through many books with me over many years—often while we walked along her beloved Daytona Beach. Every morning while I was away, I would get up at sunrise to walk that beach, do yoga and pray in the morning light, and then run back to my little beach hideaway to write for the next twelve hours! Thank you, Mary Ann.

Finally, the household in which I spend most of my time, both writing and living, during the sabbatical and in ordinary time, must get the most thanks of all. My two sons, Luke, now fourteen, and Jack, now nine, have become the anchors for me; and my daily life and conversation with them continually show me what is most important and what is not. Joy, my beloved wife and their wonderful mother, keeps life together for all of us. And her own vocation as a priest, and now "village priest" in our local community, is a great example of what it means to serve the common good. Joy, Luke, and Jack have taught me what it means to love something or someone more than anything else in the world. Together we continue to learn what it means to integrate the common good with our own personal good—and that is the spiritual foundation for this book.

Inspiring the Common Good

··· 1 ···

A Gospel for the Common Good

This is the rule of most perfect Christianity, its most exact definition, its highest point, namely, the seeking of the *common good* . . . for nothing can so make a person an imitator of Christ as caring for his neighbors.

—John Chrysostom (ca. 347–407)[1]

Our life together can be better. Ours is a shallow and selfish age, and we are in need of conversion—from looking out just for ourselves to also looking out for one another. It's time to hear and heed a call to a different way of life, to reclaim a very old idea called the common good. Jesus issued that call and announced the kingdom of God—a new order of living in sharp contrast to all the political and religious kingdoms of the world. That better way of life was meant to benefit not only his followers but everybody else too. And that is the point of it.

Christianity is not a religion that gives some people a ticket to heaven and makes them judgmental of all others. Rather, it's a call

1. Homily 25 on 1 Corinthians 11:1, quoted in Diana Butler Bass, *A People's History of Christianity: The Other Side of the Story* (New York: HarperCollins, 2010), 60 (emphasis added).

3

to a relationship that changes all our other relationships. Jesus told us a new relationship with God also brings us into a new relationship with our neighbor, especially with the most vulnerable of this world, and even with our enemies. But we don't always hear that from the churches. This call to love our neighbor is the foundation for reestablishing and reclaiming the common good, which has fallen into cultural and political—and even religious—neglect.

Judaism, of course, agrees that our relationship with God is supposed to change all our other relationships, and Jesus's recitation of the law's great commandments to love God and your neighbor flows right out of the books of Deuteronomy and Leviticus (see Deut. 6:5; Lev. 19:18). Islam also connects the love of Allah with love and responsibility to our neighbors. In fact, virtually all the world's major religions say that you cannot separate your love for God from your love for your neighbor, your brothers and sisters. Even the nonreligious will affirm the idea of "the Golden Rule": "Do to others as you would have them do to you" (Luke 6:31).

That transformation of all our relationships, especially the clear connection between loving God and loving your neighbor, has always—when lived out—been the best catalyst for movements aimed at improving the human community. But the common good is quite *uncommon* today. We seem to have lost this unifying vision in our community and public life, and especially in our politics—on both sides of the aisle. In the intensely ideological and increasingly vitriolic political battles of Washington, DC, and other world capitals, the common good is virtually ignored.

So it's time to listen again to an old but always new vision that could, and is supposed to, change our selfish behavior—*and make us happier too*. Jesus said those who live by the beatitudes of his kingdom are "blessed" or "happy" (Matt. 5:3–12). But it's a happiness different from and deeper than what we are offered by a selfish society, which actually makes us feel quite fearful and unhappy.

I am a Christian, and this book is about three clear things. First, Christian conversion involves more than just the destiny of the soul; it involves the way we live in the world. Second, faith transcends politics, and Christianity doesn't translate only into right-wing voting issues, despite what both the conservative and liberal media love to keep saying. But neither can it be repositioned into left-wing politics. We don't simply need a religious left to counter the religious right. Third, faith should be lived out in our public life for the common good. As people of faith, our challenge is to rise above political ideology and lead on moral grounds. Don't go right, don't go left; go deeper. The common good is about so much more than partisan politics. It grows out of our personal and family lives, our vocational callings, the mission and witness of our congregations, the moral power of social movements, and the independent integrity of prophetic religious leadership in our public life as we fight not just for "our" rights but for the rights of all people.

It is time to reclaim the neglected common good and to learn how faith might help, instead of hurt, in that important task. Our public life could be made better, even transformed or healed, if our religious traditions *practiced what they preached* in our personal lives; in our families' decisions; in our work and vocations; in the ministry of our churches, synagogues, and mosques; and in our collective witness. In all these ways we can put the faith community's influence at the service of this radical neighbor-love ethic that is both faithful to God and to the common good.

The Greatest Commandment

> "Teacher, which is the greatest commandment in the Law?" Jesus replied:
> "'Love the Lord your God with all your heart and with all your soul and with all your mind.' This is the first and greatest commandment. And the second is like it: 'Love your neighbor as yourself.' All the Law and the Prophets hang on these two commandments." (Matt. 22:36–40 NIV)

The summation of ethics and the religious laws, said Jesus, was to love the Lord your God with all your heart, soul, and mind, and *to love your neighbor as yourself*. Loving God comes first, and then is immediately connected to our neighbor, whom we are to love as ourselves. There has likely never been a more radical statement—that we are to love our neighbor as ourselves. There is no unhealthy or ascetic self-denial here. We *are* to care for ourselves and our families and our children, but we are asked to also care for our neighbors *as ourselves*, and our neighbor's children *as our children*. This is an ethic that would transform the world. It was supposed to, and it has.

This most fundamental teaching of faith flies right in the face of all the selfish personal and political ethics that put *myself* always *before* all others: my concerns first, my rights first, my freedoms first, my interests first, my tribe first, and even my country first—ahead of everybody else. Self-concern is the personal and political ethic that dominates our world today, but the kingdom of God says that our neighbor's concerns, rights, interests, freedoms, and well-being are as important as our own.

This ethic is not only radical and transformational; it is absolutely essential if we are to create a public life that is not completely dominated by political conflict, and if we are to articulate what might be in the interest of the common good. Perhaps, if we follow this teaching, we will even find some common ground between us.

Living out the neighbor ethic is essential to religion attaining any *credibility* again. Otherwise, the next generation is just going to move on from religion. Ask this question: Is love of neighbor the primary thing that people think about when they watch the behavior of our faith communities and institutions? Or are they more likely to see self-interest and judgment of others?

Religion makes a big mistake when its primary public posture is to protect itself and its own interests. It's even worse when religion tries to use politics to enforce its own codes and beliefs or to use the force of law to control the behavior of others. Religion does much better when it *leads*—when it actually cares about the needs of everybody, not just its own community, and when it makes the best inspirational and commonsense case, in a pluralistic democracy, for public policies that express the core values of faith in regard to how we should all treat our neighbors.

There is a deep hunger, especially among a new generation of young people, for a new ethic of loving our neighbors, in our neighborhoods and around the world. But who will offer leadership toward a new (and old) neighbor ethic for the common good? If the faith community does that, people will actually be drawn back to faith; but if we don't, our losses will continue until the majority of people will answer religious surveys with "none of the above," currently the fastest-growing affiliation.

Mr. Lincoln and Being "On God's Side"

Abraham Lincoln famously said, "My concern is not whether God is on our side; my greatest concern is to be on God's side."[2] That was probably the most important thing about religion ever said by an American president. Presidents and politicians usually want to bring God onto their side, their country's side, their party's side, and even their political policy's side. Right after the American Civil War, the most brutal and divisive war in American history, the winning side was clearly tempted to triumphalism. But Lincoln felt the shame of the horrible conflict, the sin on all sides, and the need for humble repentance if there was ever to be reconciliation and unity again. In his second inaugural address, he said:

> Neither party expected for the war the magnitude or the duration which it has already attained. . . . Each looked for an easier triumph, and a result less fundamental and astounding. Both read the same Bible and pray to the same God, and each invokes His aid against the other. . . . The prayers of both could not be answered. That of neither has been answered fully. The Almighty has His own purposes. . . . Fondly do we hope, fervently do we pray, that this mighty scourge of war may speedily pass away. Yet, if God wills that it continue until all the wealth piled by the bondsman's two hundred and fifty years of unrequited toil shall be sunk, and until every drop of blood drawn with the lash shall be paid by another drawn with the sword, as was said three thousand years ago, so still it must be said "the judgments of the Lord are true and righteous altogether."

2. The exact wording is disputed, but Rev. Matthew Simpson, in his address delivered at Lincoln's funeral, attested that Lincoln said this. See http://beck.library.emory.edu/lincoln/page.php?id=simpson16. The thought is also attributed to Lincoln in the 1867 book *Six Months at the White House with Abraham Lincoln* by Francis B. Carpenter (p. 282); see http://books.google.com/books/about/Six_months_at_the_White_House_with_Abrah.html?id=3W4FAAAAQAAJ.

With malice toward none, with charity for all, with firmness in the right as God gives us to see the right, let us strive on to finish the work we are in, to bind up the nation's wounds, to care for him who shall have borne the battle and for his widow and his orphan, to do all which may achieve and cherish a just and lasting peace among ourselves and with all nations.[3]

Lincoln had it right. The biggest problem with religion is that people, groups, institutions, nations, and all of our *human sides* sometimes try to bring God onto *our side*. When people and groups are sure they are right, they want to confidently say that God agrees with them. Divine claims of righteousness for very human behavior—and often very brutal behavior—have always undermined the integrity and credibility of religion. The much harder task, and the more important one, is to *ask how to be on God's side*, as Lincoln was suggesting. And that often means changing our minds and hearts about many things, and learning a whole different perspective from the one we already agree with.

Agreeing with God is much more important than getting God to agree with us. But that often means turning many of our own opinions upside down. As the apostle Paul said in the book of 1 Corinthians, we humans only "see through a glass, darkly" (1 Cor. 13:12 KJV), meaning that we are bound by our limitations and required to exercise the humility that Lincoln was calling for. Knowing exactly what God's side is on every issue and in every moment is very difficult for very human beings. Trying to understand God's side means being more reflective and critical of ourselves and of "our side," which we must endeavor to transcend if our "greatest concern is to be on God's side."

We have seen many tragic examples of people claiming that God is on their side. Some have flown airplanes into buildings full of innocent people. Others claim God for their wars on terrorism, which also take many innocent lives. We have seen people co-opting God for their party's political agenda, their nation's supremacy, their economic stratum's global dominance, or their tribe's identity politics. Others try to impose

3. Abraham Lincoln, "Second Inaugural Address," March 4, 1865, The Avalon Project, http://avalon.law.yale.edu/19th_century/lincoln2.asp.

their religious codes on society by legislation or by attacking people who disagree with those codes. Claiming God's special blessing for our own race, class, group, country, or even our religious community is a most dangerous example of trying to put God on our side.

On the other hand, trying to be on God's side requires much more humility and grace. It means submitting our claim of national supremacy, our economic values and practices, our tribe's special place, and even our faith's religious domination to moral scrutiny. It means seeing God's purposes ahead of our own or our group's self-interest. It means loving our neighbors, even when they are in a group different from ours, and even when they are our enemies. That kind of transformation of mindset and perspective will often take what we call *conversion*.

Being converted in this way means focusing on instead of ignoring our neighbor, letting the poor *move us* instead of *serving us*, and learning how to understand and even love our enemies instead of just hating and seeking to defeat them. On God's side we learn how compassion takes precedence over control, forgiveness over fighting, and reconciliation over retaliation. And that requires a pretty radical transformation of how we think, act, and relate to others and to God. Again, it's called conversion—to God's side.

Religion that claims God for its side is fast becoming irrelevant to solving the biggest problems the world faces today. In fact, it is actually an impediment to discovering solutions. But faith that humbly and diligently seeks the meaning of being on God's side could play a vital role in building the bridges, asking the questions, and finding the answers we most need.

A Lion, the Idolatry of Politics, and the Promise of the Common Good

What helped me rethink the questions of conversion to the common good was my encounter with a lion in a monastic community overlooking the Pacific Ocean at the beginning of the sabbatical I took to write this book. Entering into solitude and silence with monks—punctuated only by vigils, lauds, Eucharist, and vespers—can alter your perspective.

In the monastery's guest library I spotted *The Chronicles of Narnia* by C. S. Lewis and decided to reread them. Aslan the lion is the creator and leader of Narnia, the true and good king and, as many have observed, a "Christ figure" in the stories. Because I was writing about the common good and saw Jesus as an inspiration for it, I was again drawn to Aslan.

Aslan overcomes evil with good, shows the power of unconditional love, and is the cause of transformation. The lion confronts the bad but always invites everyone—friends and enemies alike—into the good. Aslan exemplifies the *common good*, making every decision and action in the best interest of the people and the land but always paying special attention to the weakest and most vulnerable creatures. Sometimes I felt like Aslan was walking beside me, up and down the coastal hills to the sea, teaching me again what it means to be a Narnian.

The lion helped inspire my hope to write a biblical and theological defense of the common good, something that has been almost lost in an age of selfishness. Yes, we need better public policies, but our deepest need is more spiritual than political. The issues are much deeper now than just public policy disputes.

My sabbatical time away was deeply needed, and good for my soul, mind, and body; I feel better than I have in years. Sunrise walks on the beach, yoga and prayer in the morning light, and running along the waves put many things in perspective. Such a wonderful time with my wife, Joy, and my boys, Luke and Jack, reminded me again of the things that are most important.

But my sabbatical took place during a US presidential election year, one that dramatically demonstrated the idol that American politics has become. Idolatry is letting other things take the place of God.

I was reminded again that people of faith should never worship at the altar of politics because we worship God, and the kingdom of God is never the same as the kingdoms of politics. It is our worship of God that must shape our engagement with politics, not the other way around. When politics shapes our religion, it distorts our true worship. Left and right are political categories—not religious ones. Attempting to mold faith to fit those labels distorts faith's meaning and power.

10

Rather than becoming the chaplains or enablers of political idolatry, the faith community should confront it. The idols of politics are legion: the idol of money over democracy, the idol of winning over governing, the idol of celebrity over leadership, the idol of individualism over community, and the idol of ideology over civility—just to name a few. Today, both political sides take a problem and do two things with it: first, they try to make us afraid of it, and second, they blame it on the other side. What they don't do is work together to confront the underlying causes of our problems and solve them for the common good.

People of faith, whether they vote conservative or liberal, should not be rallying around the kings of their party with the kind of blindly uncritical support that the political elites on both sides urge—all of them eager to protect their access, influence, and income in the present order of things. We who call ourselves followers of God should instead be raising our voices in defense of, and as advocates for, the people and principles that are essential to our faith and the true worship of our King.

Power and Powerlessness

Power is both the means and the end of politics in centers of government, but God's politics is most concerned with the *powerless*—the least of those among us, whose interests are the most absent in election years and yet are the very ones Jesus would always have us "voting" for. This means we must care most about what happens to the poor and vulnerable, especially when both parties will make their appeals to the middle-class voters and wealthy donors they desperately need. It means protecting human life and dignity and promoting the actual health and well-being of families instead of just substituting rhetorical devices around hot-button social issues in the pursuit of votes.

It means lifting up the people who have no political influence: undocumented immigrants, who are "the strangers" among us living in the shadows of a broken immigration system; low-income families and children, who face losing their nutritional and health-care support because others want to protect the subsidies and benefits to the wealthy people and interests that fund all political campaigns; and the poorest of the poor globally, who will die of hunger and preventable diseases such as malaria, HIV/AIDS, and tuberculosis because of cuts in foreign aid programs that fall out of fashion in election years.

Elections can make a difference. They can prevent or produce wars. They can protect or further devastate the poorest and most vulnerable among us. They can expand fairness, equality, and opportunity, or perpetuate further imbalances of the same, on the basis of income, race, and gender.

And yet, ultimately, how we live and what we do for the common good is much more important than just how we vote. Political affiliation with candidates, parties, and structures is waning—especially among young people—and that's good news. What will replace these traditional loyalties and structures as we move into an era of post-candidate politics, which focuses instead on moral principles and actual people and solving the problems that most impact their lives? Will it be the overwhelming power of money? Or might these changes herald a new dawn of social movements in domestic and international politics that is emerging from a pall of corruption and greed?

Rereading C. S. Lewis's *Chronicles of Narnia* while on retreat set the tone for my sabbatical. The more I focused on what "a gospel for the common good" would look like, the more I saw how foreign an idea it is in our politics today. Watching politics for the first three months of an election year, but not engaging in it, showed me how depressing (a strong but accurate word) our political discourse has become—on all sides. This book attempts a response to that discourse—trying to lift up the common good, a new civil discourse, and the hope for common ground on important issues, even among people who vote differently.

The idea of the common good is missing in politics today. Our public life is dominated and distorted by other interests—economic interests, special interests, and partisan interests. Finding what is right and what works has almost disappeared from our political discourse; solutions have been replaced by fear, blame, and an increasing vitriol. How can we renew a public interest in the common good and then restore accountability to our political leaders—all of them?

The Kind of Jesus Christians Believe In Will Determine the Kind of Christianity They Practice

Many people profess to be Christian, and if you add our brothers and sisters from Judaism, Islam, Buddhism, Hinduism, and other faith traditions, the number of citizens who say they are "religious" or "spiritual" grows even more. But what does this mean for our life together?

Religion is not exempt from the need for conversion from self-interest to neighbor-interest. But the starting point is as simple as turning the *profession* of faith into the *practice* of it. What if our faith traditions compelled us to actually do the things we say are important? Imagine the power of divisive religion converted into a spiritual force for the common good in our time. It is as close to us as the renewal or revival of genuine faith.

While the name of Jesus is still very popular, do we know or really understand *why he came*? One thing has become very clear to me: the kind of Jesus we believe in will determine the kind of Christianity we practice. Who is this Jesus? How do we learn and relearn his meaning and purpose *from his own words and actions*? And how different is that from what we see and hear in our churches? Could exploring why Jesus really came help us also to rediscover the common good? If we care about either of these questions—why Jesus came or the common good—this is a search we can make together.

I believe we can find some new directions and solutions by recovering a biblical vision of why Jesus came. Think of the very different implications of a gospel mostly for the hereafter and one also for the here and now. In the Lord's Prayer we ask that "thy kingdom come, thy will be done, on earth as it is in heaven." But do we live as if we really mean it? Is Jesus just the personal Savior of the conservative churches or the historical teacher of the liberal churches? Or is he the Living Teacher who walks among us to save our lives and the world? We will examine all of that.

13

There is the original New Testament message called the *gospel of the kingdom* (Matt. 4:23; 9:35; 24:14), which was intended to transform both people's lives and their societies; and there is a more modern message that concentrates mostly on individuals, a narrowly focused message we'll call the *atonement-only gospel*. By focusing so much on what happens after we die, we have neglected the agenda of Jesus for how we live now. Our consumer culture has quickly filled the vacuum, creating biblically flawed gospels of self-help, personal enhancement, prosperity, and parochial nationalism—all providing exclusive passports to heaven. But these self-seeking promotions have turned many away from Christian faith. I think we can invite them back if we can show that Jesus's announcement of the kingdom of God was for the sake of the world and not just for the sake of religious believers. He came to change the world and all of us with it.

The good news is that attention has been shifting away from comfortable Christians bound for heaven to an engagement that finds Jesus among the world's least, last, and lost. When Christians and their churches live in comfortable places in comfortable countries, it *takes a journey* to find the poor—in our own cities and communities or across the world. But in reconnecting to their most vulnerable neighbors, Christians are also becoming closer to Jesus again. That journey is the key to the future of Christianity. Matthew 25 was the beginning of my own Christian conversion, and I am deeply hopeful about the ways this text is now leading a new generation to set out on the new pilgrimage.

So we will start with the Gospels and the words Jesus himself spoke about how he meant to change the world along with individuals. Purely private atonement is at odds with the biblical vision of individuals who are saved into community. Salvation involves personal transformation, of course, but it doesn't stop there. The gospel of the kingdom creates disciples with public commitments. It spreads throughout the societies in which believers live, changing how they treat the poor and marginalized, setting captives free, seeking the worth and equality of all made in the image of God, encouraging good stewardship of God's creation, redefining those around them and around the world as their neighbors,

14

and even reconfiguring how they treat their enemies. Again, who Christians think Jesus is will shape how they follow him.

Essential Questions for the Common Good

We need a *practical vision*. What are the essential elements of life in the kingdom that affect the society in which its believers live—and therefore make a difference for what we now call "the common good"?

We'll look at the discussion Jesus had with his young questioner who asked, "Who is my neighbor?" and try to apply Jesus's answer to a globalized world. What does the story of the Good Samaritan, which Jesus used to teach his questioner, mean now in a world in which we are all much more closely connected? For example, are those who are involved in producing our cell phones now to be seen as our global neighbors, left on the side of the road by a global economy? Does the Good Samaritan parable suggest, for example, that economic supply chains should now also become value chains?

Another critical question is who defines our "enemy" today and how we choose to treat those labeled as "the other." If we take a realistic and biblical view of the human condition and the world, it is inevitable that we will have real enemies, those who would do us harm. But what are the most effective and creative ways of responding to them? Are the current habits of our wars of occupation really working? How might we *surprise* our enemies with different approaches, and what do the teachings of Jesus and Paul have to tell us about that? Understanding what it means to be our neighbor's "keeper" in a global context can help us better build the international conditions for more safety, security, and sustainability in our world.

What would it mean if people of faith began transferring their human identities from class, racial, and national loyalties to a global identity in a new *beloved community* created by God? What if Christians really thought of themselves as Christian first, with their other identities secondary? Am I a Christian American or an American Christian? Which comes first for us, our sociology or our theology? What's right and wrong about "American exceptionalism"? Imagine how faith

15

communities from many countries could help bring our "tribes" together when global crisis calls us to do that.

Both Liberals and Conservatives Are Needed for the Common Good

A central purpose of this book is to challenge the hateful ideological warfare between the conservative and liberal sides in our ongoing political battles, as well as their inability to listen to or learn anything from each other. I believe the best idea of the conservative political philosophy is the call to *personal responsibility*: choices and decisions about individual moral behavior, personal relationships like marriage and parenting, work ethics, fiscal integrity, service, compassion, and security. And the best idea of the liberal philosophy is the call to *social responsibility*: the commitment to our neighbor, economic fairness, racial and gender equality, the just nature of society, needed social safety nets, public accountability for business, and the importance of cooperative international relationships. *The common good comprises the best of both ideas—we need to be personally responsible and socially just.* This is key to ending the hateful conflict and beginning to understand the other side's contributions to the quality of our life together.

Our economic crisis has destroyed any sense of public trust in how financial decisions are made and in the people making them. In the economy, the gap between those at the top and the rest of us is greater than at any time since the Great Depression, and our poverty rates are the highest in fifty years. A new generation has risen up to focus our attention on the core issue of grotesque inequality, which is a fundamentally biblical matter. The 1 percent are experiencing a growing discontent coming from the 99 percent, and that is now becoming a factor of life in politics. The Occupy movement is challenging the elitism and plutocracies that now dominate our public life.

To restore the trust that has been lost in part because of such massive economic inequality, we need to replace the *broken social contracts* we have experienced with a *new social covenant* between citizens, business, and government. How do we replace market fundamentalism with a

16

moral economy, move economic thinking from the short term to the long term, shift from the interests of only shareholders to broader stakeholders, and commit to doing good while doing well?

The CEOs I talk with believe that the key to economic reform is for businesses to operate with more than financial logic and shareholder profits in mind; they must operate with a social purpose and be accountable to the enabling environment in which they function. Using business to solve social problems appeals to a new generation of entrepreneurs, but it is still a minority view that needs to be cultivated. Could business leaders who are also people of faith help lead the way? We will examine these questions of economic trust.

We will also look at the proper role of government—theologically, and not just politically. Should it be small or big, or just smart and effective? Is government good or evil, or does it have the potential to be both? What does the Bible say about all that? C. S. Lewis said that we need democracy not because we are so good but because we are not! There is a very strong case to be made for a serious political system of checks and balances because of a realistic and biblical view of our selfish human nature. But today we seem to have mostly checks (financial ones) and fewer and fewer balances. If we don't believe in either sinless government or sinless markets, how do we find some balance for the common good? What would it mean to take the mission of *public service* seriously—with a *servant government* working for the common good?

I am convinced that what happens *in our households* is as central to the common good as what happens outside them. The quality of personal, everyday life in our families, neighborhoods, and local communities is vital to shaping the quality of our public life. Being a husband, father, and Little League baseball coach has convinced me that the common good is about far more than what happens in the hallowed halls of power in Washington, DC. Restoring healthy households means making the transformation from *appetites* to *values*. Our homes must become the places where our children learn the difference between the two.

Marriage must be affirmed and supported, and parenting is an absolute key to the well-being of any society. Sexual integrity and fidelity must be taught and shown, not just preached. And the choices parents make to prioritize time with their children will always be the best investment we can make in their futures and the future of our societies. Our households are where we teach and learn family values, moral choices, and the strength of close communities. Neighborhoods must become villages, and the vitality of local connections and economies is crucial to a good society. People were made for family, community, and human flourishing, not consumerism, materialism, addiction, and empty overwork. And we learn most about that in the households and communities where we live.

Redeeming democracy will require turning consumers into citizens. If politics is now mostly about advertising, it must become more about participation—not just during elections but between them as well. Perhaps the final barrier to democracy is the power of money over politics, and to change that we will need to turn again to the historical power of movements to change the big things. And the idea that corporations are persons is a theological mistake, not just a political one.

What Religion Needs to Remember

Despite ideological efforts to politicize religion, ancient faith traditions do not fit neatly into modern political categories. When religion is manipulated for political gain, faith loses its prophetic stance. And when faith squeezes itself into narrow political categories, it loses its intended shape and is twisted to benefit partisan politics. A better role for faith is to challenge politics and hold the public square morally accountable to values derived from a position of faith—even though it must be made clear that *religion has no monopoly on morality*. And we all must learn how the wisdom from other faith, spiritual, and secular moral traditions contributes to our understanding of the common good.

Faith can subvert our worst and most dominant social narratives or, to use the biblical language, challenge our prevailing idolatries. It exposes lies that control societies and turn human beings away from their created purposes. Faith reminds us what people are created for and should confront what distracts us from that. How do we nurture both families and communities, promote a civil discourse, and approach problems with solutions and hope instead of fear and blame?

Religion must change too. How can we redirect faith communities outward? Instead of trying to dominate the public square, faith communities should seek to inform and inspire it. Faith communities should prefer authenticity over conformity, reflection over certainty, leadership by example and not control. Faith communities must be committed to "speaking the truth" while respecting the growing religious pluralism of our societies. As we move into a post-Christian world, churches can be free to live a faithful gospel lifestyle that does not require majority acceptance. And that is a great freedom indeed.

Our effectiveness in contributing to the common good will be judged not by who has the superior understanding of doctrine or the most religious adherents but by who has an authentic life, who is meeting the needs of others, who shows what neighbor-love means, who leads by example and not by dominance, who has prophetic independence from the money and power of partisan agendas, and who retains the moral authority and capacity to hold society accountable to the ethics of the common good. We can do better with the public witness of faith in our time—and we can help build a better values culture of opportunity, fairness, compassion, character, commitment, nurture, and hope.

Time to Go Deeper

Shallowness characterizes our politics, our media coverage, and our popular cultural values. If we are truly committed to discovering what it means to be on God's side, it is time to go much deeper in seeking a redemptive path forward. It's time to move beyond our superficial and even hateful politics and media. It's time to dig deeper in the places that supply our better values and instincts and to revive the practices that renew our faith traditions and ethical priorities. And it's time to do the spiritual reflection that could provide the moral compass that our politics and economics have lost and that even our religions can forget.

How do we remember that each of us is indeed our neighbor's keeper? We need to recover a personal and social commitment to the common good, and I believe a rediscovered faith can help renew the ethics and practices of it.

There is now a public and bipartisan consensus that our politics is broken. But, at an even deeper level, we must say that the ethic of the common good has been lost on all political sides. We have entered a dark and dangerous period of selfishness in both our culture and our political life. "I" has replaced "we." Winning has indeed replaced governing, and ideological warfare substitutes for finding solutions to real and growing problems.

To disagree isn't enough anymore—politicians and media pundits now attack their opponent's character, integrity, patriotism, and even faith. And the political idea of finding compromise or working across party lines has been mostly upended on Capitol Hill, where members of different parties don't have dinner or drinks anymore and don't know each other's families or even say hello or make eye contact in the hallways. Political veterans from both parties tell me this is the worst polarization they have ever seen. This paralysis is now a way of life in American politics.

Our media, especially our cable television and talk radio shows, have helped create a poisonous political environment ruled by falsehood and blatant political bias, often using the language of hate and fear. Americans, for the most part, are not turning to journalistic sources to inform and challenge them but rather to programs that will enforce and intensify their existing prejudices. As we move from one competing network to another, the political views may change, but the tone and style in which they are articulated are increasingly interchangeable.

How can we better understand the causes, challenges, and choices in the problems we're now facing and find better ways to engage in serious public discourse about them? I especially want to encourage the faith community to take on a genuinely prophetic and pastoral role in this critical discussion. Perhaps faith communities could help play some of the critical roles that the press used to fill in challenging politics and holding it accountable. We need to not just react to the shallow and strident politics and media of the election year America just came through; we need to try *to go deeper*.

The underlying issues here are deeply theological, spiritual, and cultural, and not simply political. How do we name and unmask the "idols" of politics and lay out the biblical, spiritual, and even secular foundations for an ethic of the common good? How do we move from the politics of fear and blame to the politics of values and solution? How do we build a culture for the common good in an age of selfishness? And how can we find common ground by moving to higher ground?

Our citizens are longing to see political polarization and paralysis give way to visible progress on the issues that most affect their lives. But broken systems generally cannot fix themselves; it takes a movement from outside, citizens intervening to bring about change. That many local churches are moving into community organizing is a most hopeful sign. And that the next generation is being drawn to a post-candidate politics, focused more on real people and real issues, is also a sign of change.

There are very hopeful signs among younger Christians and other believers or seekers with whom I regularly speak. They care about their world, are engaging it, and want to connect their faith or spirituality with social change. The citizens of a new generation really want to change their societies, and their question is how. What are the new questions and models? How can faith communities play a key and even catalytic role in creating and sustaining the kind of movements that have changed things in the past? Major social reform movements have always had faith communities at their center. We have done this before and we can do it again.

Baseball and the Vocation of Unexpected Hope

Here's a baseball story. I have been a Little League baseball coach for both my sons' teams over many years. And I've learned that baseball teaches us lessons of life.

Last spring, our nine-year-old's team was down 5–0, and we had already lost our opening couple of games. It didn't look good. But all of a sudden, our bats and our team came alive, and all the practice and preparation we had done suddenly showed itself. Best of all, our rally started in the bottom half of the order with our weakest hitters. Two kids got on with walks, and our least experienced player came up to the plate. With international parents, Stefan had never played baseball before, and it was clear he didn't have a clue. But somehow he hit the ball, and it went into the outfield. Our first two runs scored, and Stefan ended up on second base. Being from a polite British Commonwealth culture, he began to walk over to the shortstop and second baseman and shake their hands! "Stefan," I shouted, "you have to stay on the base!" "Oh," he said, "I've never been here before."

Inspired, other kids who had never gotten hits before either also got them now. Then the best hitters started to hit, and we came back to win 11–6. I gave Stefan the game ball. In a long team meeting afterward, the kids couldn't stop telling each other what they had learned. "We didn't give up and came back!" "Our rally started with the bottom of the order." "Sometimes you get what you need from unexpected places." "We all just kept cheering for one another." "Everybody helped us win today." Finally, our star player said, "This just goes to show you, you can't ever give up on hope. We always have to keep on hoping no matter what." *Lessons of life*. Most important, we became a team on that day. And we won most of our games after that!

I believe the same insight is central to our vocation as faith communities: *we need to offer unexpected hope to the world.*

The Christian mission is to proclaim and live the kingdom of God: "Your kingdom come. Your will be done, *on earth* as it is in heaven" (Matt. 6:10; emphasis added). That is what we pray. But while the kingdom of God was the central message of Jesus and the New Testament, it has faded as ours. Finding salvation in heaven is part of the message, getting closer to God is part of the message, but the heart of the message of Jesus was a new order breaking into history, changing everything about the world, including us.

That is why we can offer such hope to the world. The church is supposed to be *saying*, and the church is supposed to be *showing*, that *our life together can be better*. In our shallow, superficial, and selfish age, Jesus is indeed calling us to a completely different way of life that people are supposed to be able to *see*. He called it the *kingdom of God*, and it is a very clear alternative to the selfish kingdoms of this world. As we said at the very beginning, that better way of living was meant to benefit not just Christians but everybody else too. That's what makes it transformational.

When people see that kingdom of God actually being lived out, *they are first surprised by it and then attracted to it.*

They are attracted when a huge and successful church in a midwestern state's suburbs decides to take on the renovation of dilapidated and failing public schools in their neighboring urban area. Or when a church in the South's Bible Belt puts up a sign welcoming the Muslim cultural center that has just moved into their neighborhood and befriends those who were afraid of being attacked—and when the story of that new Christian-Muslim friendship is broadcast on CNN and changes the hearts of angry men in Kashmir, Pakistan. Or when a graduating seminarian decides to start a church made up of homeless people and, after ten years, almost all of the congregation's leaders literally come from off the streets.

When a Christian family farm business builds day-care centers and houses for their migrant workers, provides college scholarships for their employees' children, gives millions of dollars to Africa and Haiti, and still has the most successful apple orchard in their region, it attracts attention. When conservative Southern California Anglo churches get deeply connected to Hispanic churches in their own communities, and the two groups come to know each other's faith and families, and then together seek to fix a broken immigration system, it gets the attention of policy makers in Washington.

When Christian leaders in the US, UK, and other Western countries form alliances with their Palestinian and Jewish brothers and sisters of faith in the Middle East, it can change foreign policy. When a famous evangelical megachurch in Ohio doesn't just righteously proclaim itself to be "pro-life" but quietly takes in hundreds of low-income pregnant women every year to help them carry their children to term and settle into a better life, people feel helped and not just judged. And when faith-based organizations and denominations who might vote differently in elections make it clear to both Republicans and Democrats that they must not balance their budgets and reduce their deficits by increasing poverty, but must draw a "circle of protection" around the poorest and most vulnerable, it breaks through the self-interested politics of both parties.

All these are true stories, and this book is full of stories like these— real people, real faith, making a real difference in the world. They are all about *unexpected hope* in hopeless times.

My advice to young pastors going into ministry is: Never be content with what is predictable and never become cynical about change. Don't be satisfied with a church whose lifestyle and behavior you can predict just by looking at the culture around it. The job of the pastor is to lead a faith community whose vocation is to be unpredictable and to offer hope where nobody else does.

That is because Christians are not committed to the kingdom of any culture, class, or racial group, or to the kingdom of America or any other nation-state, or even to the kingdom of any church, but rather to the kingdom of God. That kingdom turns all the other kingdoms on their head, brings forth the unexpected, and breaks open the unpredictable. We are called to show people how to love God and their neighbors and thereby bring new hope to lives, neighborhoods, nations, and the world. The world around us is longing for that wholly unpredictable ministry of hope. And that's the side I want to be on.

... 2 ...

The Lion, the Word, and the Way

I'm on Aslan's side even if there isn't any Aslan to lead it. I'm going to live as like a Narnian as I can even if there isn't any Narnia.

—Puddleglum, in *The Silver Chair*[1]

Who we think Jesus is will determine the kind of Christianity we live. The more I have thought about this, the more I believe it is central to the current status and future of the church—and the world. If Jesus is mostly a private figure for our individual lives, our faith will be primarily personal and not much engaged in the societies in which we live. If Jesus just provides us a pathway to heaven, we won't be much concerned with what happens on this earth. Or if we create a Jesus mostly in our own image, he won't be very useful to "others" who are very unlike us.

But if Jesus came because "God so loved the world," he will be a different Jesus for us. If his message is about changing the world and not just our own lives, then our lives will reflect that message. If Jesus

---

1. C. S. Lewis, *The Silver Chair* (New York: HarperCollins, 2009), Kindle edition, locations 1861–62.

came to create a new community and not just save people, then that community's collective life in the world will be of crucial importance. And if we as individuals are so drawn to Jesus that we want to learn the ways he would have us live, he becomes the Living Teacher who walks among us. All of which brings me to a lion.

Not a Tame Lion

What has come into being in him was life, and the life was the light of all people. The light shines in the darkness, and the darkness did not overcome it. (John 1:3–5)

I spotted them while getting my food for lunch the first day, to take back to my little cell at the monastic hermitage. Three old shelves composed the monastery's library for their guests, mostly containing books on theology, church history, and prayer, as well as some novels. And the library was in the kitchen! I was pleasantly surprised to see, there on the bottom shelf, *The Chronicles of Narnia* by C. S. Lewis.

Joy and I had read the *Chronicles* to our boys before bed at night, and our family had seen the recent movies based on the stories of Narnia. But I hadn't sat down to read them myself for many years. High in the mountains overlooking a vast and stunning blue ocean, in the midst of sturdy redwoods, seemed like the right kind of place to read these magical stories again.

So I picked up *The Lion, the Witch and the Wardrobe*, thinking I would read just one book. But that quickly turned into another and another. I read them early in the mornings after vigils, at night after vespers, and during afternoon walks up and down the mountains to the sea. My other reading was in theology, New Testament, and the Psalms—a favorite for these monks of the Camaldoli order. But the *Chronicles* gave a lift to my days and my spirit and provided a mystical framework and spiritual narrative that gave even more meaning to the rest of my reading and reflection for the week.

I discovered the lion again. Aslan is not a tame lion but a great and good one, and he is commonly recognized as the Christ character in the stories about the land of Narnia, which is a very different kind of kingdom than all the ones around it. He is the true king teaching all the other kings and every other creature, from the most important to the least, about how they should live—and live together. My purpose in taking the sabbatical was to write a book about the common good, so going back to Narnia and to Aslan seemed like a good way to begin.

Friends of mine know that I have a special love for lions anyway, and we have a beautiful oil painting of a South African lion that hovers over us in our dining room at home. I am often asked if the lion in the painting is Aslan, and I just smile; but I wouldn't have bought it if I didn't think he was. His searching eyes look right into yours in the way Lewis describes his lion doing in the Narnia stories.

To the children in those stories, who are magically transported from mid-twentieth-century England to the kingdom of Narnia and who play major roles in the history of that enchanted land, Aslan is the central figure, as he is to all of Narnia's other creatures too. He is powerful but gentle, and an utterly captivating force for good over evil and for unconditional love, deep wisdom, and human transformation (animal transformation too!).

Present both at the creation of Narnia and at its end, Aslan has a presence that sings from the pages of the New Testament, such as in the opening words of John's Gospel: "What has come into being in him was life, and the life was the light of all people. The light shines in the darkness, and the darkness did not overcome it."

Aslan, the great lion king, is always in the right place, with the right person, at the right time. He influences things very large, historical, and cosmic; but at the same time he cares about things very small, individual, and practical. The lion challenges what is evil but constantly and consistently offers what is good—inviting friends and even enemies to embrace the vision of Narnia. Aslan's appeal is breathtaking, both as the *champion* of every great cause you would ever want to fight and give your life for and as the *companion* you would always want to have in very personal moments and struggles, when you are most vulnerable. He is indeed an amazingly compelling picture of Jesus. And you don't need to be religious to be drawn to Aslan.

Aslan leads and teaches the common good of Narnia. What is best for the people and the land of Narnia is always his overriding concern. Aslan is the loving and living *teacher* who instructs and inspires the creatures of Narnia as well as the "sons and daughters of Adam and Eve" from England who have all come to learn the ways that make for a good and peaceful land. They gladly become his apprentices, and under his mentorship love to wrap their arms around him, snuggle close to his golden mane, and have their faces touched by the lion's head.

Aslan often surprises the humans, challenges them, and even scolds them, but always protects and defends them. He is always pointing the way, urging them to "go further up and further in" to the real kingdom of Narnia and what it was supposed to be from the beginning. He calls them by name, knows them well, and loves them all.

Walking every day with the *Chronicles* in my hands, through a land with a beauty not unlike the descriptions of Narnia, was a highly impressive, personally emotional, and even earthshaking experience for me at times. And there were moments when it did feel like Aslan was walking right along beside me too, pushing my mind and heart and rekindling my love and longing for Narnia.

This experience made me realize again how much I want to be a Narnian rather than a part of the other kingdoms that surround it. Those long walks got me thinking in fresh ways about Jesus and how we understand him. During the retreat I was also reading on a topic that theologians call "Christology," our theology of Christ. But Aslan did more to push me to remember, reconsider, and reconfigure the meaning of *why Jesus came* than the theologians could.

In particular, the lion made me rethink how both conservative and liberal churches in America today often get their Christology wrong.

What the Conservative Churches Get Wrong

Many conservative churches still have a very hard time understanding Jesus as a *teacher*. He is instead only the Savior, the lamb that was slain for our sins, the sacrifice necessary for our atonement, the figure whose propitiation opens our way to heaven.

But as far as teaching us how to live now or how to be a follower of Jesus on this earth, we don't hear very much from the conservative churches. The one exception is in matters pertaining to sexuality, in which conservative churches have strong feelings about our behavior. But on a whole range of other issues, clear teaching and practices are often missing—even on things Jesus was most clear and persistent about, such as economics and the poor or loving both our neighbors and our enemies.

It is almost as if Jesus wasted three years with all his parables, teachings, and miracles about the meaning of "the kingdom of God," which the New Testament says he came to bring. All that becomes just a minor series of teachings and events before the one great event he came for—to die on the cross to save us from our sins. Some conservatives even say that the Beatitudes and the Sermon on the Mount, which are the charter of the kingdom and were used by the early church as the major teaching catechism for new converts, are not really meant for our time and world but for another "dispensation" that is yet to come.

As a young teenage boy in a conservative church, I was told that Jesus's teaching "blessed are the peacemakers" (Matt. 5:9), for example, was for our lives in heaven and not for now. But even as a fifteen-year-old, I couldn't figure out why we would need peacemakers in heaven but not in my racially divided hometown of Detroit or in the middle of the Vietnam War in which America was tragically engaged—neither of which was a problem for my conservative fellow church members. Such obstructions to Jesus's teachings were central to the reasons why I finally left the church, and the church's avoidance of Christ's teachings today is also why many young people are turning away from Christian faith.

The cross and resurrection are absolutely central to my faith and theology. And the central drama in *The Lion, the Witch and the Wardrobe* is when Aslan agrees to pay for another person's sin, young Edmund's, with his own life—being tortured and killed by his enemies—only to rise again and defeat the White Witch and her forces.

Christ's death on the cross does save us, and his resurrection establishes his kingship and inaugurates his kingdom. Salvation is both personal and social, both in the New Testament and in Narnia. But,

29

as I argue biblically in the next chapter, the reduction of salvation to an atonement-only gospel is a modern mistake, especially apparent in affluent and powerful countries that would feel easily threatened by a full proclamation of the kingdom of God and all its teachings. In that private gospel, what is lost is Jesus the Teacher, who shows us the ways of his kingdom. There is no powerful lion, just a sacrificial lamb.

What the Liberal Churches Get Wrong

One of the reasons that more conservative churches have been suspicious even of the term "teacher" when applied to Jesus is that some of the liberal churches have long used that language. Many mainline Protestant churches have, since the last century, preached a "social gospel," which often highlights the teachings of Jesus and tries to apply them to issues of poverty, race, war, and peace. And some have shown great courage in doing so.

But the real problem comes down to Easter Sunday and what these churches believe about it. Many of our churches' Easter liturgies have the pastor proclaim, "He is risen!" to which the congregation replies, "He is risen indeed!" The question is whether all those parishioners, or even their pastors, truly believe it. Do we really believe that Jesus is *alive* and among us? I am not sure that all of our liberal churches really do. To believe in the resurrection—that Jesus of Nazareth was crucified by the political authorities, died and was buried, and rose from the dead after three days—takes a real act of faith.

Too many liberal church theologians, seminaries, and pastors have a very hard time with that kind of faith. They have said, as put very crudely by one of their twentieth-century leaders, Rudolf Bultmann, "It is impossible to use electric light and the wireless and to avail ourselves of modern medical and surgical discoveries, and at the same time believe in the New Testament world of spirits and miracles."[2] The German theologian's description of science and technology is way out of date,

2. Rudolf Bultmann, "New Testament and Mythology," in *Kerygma and Myth: A Theological Debate*, ed. H. W. Bartsch, trans. R. H. Fuller (New York: Harper & Row, 1961), 5.

but his disbelief of things that can't be easily explained by science is still very much alive in these circles.

Contemporary theologians of that same critical tradition have described the resurrection as an important "metaphor" but not as a historical reality that can actually be believed and acted on. Just as some religious fundamentalists make the mistake of thinking that religion can explain the physical world better than science can, some liberal modernists make the mistake of thinking that science can best explain what is behind the universe. But even many of our contemporary physicists hold the door open for unexplained mystery more than some of our liberal theologians do.

But whether for reasons of science or just cynicism, if you don't believe that Jesus is really alive today, all you have is a list of teachings without the Living Teacher. And that is a very big problem. Some then add the teachings of other social leaders like Martin Luther King Jr., Mahatma Gandhi, and Dorothy Day. But as much as those three, in particular, are personal heroes to me and represent causes to which I have given my life, they are all very flawed men and women and also are very dead, even if their words and teachings live on.

It is indeed a wonderful thing to listen to the sermons of Martin Luther King Jr. (and I think I have heard most of them), or to read the autobiography and writings of Mahatma Gandhi (which take up a whole shelf in my library), or to learn the amazing story of Dorothy Day's Catholic Worker Movement (which I got to hear from her before she died). But one is still left with just a list of powerful ideas and inspiring teachings that we try to carry out as best we can.

The same can be said about the teachings of Jesus. When we no longer believe he is alive, all we have are inspiring words from someone who lived a long time ago. Take all Jesus's teachings and wish each other good luck in trying to follow them—that's a lot of hard work when we are left to do it on our own.

Having the teachings without the Living Teacher is causing many liberal churches to die. One of their denominational leaders recently described facing a "tsunami of death,"[3] as church members grow old

3. Lovett H. Weems Jr., *Focus: The Real Challenges That Face the United Methodist Church* (Nashville: Abingdon, 2012).

and nobody is replacing them. The teachings of Jesus are of course respected, but without a living relationship with the Teacher, the children of too many liberal churches are not staying—and are not remaining Christians.

The Narnia Story

Lewis tells a very compelling story with Aslan in the *Chronicles of Narnia*. The lion is powerfully present, never controllable or predictable, appearing when not expected and always at the right time and place. He protects, redirects, confronts, defeats evil, welcomes the good, and puts his students back on the right path again and again. He is the source of authority, power, and hope. He inspires and strengthens the people and the creatures to be brave, to lead, to fight for the right, to stand up to the wrong, and to find their own vocations in Narnia.

And with him they are full of joy. They laugh, eat and drink, tell stories and jokes, embrace one another, value their friends, and even look for ways to reconcile with their enemies. Care and compassion, justness and fairness, dignity and respect, honor and valor, and service and sacrifice become their values; and this is the way things are supposed to work in Narnia. The other creatures are valued along with the humans, and some of them can even talk! Throughout the story and land of Narnia, the stunning beauty and luxuriant grandeur of the natural world—the mountains and valleys, rivers and waterfalls, beaches and seas, forests and flowers, fruits and other food—are all lavishly loved and generously shared.

As one reads through the *Chronicles*, the parallels between Narnia and the kingdom of God become more and more apparent; by the end, they are very clear. In *The Last Battle*, a new Narnia is created out of the old. Says the narrator, "That had a beginning and an end. It was only a shadow or a copy of the real Narnia which has always been here and always will be here: just as our own world, England and all, is only a shadow or copy of something in Aslan's real world."[4] The new

4. C. S. Lewis, *The Last Battle* (New York: HarperCollins, 2005), Kindle edition, locations 1934–35.

Narnia was a "deeper country"[5] than the old Narnia, like what can be seen through a magical looking glass.

Lucy is the first of the children to go through the wardrobe into Narnia, is always the closest to Aslan, and is the most Narnian of all the English visitors. At the beginning of the story, the first creature she meets in the winter woods is the faun Mr. Tumnus. And at the end of the story, they reflect together. "The further up and the further in you go, the bigger everything gets. The inside is larger than the outside," says Tumnus. "I see," Lucy says. "This is still Narnia and, more real and beautiful than the Narnia down below . . . world within world, Narnia within Narnia."[6]

The Original Story

What the New Testament says, and what Christians who follow Jesus have believed from the reality of the empty tomb, is that Jesus is the Living Teacher who walks among us. Walking the hills above the California coast, I felt the spirit of Aslan offering a very different model than that offered by either the conservatives or the liberals. In another one of his books, *Mere Christianity*, C. S. Lewis has this to say about the message of the New Testament: "The real Son of God is at your side. He is beginning to turn you into the same kind of thing as Himself. He is beginning, so to speak, to 'inject' His kind of life and thought . . . into you."[7]

Jesus came to bring a new order of living called the kingdom of God. He taught it to his disciples, who were his apprentices. From his Beatitudes and Sermon on the Mount to all of his stories and parables, to his words of exhortation and correction, he was constantly trying to teach his disciples this new way of living. From the narratives of the New Testament it is apparent how hard it was for his disciples to "get it."

Their old ways, the habits of the culture in which they lived, the pressures of economics, their own religious institutions and leaders,

5. Ibid., 1948.
6. Ibid., 2051–52.
7. C. S. Lewis, *Mere Christianity* (New York: HarperCollins, 2000), 189.

and the threats and fears caused by their Roman political occupiers all weighed against the values and priorities of Jesus's new order of things. But he kept teaching, and they kept listening, following, staying with him, and experimenting, if you will, with his new way of living in the life they shared together.

But Jesus was alive, he was with them, and they had committed to being his apprentices, students, disciples. They felt his love, which had changed them forever, and each day with him opened up a whole new world for them. Their lives and world were being transformed, and they were utterly compelled by the Teacher who walked alongside them every day.

Then he was killed by the authorities and buried in a tomb, and the disciples mostly fled. Hiding together in fear, grief, and loss, they were paralyzed and stuck, completely uncertain and confused about what was next, what they would do now. What they did not do was decide to simply compile his teachings and try to live by them. There was nothing about his teachings that they remembered now that had the power to bring them back to life from death or give them strength, power, and hope. They were imprisoned in their upper room by confusion and fear.

What finally brought them back to life was the excited announcement, from the women who were less afraid than the men and had gone out to minister to the body of their beloved Lord, that Jesus wasn't dead but alive! The disciples ran to see for themselves; they saw the empty tomb and later met Jesus again. Their teacher was alive again and able to teach and lead them. And even after he left the earth, Jesus gave his disciples the Holy Spirit to live with them always, after which they hit the streets of Jerusalem and then the rest of the world. And so a new movement was born. Their proclamation was of a living Lord with a new kingdom to bring to the world, a kingdom that could change everything.

The Kingdom and the Teacher

From the Easter story we begin to understand worlds seen and unseen, smaller and larger, less real and more real, lasting and everlasting, with one trying to change the other. That's what the kingdom is: a world brought into this one to change it, God's order breaking into our own, and God's Son announcing it, teaching it, and dying for it and for all those who would join it. But now he is alive again as the Living Teacher who walks among us to show us the meaning of the new order—in things large and small.

It is exactly the transforming character of this live and active connection with the Teacher—this interaction, this relationship—that stands at the heart of the gospel and the power of the kingdom in our time. It changes us year to year, day to day, and hour by hour as we listen to what the Teacher is trying to teach us about the very biggest parts of life and also the smallest—like a golden lion who wants to accompany us through the woods and up the mountain, softly speaking to us along the way.

This personal and interactive relationship with the Teacher can sweep up people from both the conservative and liberal churches and is doing so among a new generation. Younger people from the more conservative churches are hungry to live for the kingdom "on earth as it is in heaven"[8] and not just settle for a ticket to the hereafter. And a new generation of liberal church pastors and leaders are speaking again of "evangelism" to the whole gospel of Jesus, transforming individuals *and* the world.

Without the teaching, we simply have a belief that might be good for heaven but won't do us any good on earth. And without the Teacher, the teaching will be too hard to put into practice. Having a list of beliefs for heaven or a list of teachings for earth is not enough. We need the Living Teacher to walk among us, like a great lion, whispering in our ears the things that we need to do to change ourselves and our world.

This powerful reality of a current, constant, and interactive relationship with a Living Teacher is the compelling attraction of faith in Jesus Christ. The old battles over doctrine and belief are far less compelling, especially to a new generation. The conservatives are mostly telling us what we have to believe to be saved and go to heaven. Jesus is the atoning figure, the sacrificial Savior, the one who paid the price for our sins; but he remains distant and remote, now far away in heaven waiting for

8. Matt. 6:10.

us to join him someday, or very much alive in our hearts but not in the world around us. The liberals, who don't readily embrace the talk of a living Christ, are modern skeptics of spiritual matters and just hold forth the teachings of Jesus, who also remains distant as a great figure from long ago. But the promise of a living relationship with the Teacher is something that draws people from both sides of the theological chasm.

The relationship with the Living Teacher who walks among us brings two things in particular to the center of our lives that are often missing in the rush of our existence: attentiveness and hope.

Attentiveness

In my retreat journal I wrote, "Lessons from a week with the monks: replace scheduling, rushing, and worrying with attentiveness."

The experience of retreat—both religious and not—satisfies the growing need that many people now feel to stop, slow down, be quiet, rest body and mind, think and reflect more deeply, and even pray. Retreat centers and monasteries are often booked far in advance these days with retreatants who come for a few days just to get away from their normal routines. Many feel like they've lost important things and want to regain some perspective. They want to reclaim both body and spirit and renew both heart and mind.

In an article called "The Joy of Quiet" in the *New York Times Sunday Review*, journalist Pico Iyer speaks both culturally and personally to that need. He tells stories of his busy colleagues who expressed the need for "stillness."[9] Some high-end resorts, Iyer reports, now deliberately create luxury suites with no television or internet. "In barely one generation," he observes, "we've moved from exulting in the time-saving devices that have so expanded our lives to trying to get away from them—often in order to make more time. The more ways we have to connect, the more many of us seem desperate to unplug."[10] When average office workers enjoy no more than three minutes without an

9. Pico Iyer, "The Joy of Quiet," *New York Times Sunday Review*, December 29, 2011, http://www.nytimes.com/2012/01/01/opinion/sunday/the-joy-of-quiet.html?pagewanted=all.
  10. Ibid.

interruption, more and more people desire "the chance to clear their heads and hear themselves think."[11]

Iyer quotes Nicholas Carr's book *The Shallows*, which describes how the average American now spends at least eight hours a day in front of a screen and how our time on the internet and in front of the television steadily increases. The average teenager sends or receives seventy-five text messages a day, and many a lot more. "The children of tomorrow," Iyer says, "will crave nothing more than freedom, if only for a short while, from all the blinking machines, streaming videos and scrolling headlines that leave them feeling empty and too full all at once."[12] He speaks of colleagues trying to take "Sabbaths" from the internet, cell phones, and "the breaking news," or turning to things like yoga, meditation, or long walks on weekends. Iyer sees the need for retreat as a way to regain perspective and really have something to bring to one's work and relationships. "It's only by having some distance from the world that you can see it whole, and understand what you should be doing with it."[13]

We are now flooded with information, but we lack insight. Our lives are full of communication, yet we often fail to reflect on what we are hearing. We are conformed to our culture, in part, because we are captive to its pace. The answer is not simply to withdraw from the world but to find the stillness and silence we need in order to truly engage it.

Taking the time to slow down—to create quiet space, find solitude, embrace silence, think, reflect, meditate, and pray—is a wise and time-tested spiritual practice. And many people are feeling a growing urgency to seek out such time, given that our normal lives and routines often lack it. We are looking for moral clarity, mental sharpness, and emotional maturity in our responses to the steady assault of outside messages on our lives. It is a discipline—quite different from the noise of our usual surroundings and schedules—to be content by ourselves.

After reading Iyer's article, I happened to discover that he was at the same Benedictine retreat center I was just two weeks later. In his

11. Ibid.
12. Ibid.
13. Ibid.

retreats, Iyer says, he is looking for "something deeper than mere happiness: it's joy, which the monk David Steindl-Rast describes as 'that kind of happiness that doesn't depend on what happens.'"[14] While he goes on retreats regularly, the journalist says, "I don't attend services when I'm there, and I've never meditated, there or anywhere; I just take walks and read and lose myself in the stillness, recalling that it's only by stepping briefly away from my wife and bosses and friends that I'll have anything useful to bring to them."[15]

What I find on retreat is the renewal of my "attentiveness." And in the time with *The Chronicles of Narnia*, I found myself becoming more and more attentive to the lion called Aslan as we roamed together the mountains that overlooked the expansive blue of the Pacific Ocean. As Aslan in the stories was close to his students, Aslan as the teacher felt very close and very clear to me. When I myself wasn't talking so much, I could almost hear him talking. And when the only words I heard the whole week were those of the monks reading the Scriptures and prayers, all the other words I hear from the noise of my society began to fall into place.

Walking was a big part of my slowing down and listening, because walking takes time and allows us to actually see the world that we are traveling through, instead of the way we "million-mile flyers" normally pass above it. Walking also gets us back in touch with our breath, our body, our health, and our feelings—especially when the beauty of what we are seeing sometimes makes us stop and exclaim, "Wow!"

Being disconnected from the internet and from newspapers, radio, and television during a presidential primary season was especially difficult for me. Resisting the temptation to go down the mountain and learn the results of the New Hampshire primary was important; but ultimately, in order to learn how to best respond to those and all the political "results" in a time like this, I needed to be quiet for a while.

We are very tightly bound to our schedules and results and to the expectations and approvals that others have for us and that we have for ourselves. Stepping outside of them from time to time helps us to

14. Ibid.
15. Ibid.

reexamine them. The permission to just relax and live from moment to moment is a spiritual discipline not common to our daily existence, and therefore essential to retreat.

Missing my wife and children as much as I did reconfirmed that I am not called to be a monk. At least I'm not called to their usual style of life. But as a husband and father, and as someone who is constantly expected to carry out the role of a social prophet and provide the perspective of a pastor, I do ask more often now how the monastic or contemplative perspective can also regularly manifest itself in my very busy life.

In all these roles, the key for me seems to be "attentiveness." And the interaction with the Living Teacher is the most important thing for me in that attentiveness. That interaction is exactly what the New Testament says we are offered in Jesus Christ. And it is how we make his kingdom come and his will be done "on earth as it is in heaven." The pilgrimage of our lives is learning to apply the kingdom to the biggest and most consequential of social and political events, to the most personal of our closest relationships, and to the daily interactions we have with colleagues, coworkers, neighbors, and complete strangers. The Teacher wants to teach us in all those ways.

Hope

Our relationship with the Living Teacher is also absolutely essential in keeping our hope alive against all the odds that regularly challenge it. The greatest challenge to us in a world of injustice and a culture of cynicism is how to hang on to belief in a better world that would change this one. Every day there are horrible events, arrogant claims, and incredible disappointments that undercut everything we believe about the promise of the kingdom of God.

Perhaps the most moving passage in the *Chronicles* for me comes in *The Silver Chair*. Two of the children from our world, Jill and Scrubb, enter Narnia and are on a mission to rescue a young, kidnapped prince of Narnia from a wicked witch (a queen from another land), who has entrapped him with her powers of enchantment. They enlist Puddleglum, an unspectacular Narnian creature of humorous characteristics, to help guide them.

When they free the prince, the witch returns and uses her powers against them. They are all wilting under her magic dust and enchanted words, which deny everything but her own kingdom. The wicked queen says there is no Narnia, no Aslan, but only her world of power. At that moment she stands for all the rulers of this world, who say that their power is the only reality and who deny the existence of any other claim or promise that could challenge them.

In the story, the one to stand up to the witch is not the valiant prince or the heroic children but the uncharismatic Puddleglum. With his bare foot he stamps out the fire that is releasing the evil incense of her enchantments. Then, limping up to her in his pain, he says this:

> One word, Ma'am. . . . All you've been saying is quite right. . . . So I won't deny any of what you said. But there's one more thing to be said, even so. Suppose we have only dreamed, or made up, all those things—trees and grass and sun and moon and stars and Aslan himself. Then all I can say is that, in that case, the made-up things seem a good deal more important than the real ones. Suppose this black pit of a kingdom of yours is the only world. Well, it strikes me as a pretty poor one. We're just babies making up a game, if you're right. But four babies playing a game can make a play world which licks your real world hollow. That's why I am going to stand by the play world. I'm on Aslan's side even if there isn't any Aslan to lead it. I'm going to be as like a Narnian as I can even if there isn't any Narnia.[16]

I stopped on the top of the mountain when I read that, and realized it is my statement of faith too. I believe the gospel of Jesus's new order. I believe it is real and true. But there are days that test my belief, there are events that cause me doubt, and there are statements of political reality by those who say that the only world we have is the realpolitik of the one that already exists—and everything else is a dream for children.

That's when I need to say, alongside Puddleglum, that our dreams are worth more than their realities, and that those dreams are better than

16. Lewis, *The Silver Chair*, Kindle edition, locations 1854–62.

what they want us to settle for. Sometimes it's hard to keep believing in the dream. Some days you wonder if the dream is really true. But the decision to believe the dream, even on the days when you wonder if it is true, is what keeps the hope of the dream alive. And living the dream is the best way to live anyway, even on the days when I am not sure it is true. The decision to live by the dream is the way to keep going until the days come when you know again that the dream is true. For that, I need my Teacher to help me remember and walk along beside me. That is what will inspire me to keep living the vision I believe in.

And religious or not, that is the kind of inspiration we all need in order to protect, create, and develop our visions for the common good.

Back to the Real World

When I came home from retreat, I was astonished at how much my own world seemed different to me. In particular, I noticed the incredible stress of the life that we live in Washington, DC. The day after I returned, I took my boys to school. The behavior of people exhibited a level of stress that I was much more sensitive to than usual. I saw more clearly than I usually do people rushing and pushing, jumping ahead of one another, speeding off with dismissive and even rude gestures and words. Letting drivers get just a few seconds ahead of me with a smile or wave seemed to ironically change people's attitudes and composure.

After the school drop-offs, I went for a routine appointment at our medical clinic. Again, the stress was apparent to me everywhere among both patients and staff. Just holding the elevator door open for two elderly and slow-moving women coming in from the parking lot seemed to change their whole morning. Asking staff how they were doing first, before telling them what I needed, seemed to bring them to life with bright eyes and sincere expressions of thanks.

All these gestures, which were small but made all the difference in the moment, made me realize how caught up in that daily stress we all are, and that I could easily be drawn into it again after a few days back in "the real world." The culture shock I was experiencing was taking place not after six months in the monastery but only seven days and nights! Yet it was striking how different everything seemed after just a week away from the normal routines in Washington, DC.

What the "real" world *is* is the big question here. Jesus says that the kingdom of God is the real world, and it is trying to change this one. Aslan says that Narnia is real and not just magic. And the Living Teacher is at our side, helping us to live as kingdom people in this world so that it might be changed. Our trusted connection and interaction with the Teacher is the most important thing we have. And the compelling power of that relationship is what can change all of us, whether we are from conservative or liberal churches or no church at all.

··· 3 ···

Who Jesus Is and Why It Matters

Precious Lord, take my hand, / lead me on, let me stand.

—Gospel hymn by Thomas Dorsey[1]

Jesus did not come just to save our souls. The Jesus I was told about as a child was quite different from the one I met later, years after leaving my childhood church. As much as we loved the Bible in the congregation my parents helped to found, we somehow missed the central message of the New Testament, the message that Jesus called "the kingdom of God." Jesus's *gospel of the kingdom* is much more than the gospel I was raised with, which I will call the *atonement-only gospel*—a message that was mostly about how I could get to heaven and not about a new order that had come to change the world and me with it.

The question is, why did Jesus come? The answer is, of course, fundamental for Christians. But it could also be of great interest to all who want to understand the true meaning of their nation's and the world's

1. Thomas A. Dorsey (1899–1993), "Precious Lord, Take My Hand"; melody by George Nelson Allen (1812–77).

largest religion. Are we getting it right? What would be the implication if we weren't, and, even more important, what might happen if we did get it right?

If we are asking why Jesus came, it makes sense to see what he said himself and what the New Testament says. So let's begin there. And because faith always has a lot to do with each of our stories, I will tell mine in relation to the question of why Jesus came.

Why Jesus Came

When he came to Nazareth, where he had been brought up, he went to the synagogue on the Sabbath day, as was his custom. He stood up and read, and the scroll of the prophet Isaiah was given to him. He unrolled the scroll and found the place where it was written:

> The Spirit of the Lord is upon me,
>   because he has anointed me
>   to bring good news to the poor.
> He has sent me to proclaim release to the captives
>   and recovery of sight to the blind,
>   to let the oppressed go free,
>   to proclaim the year of the Lord's favor. (Luke 4:16–19)

> The people who sat in darkness
>   have seen a great light,
> and for those who sat in the region and shadow of death
>   light has dawned.

From that time Jesus began to proclaim, "Repent, for the kingdom of heaven has come near."

As he walked by the Sea of Galilee, he saw two brothers, Simon, who is called Peter, and Andrew his brother, casting a net into the sea—for they were fishermen. And he said to them, "Follow me, and I will make you fish for people." Immediately they left their nets and followed him. (Matt. 4:16–20)

When Jesus saw the crowds, he went up the mountain; and after he sat down, his disciples came to him. Then he began to speak, and taught them, saying:

"Blessed are the poor in spirit, for theirs is the kingdom of heaven.

"Blessed are those who mourn, for they will be comforted.

"Blessed are the meek, for they will inherit the earth.

"Blessed are those who hunger and thirst for righteousness, for they will be filled.

"Blessed are the merciful, for they will receive mercy.

"Blessed are the pure in heart, for they will see God.

"Blessed are the peacemakers, for they will be called children of God.

"Blessed are those who are persecuted for righteousness' sake, for theirs is the kingdom of heaven.

"Blessed are you when people revile you and persecute you and utter all kinds of evil against you falsely on my account. Rejoice and be glad, for your reward is great in heaven, for in the same way they persecuted the prophets who were before you." (Matt. 5:1–12)

These are the words Jesus spoke at the outset of his ministry. When Jesus chose the text from Isaiah 61 to read in the temple, he was announcing his mission, as recorded in the Luke 4 text. These were the first public words out of his mouth, his first sermon, his first public appearance, his opening gig, and his mission statement. I've always called it his "Nazareth manifesto." Very clearly, justice would be at the center of his mission. He came to "bring good news to the poor." The root of the Greek verb Jesus uses there for "good news" is *evangel*, from which we get the words "evangelize" and "evangelical"; Jesus's movement was to be based on *proclaiming the good news*. Without a doubt, Jesus's gospel was always to be good news for the poor. Therefore, any of our gospels that are not good news to poor and vulnerable people clearly fall short of what Jesus proclaimed in his opening statement about why he came. In other words, any gospel that is not good news to the poor is simply not the gospel of Jesus Christ.

The promise of justice and freedom for those who are oppressed or enslaved is at the core of the Nazareth proclamation of Jesus's mission. Captives of all kinds would welcome this, as would all those who suffered under the burdens of injustice. Giving sight to the blind carries both literal and spiritual meaning, as Jesus's next steps reveal.

Evangelical theologian Scot McKnight says, "Jesus thought he was anointed by God to proclaim the gospel to the poor and to proclaim freedom for prisoners and recovered sight for the blind and to set the oppressed free. *This is why he came.* These are his words. Jesus got his job description from Isaiah. What Isaiah predicted would happen is what Jesus is saying he is doing. It's his mission."[2]

The Matthew 4 text, like the one in Luke 4, comes at the outset of Jesus's ministry. This is the beginning of his public life, so what he starts with is certainly important. In this Gospel text, the book of Isaiah is again invoked to prophesy about a people living in darkness who are about to experience a great light.

And the very first thing Jesus does is announce that his coming is literally the beginning of a new order of things called the *kingdom of heaven*, or the kingdom of God. Jesus was the herald of a whole new way of living that was, from the start, meant to change the world; and he called people to join that change, beginning with their own lives.

"Repent" here is the Greek word *metanoeite*, which doesn't mean feel "guilty" or "sorry" but rather "turn around"—you are going in the wrong direction and you need to make an about-face. Jesus was saying, "Turn around, for the kingdom of God is at hand." A new order is breaking in, and it's time to set off in an entirely new direction.

The biblical assumption is that we are on the wrong path, heading in the wrong direction, away from God. The Scriptures refer to our self-determined course as walking in sin, darkness, blindness, dullness, sleep, and hardness of heart. To repent is to make a complete turn and take a new path. And throughout the New Testament, the kingdom of God is the central theme of the gospel story.

After announcing the breaking-through of the new order, Jesus goes right ahead and begins to call individuals to follow him. *Conversion of persons*, therefore, would also be central to this new order, this new way of life. Indeed, the earliest name for Christians was "the people of the way." And these simple fishermen, whom we would likely call working class today, were the first to be invited to join Jesus and his new

2. Scot McKnight, *One.Life: Jesus Calls, We Follow* (Grand Rapids: Zondervan, 2010), 64 (emphasis added).

46

order—to be completely changed by it, to experience a transformation so profound that John (another disciple) in his Gospel would later refer to it as a "new birth" (John 3:3–8).

No aspect of human existence—the personal, spiritual, social, economic, or political—is safe from this sweeping change. Everything must change. Our choice is whether we will offer our lives and our allegiance to the kingdom of God. And making that choice requires conversion.

This is not an add-on to personal spirituality or private piety meant to merely enhance one's life. These Galileans were called to give up everything else to follow Jesus, and the Gospels report that those who were called "left their nets," their former way of life and their previous work and vocations, to follow Jesus. A new order has arrived, and if we want to participate in it, we will need to be converted to the One who brings it.

The Charter of the New Order

As the audience was beginning to swell in response to Jesus's teaching, he went up a hill, his disciples followed him, and he began to teach them the meaning of this new order. The Beatitudes and the Sermon on the Mount are the charter of the kingdom of God, the Magna Carta or constitution of the kingdom; they are the *instruction manual* for living in the new age.

In fact, the Beatitudes and the Sermon were used by the early church to instruct all new converts in what it meant to follow Jesus and enter into his kingdom. It was the church's most basic course or catechism, The Gospel 101. These radical teachings were never simply for a certain age or time; they are meant to describe and define our lives right here and right now. Yes, the kingdom has come, and yes, it has yet to be fulfilled in history. It is therefore "already" and "not yet," meant to be lived now by those who follow Jesus as a sign and community and catalyst for the new order.

Much has been written on the Beatitudes and the Sermon on the Mount, and all of that commentary should be the subject of continual study and devotion by believers.[3] It is the place to begin to understand the kingdom of God. Here is my brief summary:

3. For more on these passages, see J. H. Yoder, *The Politics of Jesus* (Grand Rapids: Eerdmans, 1972); C. Jordan, *The Cotton Patch Version of Matthew and John* (New York:

Blessed are the poor in spirit, for theirs is the kingdom of heaven.

Luke's version of the Sermon on the Mount sayings simply has "blessed are you who are poor" (Luke 6:20); so, taking Matthew and Luke together, the kingdom will become a blessing to those who are afflicted by both material and spiritual poverty. The physical oppression of the poor will be a regular subject in this kingdom (as Jesus's "Nazareth manifesto" also made clear), but the spiritual impoverishment of even the affluent will also be addressed and healed. In affluent churches and countries, the Beatitudes' focus on the materially and physically poor is often a threat and even an embarrassment, but the consistent biblical imperative cannot be denied. For the biblical writers, spiritual poverty is often the result of having too much affluence and no longer depending on God. But the message is holistic in the Gospels of Matthew and Luke—Jesus offers blessings and healing to those who are both poor and poor in spirit.

Blessed are those who mourn, for they will be comforted.

Those who have the capacity to mourn and weep for the world, those who have the compassion to care, will be comforted by the coming of this new order. What we call "empathy" is perceived not as a weakness in Jesus's new way of living but rather as one of its most important strengths. Of course, Jesus's disciples would later hear him say that to love their neighbor as themselves was one of the two great commandments (Matt. 22:39; Mark 12:31; Luke 10:27). To be able to feel the pain of the world is to participate in the very heart of God. The compassionate response of God's people to human suffering is one of their defining characteristics.

Blessed are the meek, for they will inherit the earth.

It will be the humble, not the haughty, who will be the favored ones here; this kingdom turns our understanding of the logic of power and who's on top upside down. Mary's Song, called the Magnificat, promises the same when she prays about what the coming of her son means: "he has scattered the proud . . . brought down the powerful from their thrones . . . lifted up the lowly . . . filled the hungry with good things,

---

Association Press, 1970); and G. Stassen and D. Gushee, *Kingdom Ethics: Following Jesus in Contemporary Context* (Downers Grove, IL: InterVarsity, 2003).

and sent the rich away empty" (Luke 1:51–53). And when Jesus is asked by his disciples who will be first in his kingdom, he tells them it will be the servants of all. Humility is one of the most underappreciated values in our intensely competitive culture, economy, and politics.

Blessed are those who hunger and thirst for righteousness, for they will be filled.

To be hungry for "righteousness," a word in the Scriptures that is often synonymous with "justice," will be a leading characteristic of Jesus's new order. While religion has often covered up and even benefited from injustice, this kind of faith will overcome it. Justice—social, economic, racial, and gender—is at the core of the kingdom of God. Those who love the kingdom will both seek and pursue it. And those who long for the presence of justice, who are hungry and thirsty for it, demonstrate that they belong to a God who promises it.

Blessed are the merciful, for they will receive mercy.

Those who have the grace to show mercy and forgiveness will be an example now. If you want to be shown mercy, or if you need to be forgiven for anything (and who doesn't, in all honesty?), the only way to receive it is to also offer it, says Jesus. In a world of such enormous pain and violence, and all the hurt and scars that come from it, it is critically necessary for us to learn the ethics of forgiveness—a key to this kingdom. There is no way that all our conflicts and sins against each other can be rectified in this very human world, but those who have learned to forgive by practicing "truth and reconciliation"[4] herald the coming of the kingdom of God.

Blessed are the pure in heart, for they will see God.

"Pure in heart" is another way to say "having integrity," something that seems to be sorely lacking in cultures that encourage us to get away

---

4. Two biblical words used in naming the South African Truth and Reconciliation Commission, which put forgiveness into practice after the incredible injustice and violence of the apartheid regime—a practice that likely prevented the prospect of great retaliatory violence. Forgiveness, but not the weak kind that obstructs the truth, is always a herald of the kingdom of God.

49

with anything we can. We long for people who have an inner quality of truthfulness, honesty, goodness, and honor. We want to trust them because we know we can depend on them. And they will be both admired and trusted in this kingdom. Little is more countercultural in our society than to teach such integrity to our children, and nothing will better demonstrate the quality of true leadership. Such leadership is the only kind that will be trusted today.

Blessed are the peacemakers, for they will be called children of God.

Conflict is found in every corner of our world, and violence is the habitual way of resolving our grievances and disputes. Even being "for" or "against" wars becomes just another confrontation. What we need most are not just *peace lovers*, who talk against all the violence, but *peacemakers*, who actually learn how to resolve our endless and inevitable human conflicts without recourse to such destructive methods. The practices of conflict resolution are urgently needed in both our personal and political battlegrounds and will be the only way to break the tragic cycle of violence. In this new order, those who show the skills, behaviors, disciplines, and courage of peacemaking will have the honor of being called "children of God."

Blessed are those who are persecuted for righteousness' sake, for theirs is the kingdom of heaven.

There is always a special and honored place for those who are persecuted or who end up giving their lives for the cause of right. We remember them as our heroes, and our children look up to them as role models. Even in death, their spirits seem to live on and inspire others to follow in their steps. Those who are persecuted for the sake of what is right and just will inherit the kingdom, says Jesus.

Blessed are you when people revile you and persecute you and utter all kinds of evil against you falsely on my account. Rejoice and be glad, for your reward is great in heaven, for in the same way they persecuted the prophets who were before you.

The assumption is that if you live by Jesus's new order, you will be persecuted for it—by all those who feel threatened and challenged by its values and practices. You may be reviled, attacked, and falsely accused of many things, all on account of Jesus and his kingdom. But don't worry, you will find good company with the biblical prophets, who were often persecuted for proclaiming the word of God. Instead, rejoice and be glad, for you will be rewarded by God for such good and world-changing behavior.

The rest of Matthew 5, 6, and 7 is all the Sermon on the Mount. Its words are among the most elegant in all of Scripture and show how the kingdom that Jesus brings will turn the world upside down. And those who truly follow it will become the "salt of the earth" and "the light of the world" (Matt. 5:13, 14). Jesus comes not to "abolish" the law and the prophets who came before but to "fulfill" them (Matt. 5:17). Over and over, we hear him say, "You have heard it said . . . but I say to you,"[5] and then take everything said before to a new and much deeper level. He connects anger with murder. He brings moral clarity to personal choices like adultery, lust, and divorce, and in ways that especially protect women. His instructions about retaliation call for revolutionary tactics of nonviolent resistance, and he follows that by giving us the most radical command ever—to love our enemies.

Prayer and giving are to be done quietly, before God, not in a trumpeting of piety and philanthropy. Where we have invested our "treasure" will show where our "heart" truly is (Matt. 6:21): either on earth or in heaven. And don't worry so much about what you eat, drink, or wear, or how you look; in other words, pay absolutely no attention to the entire message of modern advertising. "Look at the birds of the air. . . . Consider the lilies of the field," and see how "your heavenly Father" looks after them (Matt. 6:26, 28). Don't "strive for all these things," but do trust God, and "strive first for the kingdom of God" (Matt. 6:32–33). And remember the key choice Jesus gives us here: "You cannot serve God and wealth" (Matt. 6:24). A serious look at these teachings would turn most churches upside down, not to mention Wall Street and the economy, which is likely why these teachings are seldom seriously studied, even in our congregations.

5. E.g., Matt. 5:21–22, 27–28, 33–34, 38–39, 43–44.

We are also told in this sermon not to judge others, so that we won't be judged in the same way—advice that would save our religious communities a lot of time and effort. And then we are confronted by the most chilling challenge to hypocrisy ever written: "Why do you see the speck in your neighbor's eye, but do not notice the log in your own eye?" (Matt. 7:3).

The Sermon also contains what was later named "the Golden Rule": "In everything do to others as you would have them do to you" (Matt. 7:12). There has likely never been a better formula for the common good spoken or written in history.

Jesus warns against false prophets who will come to us as wolves in sheep's clothing. He suggests we evaluate so-called prophets by what they do and how they live, not just by what they say. And he says not everyone who calls him "Lord" will enter into this kingdom. In fact, Jesus tells us, there is a broad gate and easy road that leads to destruction, but "the road is hard that leads to life, and there are few that find it" (Matt. 7:14).

The Sermon concludes by predicting that those who don't heed these words of Jesus are like foolish people who build their houses on sand; they will be blown away when the storms of life come. But, he says, "everyone . . . who hears these words of mine and acts on them will be like a wise man who built his house on rock. The rain fell, the floods came, and the winds blew and beat on that house, but it did not fall, because it had been founded on rock" (Matt. 7:24–25).

Of course, the Sermon on the Mount contains the Lord's Prayer, which many churches ritually repeat every Sunday in worship liturgies. But do we really listen to it, believe it, take it seriously, or honestly act on what it says? "Your kingdom come. Your will be done, on earth as it is in heaven" (Matt. 6:10). That's what Jesus asks us to pray—for his kingdom to come "*on earth* as it is in heaven." That means now, in this life, in this world—in our lives, families, churches, neighborhoods, and nations.

The Personal Stories of Theology

The biblical texts I cited above are Scriptures I heard almost nothing about in all my formative years in church. And the commentary I just offered on them was never even vaguely discussed in any sermon or Sunday school lesson I received. The fact that many other Christians in the second half of the twentieth century could say the same thing points to a very serious theological and spiritual crisis in our church history. While the kingdom of God is central to the New Testament, it was never central in the churches that many of us grew up in. Instead, in our conservative churches, *the gospel of the kingdom* was replaced by an *atonement-only gospel*.

Let me try to reveal that tragic story by telling my own.

Four decades after leaving my seminary, I went back there for a debate on the question, "Is social justice an essential part of the gospel and the mission of the church?"[6] Trinity Evangelical Divinity School is a very "evangelical" school and one, like many other evangelical institutions, that is trying to correct mistakes of the past.

It was great to be back at the place where our *Sojourners* magazine and movement had begun. I still have many fond and powerful memories from those days when we were young seminarians wrestling with these very issues of social justice and the church's mission. I looked out over a packed chapel and was told that this Trinity Debate had the largest audience of any in ten years.

I was debating a leader from the Southern Baptist Convention who is a seminary president. I argued yes, that justice is *integral* to the gospel, while he said no. Dr. Albert Mohler argued that social justice was important but that "the gospel" was the atonement brought about in Christ that saves us from our sins and secures our souls for heaven. It was a very civil and respectful conversation because Al and I know each other and because both of us wanted to demonstrate a kind of discourse different from what now prevails in our culture and politics. But we did disagree, and our disagreement is at the heart of very different visions today for the future of the church. The big question is, what is the gospel?

I spoke about the "gospel of the kingdom," outlined in Jesus's initial proclamations in Matthew 4 and Luke 4, with the meaning of the

---

6. Jim Wallis and Dr. R. Albert Mohler, "Is Social Justice an Essential Part of the Mission of the Church?," The Trinity Debates, October 27, 2011, http://www.henrycenter.org /programs/trinity-debates/.

kingdom then elaborated in Matthew 5, 6, and 7 in the Sermon on the Mount—just as I have discussed it above. I believe that Jesus's own words are very clear when it comes to answering the question posed at the Trinity Debate.

Dr. Mohler said he agreed with everything I was saying about the biblical imperatives for justice, but that it was only an *implication* of the gospel and not the gospel per se. The gospel, he said, is about the singular issue of substitutionary atonement and personal redemption outlined in the Pauline Epistles.

I find Paul's later teachings on justification by faith fully consistent with and complementary to Jesus's gospel of the kingdom. But I agree with Paul himself that we should interpret Paul in light of Jesus, and not Jesus in light of Paul. Thus, for me, "social justice" is integral to the meaning of the gospel—a holistic message that includes both personal salvation and social transformation. This is the gospel of the kingdom, not an atonement-only gospel. In the latter, it almost seems that Jesus wasted his first three years with all those teachings, parables, and healings. He might have just gone straight to the cross to make atonement for our sins. In that case, why worry about this world? Why not just focus on heaven?

Red and Yellow, Black and White, They Are Precious in His Sight

I shared with the young Trinity seminarians the story of my evangelical church's "atonement-only gospel." I thought that, as part of a new generation of evangelicals, they might be looking for something different from what I was raised with and what was very prominent in my own seminary years.

I still vividly recall being put on the front row one Sunday night when our church hosted a revival preacher. I was there because all the "unsaved" kids had to be, and my parents were concerned that I had yet to be "saved," as I was getting up in years. I was six.

It felt like the fiery evangelist was pointing his finger right at me when he said, "If Christ came back tonight, your mommy and daddy would be taken to heaven, and YOU would be left ALL BY YOURSELF" (emphasis added based on how it sounded to me at the time). He got my attention. I knew I had a problem if that were to happen: I would be a six-year-old with a five-year-old sister to support. My mom was good at fixing things, so I went to her. As was her way, she didn't tell me about the wrath of God, but that God loved me and wanted me to be his child.

That all sounded pretty good to me, so I signed up. It wasn't very deep, but it was real enough for a six-year-old child. After "adult baptism" when I was eight, I went through the usual evangelical church pilgrimage: church every Sunday all day, Sunday school, vacation Bible school, summer Bible camp, and eventually the youth group. I was very good at "sword drill" competitions, in which the object was to see who could most quickly find a Bible verse and read it aloud. And every Sunday night, I was usually the youngest at the men's prayer meetings before the evening service, which got me lots of pats on the back and hopes for my future spiritual leadership.

But when I reached my teenage years, other questions began to grow inside of me. Mostly they were questions about what was happening outside of me and outside of our church in the city of Detroit. My hometown, the Motor City, was completely segregated and deeply divided by race—and the tensions were on the rise. In my Sunday school, they had taught us kids a song whose lyrics went, "Jesus loves the little children, all the children of the world; red and yellow, black and white, they are precious in his sight; Jesus loves the little children of the world."

But the only children in our sight were white kids; we never saw any black people at all, except when we would pass by them downtown and my grandmother would have us wash our hands afterward. I had heard there were black churches in Detroit, but we never went to them or knew much about them. We also never had a black preacher or even a black choir in our all-white church.

We were called the Plymouth Brethren, a small evangelical group that came to America after breaking off from the Church of England many years ago. We believed that most other churches were likely not really Christian, but the closest to us were probably the Baptists. Plymouth

Brethren didn't have ordained ministers but relied on laypeople to lead and preach.

My father was the head "elder" and pastor in our church. He was an engineer and businessman for Detroit Edison but rose every day early in the morning to read and study his Bible before we all got up for work and school. My mother—really a pastor too, if you count taking care of everybody as the role of a pastor—couldn't be recognized in any official church leadership role because she was a woman. (But her memorial service was the largest event in our church's history, rivaled only by my father's several years later.)

I learned that there were actually black Plymouth Brethren churches in Detroit, but we were never told anything about them. We loved the same Jesus, read from the same Bible, and sang from the same hymnals (though we never sounded as good as they did). They knew about us, but we didn't know about them.

I began asking questions about the things I was hearing and reading. Why were there hungry people in Detroit? Why were so many black people poor? Why were there so many black men in jail? Why were we all so separate? Why didn't we know any black Christians or ever go to their churches or have any of them come to ours? And who was this minister in the South named King? What was he up to?

The questions led to trouble, as questions from young people often do, and nobody wanted to or could answer them. We lived in a white suburb, but I began to go into the city by myself when I could. I eventually found some of those black Christians and churches, who took me in and began to answer some of my questions. Then I started to take jobs in the city to save money for college, alongside young black men who were using their salaries to help their families survive. We began to talk to each other, as young people do, about our lives. And I began to understand that we had been born and raised in different countries, even if we lived in the same city.

I was discovering that something was terribly wrong in my city and my country. So I pressured my church elders to have a church meeting to discuss the problem, and after a long time, they finally agreed. They asked me to take the "side" of the blacks, and they had some church elders defend the way things were. I studied hard, learned lots of facts, and read the Bible where it seemed to apply. But it didn't matter. The church meeting did not go well, and the majority opinion was that blacks had to "pull themselves up by their own bootstraps," as all of "us" had done. "Would you really want your sister to marry one?" was the question I most remembered. Nobody except me mentioned the Bible much or cared much when I did.

The culminating conversation came when a church elder later took me aside and said, "Son, you have to understand that Christianity has nothing to do with racism; that's political, and our faith is personal." I think that was the night that I left my church—at least in my head and heart—and, after a little more time, I was off to university and away from my childhood faith and church, much to my liking and to theirs. I found my new home in the civil rights and student movements of my generation. My old church members weren't "political," they said, but most were against the civil rights movement and ministers like Dr. Martin Luther King Jr.

So what happened was this: a young Christian became slowly aware of the momentous moral issues of justice and injustice that surrounded him, his nation, and his church. He tried to apply his faith to them, but the church shut that down. He wanted to change the world *because* of his faith. But the church told him that faith was not supposed to change the world, just to change *us* and get us to heaven.

The great lesson I learned from all that, many years later after coming back to faith, is a message I now say over and over again: *God is personal but never private.* I believe in a God who wants relationship with every one of us and then wants to sign us up for God's purposes in the world. And ever since, I have been distrustful of private gospels and theologies that refuse to address the world and its need to be changed.

The theology that deals only with the atonement, one of personal salvation and the life hereafter, was the theology of both my Plymouth Brethren church and Al Mohler's Southern Baptist church. Both churches, mine and his, missed the greatest moral issue of our time. We missed the civil rights movement, and most of our white Christian brothers and sisters were on the wrong side of it.

When a church gets something that big that wrong, it certainly raises very deep questions about its theology. The theology of our churches made the church complicit with white racism, opposed to the civil rights movement, and completely unsupportive of our brothers and sisters in the black church. That enormous moral failure drove me and many other young people away from the churches and faith of our childhoods.

At our debate Dr. Mohler admitted that his Southern Baptist tradition had failed on the issue of race and had been on the wrong side of the civil rights movement. He also affirmed the role and leadership of the black churches in America, just as I had. But he said the gospel was still about atonement, and we just needed to do a better job of making the *implications* of the gospel clearer—helping Christians become disciples committed to social justice, along with their primary preaching of personal salvation.

The Gospel of the Kingdom versus the Atonement-Only Gospel

I came back to my faith only after reading Matthew and Luke and discovering the gospel of the kingdom, which wasn't just about "me and the Lord" but about a new order breaking in to change the world and us with it—an integral gospel inclusive of justice.

And my post-debate reflection was this: if the atonement-only gospel churches in America—like my Plymouth Brethren church and Dr. Mohler's Southern Baptist church—were on the wrong side of the civil rights movement and are still generally less involved in issues of justice, maybe something is wrong with their *theology* and not just their practice.

The same was true of white South African churches that also had an atonement-only definition of the gospel. They too were on the wrong side of justice and were the bulwarks of the brutally oppressive apartheid system. They were completely opposed to inspirational and prophetic Christian leaders such as Archbishop Desmond Tutu, just as white evangelicals in America were opposed to Rev. Martin Luther King Jr.

Conversely, the churches that have been on the side of justice, such as black churches both in the United States and South Africa, were always the ones to say that justice was *integral* to the meaning of the gospel and not just an *implication* of it. That should tell us something.

If justice is only an implication, it can easily become optional and, especially in privileged churches, almost nonexistent. In the New Testament, conversion happens in two movements: repentance and following, belief and obedience, faith and discipleship, personal conversion and social justice. It's all part of the biblical vision of conversion to the kingdom of God.

Atonement-only theology and its disciples are in serious jeopardy of missing the vision of justice at the heart of the kingdom of God. Their gospel is simply too small, too narrow, too bifurcated, and ultimately too private. And, in the end, it is (as we evangelicals are prone to say) not *biblical*.

Here is what it comes down to. A gospel message that doesn't try to change the world and that concentrates only on individuals works only for those who don't *need* the world to be changed. Therefore, it ends up being too white, too privileged, too male, and too American.

Today, many in the worldwide evangelical movement are rejecting the atonement-only gospel. The clearest examples of this can be found in the global South, where "good news to the poor"[7] must be central to the gospel; in the international Lausanne movement, which advocates a holistic gospel; and in the World Evangelical Alliance as well as the National Association of Evangelicals, which both see poverty, creation care, and peacemaking as essential to the gospel and the mission of the church.

A new generation of evangelicals and young believers across theological boundaries is seeking a gospel that can change both them and the world, because they too have become aware of things in the world that tear at their hearts and cry out for their commitment, just as I did when I was their age. I know that feeling as a young believer, and I don't want the church to shut them down this time, as it did me. Rather,

7. Luke 4:18.

we need to welcome that energy and passion and say to them: Come, young brothers and sisters, and help us change the world, for the sake of Christ and his kingdom.

For God So Loved the World

It was "the world" that was missing in the church that I grew up in. The world never came up much, except for the constant exhortation not to be "worldly." Ironically, the biblical text most famous in our evangelical churches was from the Gospel of John, chapter 3, verse 16. These were the words of Jesus, too: "For God so loved the world that he gave his only Son, so that everyone who believes in him may not perish but may have eternal life." We've all seen John 3:16 signs held up in the end zones on televised football games—a witness of Christians to their favorite text. It was the first verse I ever memorized.

But somehow, all we got from that passage was assurance for our "eternal life" in heaven someday. And we missed the entire beginning of the text: "For God so loved the world." God loves the *world*. As already mentioned, Jesus also told us to pray these words: "Our Father in heaven, hallowed be your name. Your kingdom come. Your will be done, on earth as it is in heaven" (Matt. 6:9–10). I believe the life that Christ brings us is "eternal," but it is also for this world, this earth, right here and right now.

The crowd and conversation at Trinity Divinity School that night showed me again how much the evangelical movement is changing and how much my seminary had changed since I started there almost forty years ago. Too many churches today are still tragically split between those who stress conversion but have forgotten its goal and those who call for Christian social action but have forgotten the necessity of personal conversion. It's time for seminarians and pastors from both our evangelical and liberal churches to get this right. And a new generation may help do that.

All the ways the New Testament epistles and the early church described what happened on the cross must not be reduced to narrow teachings that avoid the reality and meaning of the kingdom of God.

Human sin is very real, as we have all painfully experienced and seen. Our selfish sins separate us from God, from others, and even from creation itself. And the consequence is indeed the reality of guilt and a spiritual death that affects us even now. But Christ comes to bring us back to life!

The Creator of all chose to make the sacrifice of his only Son to bear and forgive all the sins committed against a loving God, the rest of humanity, and the natural order. It is the most unbelievable and powerful story in all history. But how our great sin debt was overcome is part of what the New Testament calls the mystery of faith—"not some legal transaction that turns God into a combination of rigorous accountant and tough policeman," as a pastor friend of mine, Bob Smith, put it in his Bethel Bible class called "Jesus the Savior."

The word and image that most attracts me and stirs my imagination about that New Testament mystery of salvation is *reconciliation*. In his Second Epistle to the Corinthians, the apostle Paul says, "So if anyone is in Christ, there is a new creation: everything old has passed away; see, everything has become new! All this is from God, who reconciled us to himself through Christ, and has given us the ministry of reconciliation" (2 Cor. 5:17–18). In Christ, everything that has been broken and divided is reconciled, and now we are "ambassadors for Christ since God is making his appeal through us; we entreat you on behalf of Christ, be reconciled to God" (2 Cor. 5:20). I've talked to pastors, like Will Campbell from Tennessee, who used that text to minister to the most racist whites in the South, even during the heart of the civil rights movement. We are all sinners, said Will, and we can all be reconciled to God in Jesus Christ.

But this salvation is never just private. It runs from the personal to the cosmic in the New Testament. It saves us from our alienation and separation from God, from the power of sin and guilt, and from spiritual death; but it also saves from injustice, oppression, captivity, violence, and fear. And from a biblical perspective, salvation extends far beyond the personal, to seeing God acting in the world to redeem and restore the whole of creation—persons, relationships, institutions, and the natural environment itself.

This was always God's intention, and the coming of the kingdom in Jesus Christ is the pivotal event in that history. Paul describes the cosmic dimensions of salvation in one of my favorite texts:

> For the creation waits with eager longing for the revealing of the children of God . . . that the creation itself will be set free from its bondage to decay and will obtain the freedom of the glory of the children of God. We know that the whole creation has been groaning in labor pains until now; and not only the creation, but we ourselves. . . . For in hope we were saved. (Rom. 8:19–24)

Spiritual revival always begins with conversion. And the revivals I am most drawn to are the ones that aim their personal conversions at the changing of the world and the overcoming of the great injustices of their time. In fact, some church historians actually say that spiritual "renewal" doesn't get to be called "revival" *unless* it addresses the issues of the day—changing society as well as the hearts of its converts.

"Altar calls" were historically used by evangelists to call people to faith. Walking down the aisle to the "altar" to give your life to Christ was the practice. But in the eighteenth and nineteenth centuries, altar calls in both British and American revivals signed up their converts, on the spot, to join the abolitionist movement to end slavery! A renewal of faith brought black and white Christians into the civil rights movement and antiapartheid struggles in the United States and South Africa. Today, that engaged vision of faith is enlisting a new generation of believers in campaigns against global poverty, pandemic diseases, the exploitation of labor, and human sexual trafficking.

In the Bible and church history, conversion is always historically specific. What the gospel means in relationship to *our times and our issues* is always key. What we are *turning from and turning to* defines what we mean by the gospel.

Jesus's last words to his disciples are called the Great Commission. In it, he simply instructs them, "Go therefore and make disciples of all nations . . . teaching them to obey everything that I have commanded you. And remember, I am with you always, to the end of the age" (Matt.

28:19–20). We go out, teaching "all nations" about the kingdom of God and the new way of living Jesus has invited us into. We go out, teaching what he taught us—all those beatitudes and parables and lessons. And, as we go out into the world, the Teacher will always be with us.

···4···

Lord, Help Us to Treat You Well

Lord, we know you'll be coming through this line today; so help us to treat you well.

—Mary Glover, Washington, DC

So if Jesus is who he says he is, what does that mean, not only for Christians but also for the common good? And if the priorities of the new order he came to bring—the kingdom of God—are so different from those of the other kingdoms of the world, how might that new order help change those other kingdoms?

One of the key gospel texts that helps answer those questions is from the twenty-fifth chapter of Matthew's Gospel.

Matthew 25 may have the most challenging message in the Bible, and it was also my conversion text. Reading this passage as a university student brought me back to Jesus Christ and to my faith as a Christian. It is the text that rises above politics and calls us all to something greater than what is merely in our own self-interest. Its focus on caring for the poorest and most vulnerable is a key indicator of our own faithfulness to the gospel, and it is the central principle of the faith community's role in politics. It is also the way we can come together across our other theological and political boundaries and best serve the common good. The words of Jesus in this Scripture are the test we must put to all the leaders of the world who easily forget "the least of these" (Matt. 25:40).

In this chapter I will offer two very contemporary and significant examples of how this text is both confronting and changing traditional politics, and of the faith community's role in that change. In very important and hopeful ways, a growing unity among religious leaders in protecting the most vulnerable is causing political leaders to take notice and make public policy changes that serve those on the margins. Both of these examples are very real and in the news and will affect people's lives for years to come.

But let's first read the whole text and then unpack it.

A Conversion

When the Son of Man comes in his glory, and all the angels with him, then he will sit on the throne of his glory. All the nations will be gathered before him, and he will separate people one from another as a shepherd separates the sheep from the goats, and he will put the sheep at his right hand and the goats at the left. Then the king will say to those at his right hand, "Come, you that are blessed by my Father, inherit the kingdom prepared for you from the foundation of the world; for I was hungry and you gave me food, I was thirsty and you gave me something to drink, I was a stranger and you welcomed me, I was naked and you gave me clothing, I was sick and you took care of me, I was in prison and you visited me." Then the righteous will answer him, "Lord, when was it that we saw you hungry and gave you food, or thirsty and gave you something to drink? And when was it that we saw you a stranger and welcomed you, or naked and gave you clothing? And when was it that we saw you sick or in prison and visited you?" And the king will answer them, "Truly I tell you, just as you did it to one of the least of these who are members of my family, you did it to me." Then he will say to those at his left hand, "You that are accursed, depart from me into the eternal fire prepared for the devil and his angels; for I was hungry and you gave me no food, I was thirsty and you gave me nothing to drink, I was a stranger and you did not welcome me, naked and you did not give me clothing, sick and in prison and you did not visit me." Then they also will answer, "Lord, when was it that we saw you hungry or thirsty or a stranger or naked or sick or in prison, and did not take care of you?" Then he will answer them, "Truly I tell you, just as you did not do it to one of the least of these, you did not do it to me." And these will go away into eternal punishment, but the righteous into eternal life. (Matt. 25:31–46)

I was deeply involved in the student movements of my generation and was right in the midst of them when I discovered this Scripture. Race, poverty, and war were our passions. I found my vocation and honed my skills as an activist in the civil rights and antiwar movements of the late sixties and early seventies. I still remember how it felt in Michigan, and at my own Michigan State University, where we had the capacity to bring ten thousand people to the streets in just a few hours. Our marches down Michigan Avenue from campus led us right to the state's capitol dome in Lansing. During my college years, we drew people from all over the state to join us in our student-led protests. I led marches alongside university presidents, state legislators, and moms with kids. Often along the way, elementary school teachers would bring their young students out to the sidewalk and cheer us on as we passed by. We aimed our protests at the powers that be—and the federal government in particular—on behalf of people who were poor, who were experiencing racial discrimination, and who were the victims of the war in Vietnam.

But the student movement was not answering all of my personal, spiritual, or even political questions. And it didn't provide an adequate basis or strong foundation for the life of an activist to which I was being drawn. Like many of my generation, I was now reading beyond Martin Luther King Jr. to authors like Franz Fanon, Che Guevara, Ho Chi Minh, and, yes, Karl Marx. Their searing critique of the structures of oppression was compelling, but to me they lacked convincing solutions, had insufficient philosophical assumptions, and had no spiritual foundations or undergirding. And when I saw some of the results of the movements and governments that had embraced the ideologies of Marxism, I wasn't impressed or convinced that they held the way forward. Indeed, they created new injustices and terrible tyrannies.

But the witness of the campus Christian groups was not compelling either, at least to me. I remember helping organize an antiwar rally held at "the rock," a central gathering place outside the MSU Student Union. Stirring speeches were given and lots of enthusiasm was to be found on that sunny afternoon. I had just stepped down from the stage when several of our "marshals" brought a couple of students to me backstage. "We found these Christians being parasites on our rally, passing out their reactionary leaflets, and we think we should beat the hell out of them!" I gently reminded our marshals that they were supposed to be "peacekeepers" and that we were leading a "peace movement," and I suggested they leave the trembling Christians and their leaflets with me.

I asked the Christian students who they were and what they were trying to do that day. "We are from Campus Crusade for Christ," they said, "and we are here to say that real peace is through Jesus." I actually understood them better than they might have imagined because of my own religious background, but I asked, "What is your position on the war in Vietnam?" To which they replied, "Real peace is through Jesus!" This went back and forth for a while, with me posing questions about the war and them replying with their slogan about real peace through Jesus. Finally, I asked how they felt about the three hundred civilians killed that day, and every day, in Vietnam by US warplanes. One of them replied, "I think we should bomb those Communists to hell!" And so I learned what "real peace through Jesus" actually meant—at least to them.

I also met some more moderate evangelical Christians from Inter-Varsity Christian Fellowship, who assured me that they were "praying about the war." But apparently they never finished their prayers about the war in Vietnam because they never joined our protests or took the pro-war side. They kept praying and stayed neutral. There were a few liberal campus ministers who would occasionally come up to me and say something like, "You are the real church, and you can use our facilities for your events!" But we were not "the real church," and we had many questions—personal, philosophical, and even theological—and nobody to talk to about them.

While I had left my childhood faith and church behind (or they had left me), I had never quite gotten shed of Jesus. And in hindsight, he never got shed of me. So after a particularly intense period of activism that included the national student strike in the spring of 1970, I began to read through the New Testament again—quietly and privately.

First, I was startled by the upside-down kingdom of the Sermon on the Mount, found in Matthew 5–7, which we discussed in the last chapter. And I wondered why in the world I had never heard a sermon on that sermon—*ever*—in my evangelical church. But it was reading the twenty-fifth chapter of Matthew that led to my dramatic conversion to Christ. Again, I hadn't remembered any reference to that Scripture in my entire church upbringing. But there it was, and as I read this text over and over again, it astonished me—and then converted me. I decided I wanted to follow this Jesus.

The Journey Back to Faith Goes through the Poor

What Jesus says in Matthew 25 reverses the logic of the world. It is the common and unquestioned practice of humanity to treat those at the top of the world's pyramids of wealth and power with the greatest deference and respect (or fear) and grant them the most influence. It is even the most common practice in most of our churches and religious institutions. We all know this.

Modern presidents of the United States are all millionaires; most senators are millionaires too, and all are dependent on millionaire donors (and members of Congress are moving in the same direction). All of our political campaigns are now controlled by money, and mere handfuls of incredibly wealthy people decide which candidates and campaigns will be viable. The Occupy movement has focused our attention on the top 1 percent who rule our economic structures; today the enormous gaps between the top and the bottom (and even the middle) of our societies continue to grow. When CEOs make five hundred times as much as their average workers, it's clear that the logic of the world remains intact about whom we regard as the most important.

Of course, the celebrities, entertainers, athletes, and now even the daily media personalities who command our cultural attention are all multimillionaires too, and their way of life is held up for the rest of us to watch and envy. Even in our churches, who are the most influential members? Are they the poorest and neediest or the ones with the money to keep the institutions going? And how many religious leaders are best known for their focus on poverty?

Matthew 25 completely reverses this worldly logic. Read it carefully. Jesus says that the way we treat those who are "the least of these" will be regarded as the way we treat *him*! I was stunned when I read that for the first time, and four decades later I still am. The Son of God, sitting in judgment, as the text says, is instructing his followers and separating them like sheep and goats on the basis of how they treat those at the *bottom* of their societies. "I was hungry," says Jesus. "I was thirsty." "I was a stranger." "I was naked," meaning "stripped" of everything. "I was sick." "I was in prison." Therefore, says the Son of God with earthshaking clarity, *As you have done, or not done, to them, you have done, or not done, to me*. In effect, *I will know how much you love me by how you treat them*. A paraphrase of the text in Eugene Peterson's *The Message* summarizes it well: "I was hungry . . . I was thirsty . . . I was homeless . . . I was shivering . . . Sick and in prison. . . . Whenever you failed to do one of these things to someone who was being overlooked or ignored, that was me—you failed to do it to me" (Matt. 25:41–43, 45 Message).

There are very few passages of *judgment* in the New Testament, but this is one of them. Jesus, unlike our religious institutions, continually speaks out against *judgmentalism*. But the only time Jesus is judgmental himself is on the subject of the poor. I still find that extraordinary. That is very good news for the poor, news that, as I pointed out in the last chapter, is central to the mission Jesus announced in his Nazareth manifesto.

And it's clear from the text that all those who are listening to Jesus, the sheep and the goats, *actually believe they are his followers*. These are not unbelievers or his opponents. They regard themselves as his adherents and supporters, and they will someday be shocked by what he will say to them. "When did we see *you* hungry, or thirsty, or without clothes, or a stranger, or sick, or in prison!" they will gasp incredulously. "We didn't know that it was *you*! Had we known it was you, we would have done something; but we just didn't know it was you that we ignored! We didn't know those people were important—and especially so important to you."

It is also very significant that the text uses the term "nations" to describe those who are gathered for judgment before the Son of Man. The Scripture clearly has massive implications for any who believe they are followers of Jesus, but it isn't just addressed to individuals. "Nations" are also being held accountable. This is, of course, not about "nation-states," which are a more modern development, but rather people groups or tribes, which were common at the time. Therefore this is about not merely individual decisions alone but also corporate or collective ones made by "nations" about who or what is most important.

Jesus's response to the shocked listeners is not very forgiving here; he doesn't just tell them all to try and do better next time, now that they know it was also he whom they were treating so badly. Instead, he separates these would-be followers into two groups, the sheep and the goats, and, depending on their treatment of the least of these, sends them to "eternal life" or "eternal punishment." That's extraordinarily strong. Let's be clear that Christ's judgment here is not about having the wrong doctrine or theology; it's not about sexual misdeeds or other misbehaviors, or any other personal sin or failure. The everlasting judgment here is based on how we have treated the poorest and most vulnerable in our midst and in the world. Christ himself regards the good or ill we have done to them as the moral equivalent of how we have treated him.

The transformative power of Matthew 25 is not just in learning to avoid judgment but in changing priorities, changing perspectives, changing lives, and even changing nations. And, ultimately, it is about how and where to really find Jesus.

Finding Jesus

The people who raised me in my little evangelical church really wanted me to come to Christ. But their whole style of life was pushing Jesus away, in the form of the "least of these," and made it very difficult for them to really know or understand where Jesus was or even who he was. Instead, they were captives to the culture around them and the logic of the world, which caused them to treat those left out and left behind in the same ways their culture did. So, in the end, they didn't really know Jesus very well and couldn't tell their children how and where to find him.

For me, it took leaving or being pushed out of the church to get on a path that would ultimately bring me back to Jesus. I wasn't looking for Jesus, but I found him where I ended up. When I first began to go into the inner city of Detroit, I began to see things, learn things, understand things—and, most important of all, meet people—I had never known before. And I could see that the friendships I was making were completely changing my perspective about the world I lived in and the priorities I had. Both Mother Teresa and Dorothy Day of the Catholic Worker Movement talked about finding Jesus in "the distressing disguise of the poor."[1] And that was my experience. I met young black men when we worked alongside each other as line workers in factories or as janitors in downtown office buildings. In getting to know them and their families, I realized that we had been born and raised in different cities—really, different countries—just miles apart. *There were really two Detroits and two Americas.*

Meeting and coming to know people who were in the categories Jesus used as examples of "the least of these" has changed my life over and over again. And I now know it was always supposed to be that way; that's why Jesus spoke the way he did in Matthew 25.

Clearly, Jesus loves us all—and we are all God's children. Matthew 25 doesn't suggest otherwise. But in this text, Jesus is reminding us of his love for *all* God's children by particularly focusing on the ones he calls "the least of these," because they are the ones most easily and

1. See, for example, Mother Teresa, *In the Heart of the World: Thoughts, Stories, and Prayers* (Novato, CA: New World Library, 1997), 23, 33.

often forgotten by the logic of the world. Jesus wants us to reject that logic and remember those whom the world teaches us to ignore and forget. So the least of these, the ones left out and left behind, become *the barometer of our love of all humanity*. When the most invisible ones, instead of the most visible ones, become the test of our reality, it changes our perspective and alters our priorities.

In the process, we find Jesus in new ways. In my case, it brought my faith back to life. The journey of Matthew 25 has led me to the inner city of Detroit, caused me to focus on the rural villages in Southeast Asia, called me to live in the urban neighborhoods of Chicago and the poorest and toughest neighborhoods of Washington, DC, and taken me to the war-torn countries of Central America, the rice paddies and brothels of the Philippines, and the segregated townships of South Africa. It has brought me to the poorest precincts and racial districts, the most dangerous neighborhoods, and the "bush" areas of the cities and countries I have traveled to all over the world. Every place has changed my life in some way. Every new relationship has its own revelations about the meaning of following the One who tells us to go into those places. The encounters with people at the bottom by the logic of the world are what most help convert us to Jesus Christ.

"Help Us to Treat You Well"

It is often the more invisible Christians in the world who have understood the twenty-fifth chapter of Matthew best, and it is likely they who make the most difference in the kingdom of God. They are the glue that holds whole neighborhoods and villages together around the world—simply with the strength of their love. That description fit my friend Mary Glover, whom I quoted at the beginning of this chapter.

Mary was an older woman, poor herself, working as a day-care-center cook in our neighborhood of Columbia Heights in Washington, DC, back when it was a very tough and violent place filled with people who are considered the "least of these" by the world's logic. Sojourners Community lived there and began many projects with local people, including a food program that shared bags of groceries to help get families through the week. The line formed early on Saturday mornings, only twenty blocks from the White House, in a dramatic example of Washington's tale of two cities.

Mary was a consistent volunteer leader in helping get the food ready in our neighborhood center, and she always said the prayer just before about two hundred families started coming through the door. That's because she was our best pray-er, from the black Pentecostal tradition of praying. We would hold hands, and Mary would thank the Lord for waking us up that morning and that we were all still alive: "Thank you Lord for another day! That the walls of our rooms were not the walls of our graves! And our beds were not our coolin' boards!" Then Mary always ended her prayer by saying, "Lord, we know you'll be coming through this line today; so help us to treat you well."

I got up most every Saturday morning just to hear Mary say her prayer. It was the best commentary I had ever heard on Matthew 25. Mary Glover was an elder to me and a God-appointed missionary in our neighborhood. When we would walk those streets together, she would tell me her mission strategy. "When I see people for the first time, I just smile, not wanting to scare them off. The next time I see them I just say 'Hello' or 'How you doing?' The next time, I slow down a bit and give them a chance to answer back. Then it begins and I learn how they need help."

The Mary Glovers of the world have read the twenty-fifth chapter of Matthew's Gospel, and they love their Jesus by loving all of the "least of these" that God puts in their midst.

And they are at the heart of the church's mission in the world. Everywhere I go now, that gospel presence among the poor is growing with people of faith. In Catholic parishes and charities; in evangelical churches and their faith-based ministries; in the urban and rural projects of our major denominations; in student groups like InterVarsity Christian Fellowship and Campus Crusade for Christ; in the global engagement of groups like World Vision; in prison ministries, homeless shelters, medical clinics, food pantries and soup kitchens, immigrant services, and transformational community economic development by groups like the Christian Community Development Association

(CCDA)—in all these ways and others, faith is reaching out again to the One who said he was hungry, thirsty, naked, a stranger, sick, and in prison. Having been to as many places as I have now, I can testify to how these quiet and humble faith-inspired efforts are what hold many cities, communities, and even countries together.

Now, all over the country and around the world, I see a new generation that is reliving what happened to me many years ago. These young people are traveling to places they had never been before, being stunned by what they see—and, through a spiritual pilgrimage of pain, confusion, anger, and discovery, they are both deepening and broadening their previously narrower faith. What they all tell me is that they are finding Jesus again or, in some cases, for the very first time.

Whether helping to renovate urban schools in their own city, tutoring poor children, building houses for low-income families, digging wells in sub-Saharan Africa, or fighting sexual trafficking in Asia, many young believers are having life-changing experiences and coming away with a new sense of who Jesus is and what their relationship with him is becoming. I see it in the college students I teach and in my own sons as they enter their first community service projects. Joe Scarborough, the television host of *Morning Joe*, describes these young Christians like this:

> The modern Christian movement is changing, especially among the young. Even conservative, ideologically conservative young Christians are what I would call Matthew 25 Christians—worrying about the poor, feeding the poor, clothing the naked, visiting people in hospitals and jails. This is a quiet revolution in the church that has happened over the past twenty years that I think a lot of people in mainstream media have not seen. . . . Conservatives, moderates, liberals are coming together under this concept.[2]

And what can happen when Christians and their churches come together around the teaching of Jesus in Matthew 25 and even let his concern for "the least of these" transcend their own politics? Extraordinary

2. Joe Scarborough, *Morning Joe*, July 21, 2011, http://www.msnbc.msn.com/id/3036789/#43838877.

things. Let's take two very contemporary examples of how this text and the faith community's response to it are both changing politics and serving the common good.

The Circle of Protection

In America both Republicans and Democrats have a religion problem, and it has nothing to do with same-sex marriage, abortion, or religious liberty. Rather, their serious stumbling blocks are budgets, deficits, and debt-ceiling deadlines.

That's right, in a city deeply divided between the political right and left, there is a growing consensus from religious leaders that we must get our fiscal house in order *and* protect low-income people at the same time. Together, many of us are saying that there is a fundamental religious principle missing in most of our political infighting: the protection of the ones about whom our Scriptures say God is so concerned and who are the subject of the twenty-fifth chapter of Matthew.

Indeed, the phrase "a budget is a moral document" originated in the faith community and is often invoked in discussions about our nation's finances. Those most in jeopardy during Washington's debates and decisions are precisely the people the Bible clearly instructs us to protect and care for—the poorest and most vulnerable. In comparison to the power players of the political system, they have virtually no one lobbying on their behalf in these hugely important discussions about how public resources will be allocated.

For us, this is definitely not a partisan issue but a spiritual and biblical one that resides at the very heart of our faith. It is the singular issue that has brought together the US Conference of Catholic Bishops, the National Association of Evangelicals (NAE), the Salvation Army, Bread for the World, Sojourners, and the leaders of church denominations, congregations, and faith-based organizations across the nation.

Here is the principle still absent in our current political debate: *We must agree not to reduce deficits in ways that further increase poverty and economic inequality by placing the heaviest burdens on those who are already suffering the most.*

Religious leaders do believe that *massive deficits are moral issues* and that we must not saddle future generations with crippling debt. But we believe that *how we resolve deficits is also a moral issue.* And our society must not take more from those who already have much less than the rest of us.

We understand the politics of this debate. We know that Republicans will resist reforming the private sector because that is where their core constituencies and money lie. We understand that Democrats will resist reforming the public sector because that is where *their* key constituencies and money are.

We also understand that neither party wants to risk actually examining bloated Pentagon spending out of political fears that they might appear unconcerned about national defense or our military personnel. During elections, both Republicans and Democrats are almost entirely focused on middle-class voters and wealthy donors who all have special interests in the outcome of how government financing is determined.

And then there are the pollsters who tell both parties that talking about "poor people" and "poverty" will not be popular.

But we must agree with what a Catholic bishop told President Obama when a number of us as religious leaders met with him in the White House, as the 2011 debt-crisis deal was being decided: "Mr. President, our scriptural mandate from Jesus does not say, 'As you have done to the middle class, you have done to me.' It rather says, 'As you have done to the least of these, you have done to me.'" The president knew the Matthew 25 text and, an hour after our meeting, the White House called to say the president had decided to protect poor and vulnerable people in the final deal.

Christians have no real choice as to what our position will be in these debates. We are telling the leaders and legislators of both parties that they must form "a circle of protection" around the most effective and vital programs that help the lowest-income families survive in such difficult economic times. With one clear voice we also are telling lawmakers that the global efforts that quite simply mean life and death to the poorest around the world—those who are assailed by utterly preventable hunger and diseases such as malaria, tuberculosis, and HIV/AIDS—must be protected.

Some cuts kill. Others will destroy the small opportunities families have to lift themselves out of poverty. To make those cuts in spending, while leaving the other money protected by powerful interests alone, is simply immoral from a Christian point of view.

We are telling our legislators, for example, that if they really decide to take *most* or *all* of their proposed agricultural cuts from proven and successful nutritional "food stamp" programs that go mostly to working families with children, while taking *nothing* from the rice, corn, and sugar subsidies to rich agribusiness, they should expect to hear voices like Old Testament prophets standing outside their halls.

Or, when they plan to cut poor children's health care or take away the chance for students from poor families to go to college for the first time, but block any increased taxes on the wealthiest and keep corporate welfare checks flowing, they should anticipate having to listen to the faith community's very different priorities.

And if they cut "Meals on Wheels" feeding programs to our most vulnerable senior citizens but keep paying for the wheels on outdated and useless weapons systems, they should expect to hear some words from the Scriptures about defending the poor and not trusting in "horses and chariots."

Those who are often praised for making the "tough choices" in slashing government spending are usually not making tough choices at all. They are not making the really *tough choices* to cut wasteful military spending and stop unnecessary and bad wars. They are not cutting the enormous public benefits and subsidies to huge corporations, including bailouts to the biggest banks. They are not challenging the special interests who control so many government expenditures. They are not asking hard questions about rising health care costs that will not be ultimately sustainable. And they are not asking the wealthiest among us to pay the same portion of their income in taxes that even their middle-class employees do. Those would be the tough choices. But to instead destroy critical programs for the poorest and most vulnerable people, who have no lobbyists to defend their interests, is in fact an *easy choice* for these budget cutters to make. And, from a Christian point of view, it is also the wrong and immoral choice, completely conformed to the logic of the world employed by the most powerful and completely contrary to the biblical logic of the kingdom of God and Matthew 25. It's time to make the real tough choices and not just the easy ones that cause even more suffering for "the least of these."

An untold story in much of the media is how faith community leaders protected low-income entitlements in the sequestered automatic cuts agreed to in the August 2011 debt-ceiling deal (which would occur if legislators could not agree to a final solution—which they didn't). When the president and his team were sitting at the long wooden table in the West Wing's Roosevelt Room across from a wide cross section of Catholic, evangelical, mainline Protestant, African American, and Hispanic church leaders who told them that it was our faith imperative to protect low-income people, he got the message. When Republican legislative leaders who are Catholic or evangelical were told by the same religious leaders that exempting low-income people from brutal budget cuts is an imperative of Catholic social teaching and biblical faith, they privately conceded they would not try to block that. When the leaders of both parties saw full-page advertisements in Washington's newspapers that said "God is watching" the outcomes of their budget debates, it made them uncomfortable. And when the results of those budget deals were announced, including the exempting of many low-income programs within our "circle of protection," the faith leaders were told that it was only their relentless persistence that protected the programs. As one of Washington's most influential political insiders told me, "If it wasn't for the constant and consistent pressure of you and your faith colleagues, those low-income people would not have been protected, because there are no champions for the poor in these houses of government."

In the past, our country has successfully reduced deficits and poverty at the same time. There have been bipartisan agreements to defend the means-tested programs for low-income people against major cuts. And for the past twenty-five years, every automatic budget-cut mechanism has exempted core low-income assistance programs. Both Republicans and Democrats could and should agree to the principle of protecting the most vulnerable—as budget-cutting processes have in the past and some current recommendations that have had bipartisan involvement do even now.

Then the parties could have their private/public-sector debates and reach the compromises necessary to find fiscal integrity. But church leaders and pastors from both sides of the political and religious spectrum will be telling them to defend the ones to whom God commands us to give special care. Everything else may be on the table, but the fate of the poor and vulnerable should not be.

In these endless fiscal and budget debates, the markets are watching, the Republicans are watching, the Democrats are watching, the media are watching, the pollsters and pundits are watching, and the special interest groups are really watching. The public is watching too and is generally disgusted with Washington, DC. And when it comes to the bitter and ultrapartisan battles over the budget, the deficit, and deadlines for America to avoid defaulting on its financial commitments, the world is now watching.

But God is watching too. Others are watching to see how their self-interests will benefit in the final deal. Or they are watching to see who's up and who's down, who will get the political win, and whose election chances will be better afterward. The ones who usually win the battles over the budget and deficit are the ones who are watching most closely. As the book of Proverbs teaches, "the poor are shunned . . . but the rich have many friends" (Prov. 14:20 NIV).

But the religious community is starting to change this. We have formed a "Circle of Protection" to defend the most effective antipoverty efforts both at home and around the world. Of course, programs that help the poorest can always be reformed and made more effective, but they should not simply be slashed to allow budget savings to be made while we protect other areas with powerful special interests behind them. Faith leaders rightly say God is biased in such matters—that God prefers to protect the poor from more hurt and instructs the faithful to do the same.

Neither political party in the House, Senate, or White House has clearly and publicly committed to protect the poor and vulnerable in these fiscal debates and decisions, even though religious leaders have persistently pressed them all to do so. And we will continue to do so because of the twenty-fifth chapter of Matthew.

Faith leaders are watching the political leaders in their debates over budgets, deficits, and debt ceilings. And we believe God is watching us all.

Uniting to Defend "The Stranger"

Something very important is happening in regard to immigration, unity, morality, and common sense. I am going to describe seven days in Washington, DC, between June 12 and June 19, 2012, one week in which a public policy discussion was turned around. Both George W. Bush and Barack Obama had tried to pass comprehensive immigration reform but were blocked in the Congress by political maneuvering. But a movement rose up among people of faith in solidarity with millions of undocumented immigrants in America who we believed fell into the category of "the stranger" that Jesus talks about in Matthew 25. Those words changed us and are now changing politics in the United States. Here is the seven-day story.

June 12, 2012, was a big day in Washington. I am used to very ordinary days in the nation's capital; but this was an extraordinary one. After more than a year of hard and patient work, a new "table" had formed, and nearly 150 evangelical leaders signed the "Evangelical Statement of Principles for Immigration Reform." Signers came from across the spectrum of evangelicalism, from the leaders of top Hispanic evangelical organizations, such as Luis Cortes, Sam Rodriguez, and Gabriel Salguero, to Anglo pastors such as Max Lucado, Bill Hybels, and Joel Hunter. The president of the NAE, Leith Anderson, was there, as was Richard Land from the Southern Baptist Convention; and Jim Daly, president of Focus on the Family, was among the signers.

No, that isn't a typo. Sojourners stood side by side with the Southern Baptists and Focus on the Family to draw attention to the plight of millions who have been caught up in our broken immigration system and to launch our common principles for comprehensive immigration reform. It was exciting to see such unity across the traditional political spectrum, something that rarely happens in Washington.

Make no mistake: there are still big gaps and differences in politics among those in this group. But this day wasn't about politics. Rather, we focused on the things we agreed were fundamental moral issues and biblical imperatives. This coming together to seek a solution to a broken immigration system on behalf of those who suffer most in it is just what politics needs and could begin to affect other issues as well.

Instead of dividing over *ideology and politics*, we came together for the sake of *morality and common sense*. We came together because families were being broken up and because the people Jesus told us to protect were being assaulted. That's what leaders are supposed to do. And we had all read the twenty-fifth chapter of Matthew's Gospel.

As I stood in front of the press and others who gathered to hear us speak that day on Capitol Hill, this is what I said:

> Big things don't change in Washington first; they change in the nation's capital last. You'd think that with all the lobbyists on K Street and the billions of dollars being spent, that Washington is the most important place. But this is the place where things *don't* change, where politics maintains the status quo and the special interests maintain their own interests.
>
> Things change when hearts and minds across the country change. Things change when social movements begin, when people's understandings change, when families rethink their values, when congregations examine their faith, when communities get mobilized, and when nations are moved by moral contradictions and imperatives.
>
> Things change when people believe that more than politics is at stake, but that human lives, human dignity, the well-being of moms and dads and kids, and even faith is at stake.
>
> And when moral values change, culture changes; and then change comes to Washington.
>
> The immigration system in America is utterly broken, and politics hasn't changed that. Both sides, Republicans and Democrats, are responsible for this failed system. They are more concerned with their political

bases and their votes than with the people and families whose lives are being crushed by a broken system.

There are two invisible signs up at the border between Mexico and the United States. One says "No Trespass!" The other says "Help Wanted." And up to twelve million vulnerable people have been trapped between those two signs.

But the Bible says that these people fall into the category of "the stranger," and Jesus says how we treat them is how we treat him. They are not the political pawns of Washington, and many of them are our brothers and sisters in the body of Christ. We have come to know them, and to love them: we've come to see how their families are being torn apart, and their lives are in great danger. And we believe that breaks the heart of God and calls us to action.

Look who is here today: Christians from across the political spectrum. The NAE, Anglo churches and Hispanic churches whom God has brought together, the Southern Baptists, Focus on the Family, Sojourners. Has that ever happened before?

We realize our work is stronger together than as individual leaders. An effort for immigration reform of this size and diversity has never been attempted in the evangelical community. In the months and years ahead, the principles we release today will serve as the basis of outreach and communications work across the nation.

Together, we will create a national groundswell for immigration reform by reaching out to our fellow evangelicals in the body of Christ, to students at Christian colleges and seminaries, and to our churches, both Anglo and Hispanic; because God is calling us to stand together now in faith, in truth, and in the power of the Spirit—which is even stronger than the powers of Washington, DC.

Together we are much stronger than divided. We represent large constituencies of Christians across America, and we are here to tell our political representatives that it is time to shed your partisan behavior and implement a moral and biblical imperative; fix this broken system and pass comprehensive immigration reform! It is time to transcend politics and do what is right.

Together, we make a prophetic announcement today. Washington will change on this issue. Washington will enact comprehensive immigration reform . . . because the people of God have come together to begin that change in our own lives and our own churches. And every Sunday we pray, "Thy kingdom come, they will be done, on EARTH as it is in heaven." We mean that. Amen.[3]

We called for a bipartisan solution on immigration reform based on these six principles:

1. Respect the God-given dignity of every person
2. Protect the unity of the immediate family
3. Respect the rule of law
4. Guarantee secure national borders
5. Ensure fairness to taxpayers
6. Establish a path to legal status and/or citizenship for those who qualify and who wish to become permanent residents[4]

These, we believe, are moral and commonsense principles for fixing our broken immigration system.

The press coverage of the faith leaders event in the nation's capital was enormous, in both English- and Spanish-speaking media. That same day, our delegation of evangelical leaders had a long meeting at the White House, and we followed up the next day with more meetings on the Hill with both Republican and Democratic senators and members of Congress. Our message was the same: it's time to rise above our partisan political deadlock. And we told the White House and elected leaders up on Capitol Hill that it was time to show some courage and do the right thing.

Early that Friday morning I got a call from the White House telling us that the president had decided to make a major announcement that day: young people under sixteen years of age who had come to this country illegally but when they were only children would no longer be subject to deportation. If they were law-abiding and had been to school, they would instead receive work permits that could be renewed every two years. It was similar to, though not as expansive as, the Dream Act, which Congress had previously voted against, and which also allowed a

---

3. The full press conference can be viewed at http://www.evangelicalimmigrationtable .com.

4. Evangelical Immigration Table, "Evangelical Statement of Principles for Immigration Reform," http://www.evangelicalimmigrationtable.com.

path to citizenship for college students or those in the military. I made
the following statement:

> The announcement from the White House today is very good news for
> almost one million young people who have a dream of staying in the
> country where they have lived most of their lives. Instead of being placed
> in the deportation pipeline, they will receive work permits enabling
> them to contribute to the nation and help build America's future. This
> is an important step but only a beginning toward comprehensive reform
> of an utterly broken immigration system. This week a very broad and
> deep table of evangelical leaders called on the political leaders of both
> parties to fix that broken system and protect "the stranger" whom
> Christ calls us to defend. As evangelicals we love the "good news" of
> the gospel, and today we affirm this good news that gives hope and a
> future for young immigrants who are an important part of both the
> church and this country.[5]

Many other evangelical leaders stated their support. "This new policy is
good news for America and is good news for undocumented young adults
who came to America through the choice of others. It is the right thing
to do," said Leith Anderson, NAE president. "I hope that the Congress
will quickly follow with a just and compassionate reform of our entire
system of immigration. Our country has already waited a long time
to get our immigration laws fixed. This is an encouraging first step."[6]

Two days later, on Sunday, there was great joy in churches across
the country, with reports of many celebrations of Christians, both
Hispanic and Anglo—often together—singing, dancing, and praising
God. It was also Father's Day, and many immigrant fathers felt for the
first time in their lives the relief of not having their children living in
the shadow of fear. And from almost a million young immigrants in
the United States, there were many grateful tears.

On Monday and Tuesday, the media pundits assessed the political
situation. Contrary to many expectations, the Republican opposition
to the president did not offer much pushback to the administration's

5. "Prominent Evangelicals Praise Immigration Policy Change," *Sojourners*, June 15,
2012, http://sojo.net/press/prominent-evangelicals-praise-immigration-policy-change-0.
6. Ibid.

announcement. Rather, some conservative Republican commentators supported the action, described it as a good policy decision, and said it should have been done sooner—which, of course, it should have been. By Tuesday, a poll showed that 70 percent of all Americans supported the decision to no longer deport young people who had lived here all of their lives and instead allow them to contribute to their real home country; and only 30 percent opposed the move.[7] Most Republicans said that politics was involved, as it is in every moment in Washington, DC. But politics had just been changed after evangelical leaders went to the capital.

Both political sides and the media said that the statement by such a unified and influential group of evangelical Christian leaders made an "enormous" difference and created the "space" and "support" for political leaders to do the right thing. The week had opened the door for a new bipartisan hope for immigration reform. But bipartisan results in politics are increasingly difficult to accomplish. This result took moral pressure from outside the political system to get the system to slowly begin to work. And that is often the way that politics changes, especially on the "big things."

These experiences, and events like them around the world, have taught me the bottom line of politics for people of faith. There are always political arguments to support what we have called the logic of the world, and those arguments often lead to putting aside the interests of the ones Jesus called the least of these. But when the faith community simply and strongly says a forceful no, persists in lifting up the cause of the vulnerable, and promises to protect them as Jesus instructs his followers to, it is a line in the sand that we will not cross. And when that becomes a bottom line for many of us, politicians slowly learn that they need to respect it or they will have to face the righteous anger of the faith community—which few of them want to do. Even better is when the faith community can inspire a culture and its political leaders to defend those who have no protection and include them in our communities.

7. "Obama Immigration Policy Favored 2-to-1 by Likely Voters," *Bloomberg News*, June 19, 2012, http://www.bloomberg.com/news/2012-06-19/obama-immigration-policy-favored -2-to-1-by-likely-voters.html.

The good news is that the attention of the church is shifting from the pursuit of the comforts of heaven to an engagement that finds Jesus in the world's least, last, and lost and recognizes what his mission means for the poorest and most vulnerable. For all of us who are moving in that direction, the prophet Isaiah has a word of encouragement:

> If you remove the yoke from your midst, the pointing of the finger and speaking wickedness, and if you give yourself to the hungry and satisfy the desire of the afflicted, then your light will rise in darkness and your gloom will become like midday. And the LORD will continually guide you, and satisfy your desire in scorched places. (Isa. 58:9–11 NASB)

··· 5 ···

The Good Samaritan Goes Global

I remember when Mrs. King and I were first in Jerusalem. We rented a car and drove from Jerusalem down to Jericho. And as soon as we got on that road I said to my wife, "I can see why Jesus used this as the setting for his parable." It's a winding, meandering road. It's really conducive for ambushing. . . . That's a dangerous road. In the days of Jesus it came to be known as the "Bloody Pass." And you know, it's possible that the priest and the Levite looked over that man on the ground and wondered if the robbers were still around. Or it's possible that they felt that the man on the ground was merely faking. And he was acting like he had been robbed and hurt, in order to seize them over there, lure them there for quick and easy seizure.

And so the first question that the priest asked, the first question that the Levite asked was, "If I stop to help this man, what will happen to me?" But then the Good Samaritan came by. And he reversed the question: "If I do not stop to help this man, what will happen to him?"

—Martin Luther King Jr.[1]

1. Martin Luther King Jr., "I've Been to the Mountaintop" (speech, Mason Temple, Memphis, Tennessee, April 3, 1968), http://www.americanrhetoric.com/speeches/mlkivebeen tothemountaintop.htm.

Almost everybody knows the story of the Good Samaritan, and how Jesus told it to answer a question somebody had asked him: "Who is my neighbor?" That is always a good question. But we need to ask it in the right context. Helping a man in need by the side of a dangerous road was the example Jesus used to show who our neighbor is and how to help him or her. Who is our neighbor? In our increasingly connected global world, this ancient moral question takes on a whole new context. What does it mean for the Good Samaritan to go global?

The Lawyer's Question

Just then a lawyer stood up to test Jesus. "Teacher," he said, "what must I do to inherit eternal life?" He said to him, "What is written in the law? What do you read there?" He answered, "You shall love the Lord your God with all your heart, and with all your soul, and with all your strength, and with all your mind; and your neighbor as your-self." And he said to him, "You have given the right answer; do this, and you will live."

But wanting to justify himself, he asked Jesus, "And who is my neighbor?" Jesus replied, "A man was going down from Jerusalem to Jericho, and fell into the hands of robbers, who stripped him, beat him, and went away, leaving him half dead. Now by chance a priest was going down that road; and when he saw him, he passed by on the other side. So likewise a Levite, when he came to the place and saw him, passed by on the other side. But a Samaritan while traveling came near him; and when he saw him, he was moved with pity. He went to him and bandaged his wounds, having poured oil and wine on them. Then he put him on his own animal, brought him to an inn, and took care of him. The next day he took out two denarii, gave them to the innkeeper, and said, 'Take care of him; and when I come back, I will repay you whatever more you spend.' Which of these three, do you think, was a neighbor to the man who fell into the hands of the rob-bers?" He said, "The one who showed him mercy." Jesus said to him, "Go and do likewise." (Luke 10:25–37)

This, of course, is the very famous parable of the Good Samaritan, widely understood as one of Jesus's key teachings on ethics. And it concerns a question that was fundamental in ancient times and remains so in the modern world: Who is my neighbor? With our world now becoming so globalized and closely connected, it is a question we will need whole new ethical perspectives and patterns to deal with. This story can help us.

As you see above, Martin Luther King Jr. spoke about this parable, about the plight of those robbed and beaten on the roadways of life and the self-protecting avoidance of those who pass by on the other side—even religious leaders. Just as Jesus did, King was calling for a radical extension of the idea of the neighbor, well beyond the boundaries that people use to justify their lack of response to human suffering.

And that is what this parable is all about: expanding and extending the identity of "our neighbor." There is no doubt that most human beings believe they have obligations and responsibilities to their neighbors. But they also believe in boundaries, and many people fall outside of them to become *nonneighbors*. It's much easier when our neighbor is a relative, or friend, or member of our group and very much like *us*. But when we have to cross boundaries—like race, religion, neighborhood, region, culture, class, tribe, country, and often gender, even within those other boundaries—the justifications begin for our having ignored somebody or some group of people.

That is exactly what the lawyer in the story is doing—trying to justify himself. This isn't a sincere query by a humble man ready to confess his failure and find the strength to walk a new path. This is about how to get out of responsibilities, which is often how this conversation plays out in the politics of the public square: "Am I my brother's or sister's keeper?"[2] or "Who is my brother or sister?" And again, it is often our lawyers, or politicians, who want to put up the boundaries that stand in the way of our being our brother's keeper. The lawyer, or politician, in the story had to agree to what the law says about loving the Lord your God and loving your neighbor as yourself—which he can't get around because that is what the law says. So all that is left for him is to try to narrow whom that might apply to, whom he really has to love. He asks

2. See Gen. 4:9.

with this clear tone and meaning in his voice: "Okay then, just who is my neighbor anyway?"

In reply to the lawyer's attempt to evade and avoid his responsibilities, Jesus tells this compelling and convicting story in front of a whole audience of people listening to the question and to Jesus's answer.

One of the first things to notice is what New Testament scholars tell us about the scene and context of this story. Because the man was beaten, stripped, and left for "half dead," he couldn't be identified in the usual ways by his dress and his speech or dialect. Nobody could tell who this man was just by looking at him, lying mostly naked on the ground and likely unconscious. His terrible state demonstrated no identity, status, or position. He was devoid of any social background or cultural connection. He was nobody and could be anybody. He might also have been dead or almost dead. So it was hard to tell if this man was a "neighbor" in all the usual categories because he could not be identified.

First a priest passes him by and then a Levite. Why do they not stop? Many suggest it has to do with issues of "ritual purity" and the "holiness code," especially involving the religious leaders.[3] If the man on the side of the road was not Jewish, contact with him could risk defilement for a priest. The law was even stricter if he was actually dead; a priest was not to come within six feet of a corpse.[4] In Jesus's culture, contact with a dead body was commonly understood to defile a person. And for the priest and Levite, to ritually purify themselves again would take time, money, and inconvenience. There is debate about whether the law could have been interpreted or used in other ways to justify helping the man; for example, there could be legal exceptions for "neglected corpses" and other technicalities. In this case, the priest and Levite chose purity over compassion, perhaps letting their religious rules become their excuse for not helping.[5] Ever seen or heard of that before? But as New Testament scholar Klyne Snodgrass puts it, "The

---

3. Klyne Snodgrass, *Stories with Intent: A Comprehensive Guide to the Parables of Jesus* (Grand Rapids: Eerdmans, 2008), 355.

4. Ibid.

5. Greg W. Forbes, *The God of Old: The Role of the Lukan Parables in the Purpose of Luke's Gospel* (Sheffield: Sheffield Academic Press, 2000), 63.

parable is one more example of Jesus substituting the mercy code for the holiness code."[6]

Maybe the priest and the Levite were also afraid. It was a very dangerous and treacherous road, where robbers often attacked without warning. Perhaps the thieves were still around and would pounce on anyone else who stopped. Or, as Dr. King wondered, maybe they feared the man was faking and might be part of a plot to trap them. Stopping to help would certainly put them in touch with this man, this other human being, and that could entail some time, risk, and vulnerability—just as stopping to help people today usually does. Hurrying along would be safer than stopping. So to avoid the problem, to keep both pure and safe, the first two passersby—the religious leaders—crossed to the other side of the road, ignored the suffering man, and kept going about their business.

Too Busy to Help?

Some have also proposed another possible reason: that these men were just too busy! The religious leaders might have been in a real hurry, with too many important things and people on their minds, and perhaps on their way to very important meetings. These were leaders with tight schedules; they hardly had the time to see what was going on around them on their way to their next appointment, and certainly had no time to stop and be diverted from their prearranged plan for the day. Perhaps the Samaritan who stopped was in less of a hurry.

A fascinating experiment related to the Good Samaritan story, conducted at Princeton Seminary, may shed some light on this theory.[7] Seminary students were invited to participate in a project on religious education. After filling out a survey of religious questions about themselves, they were asked to travel from one building to an-

6. Snodgrass, *Stories with Intent*, 358.
7. J. M. Darley and C. D. Batson, "'From Jerusalem to Jericho': A Study of Situational and Dispositional Variables in Helping Behavior," *Journal of Personality and Social Psychology* 27 (1973): 100–108, summarized at http://faculty.babson.edu/krollag/org_site/soc_psych /darley_samarit.html.

other on campus to give prepared talks on different topics and have the talks recorded when they arrived at their final destination. But on their way, they encountered a young actor, lying in an alleyway right in their path, playing the part of somebody who was hurt and in distress, his condition unknown.

The researchers wanted to test three questions: (1) whether people thinking "religious" and "helping" thoughts would be likely to stop; (2) whether people who saw mostly a personal gain from religion would respond differently than those who saw it as having a value of its own for finding meaning in their lives; and (3) whether people in a hurry would be less prone to help. There were three variables: topic, identity, and urgency. One group was told to prepare a talk about seminary jobs, the other about the Good Samaritan. Some were told they were almost late for the next task, others that they would arrive early but might as well get over there anyway. In the alley, they all passed the man sitting slumped in a doorway, and he was to moan and cough—twice—as they walked by. After they arrived at the second site, the seminarians gave their talk and answered a "helping behavior questionnaire."[8]

The results from the experiment were very clear: "The only one of these variables that made a difference was how much of a hurry the subjects were in. Sixty-three percent of subjects that were in no hurry stopped to help, 45 percent of those in a moderate hurry stopped, and 10 percent of those that were in a great hurry stopped. It made no difference whether the students were assigned to talk on the Good Samaritan parable, nor did it matter what their religious outlook was."[9]

I was very struck by what the study concluded: that a person in a hurry is less likely to stop and help someone in trouble, even if the passerby is about to teach the parable of the Good Samaritan! Princeton reported that some of the seminarians literally stepped over the actor in order to continue on their way—to preach Jesus's Gospel story of what it means to be a neighbor. What does that tell us about our ethics and our actions, and about how being hurried and terribly busy all the time affects our ability to do the things we say we believe? Princeton

8. http://faculty.babson.edu/krollag/org_site/soc_psych/darley_samarit.html.
9. Ibid.

reported that many students who didn't stop to help the man in the alley didn't even seem anxious or worried about it after they arrived. Were they just too busy to even notice a person in real trouble? They were facing a conflict between the time demands being imposed on them and the possibility of ethical behavior that presented itself on their way. The study report surmised that "conflict rather than callousness can explain the failure to stop."[10]

The priest, the Levite, and most of the seminarians in the Princeton study were motivated either by a desire to maintain their holiness to please God or by a commitment to following the rules and timetables of their busy schedules; but the Samaritan decided to act in response to the needs of another human being. And he is the example Jesus uses to say, "Go and do likewise."[11] So what can we learn from the nature of the Good Samaritan's response?

The Costs of Compassion

The very fact that Jesus chose a Samaritan as his positive example in the story would have been a shock to his Jewish audience. Samaritans were of mixed race—Jewish and another race of occupied people in their region—and the Jewish-Samaritan relationship was "notoriously bad," according to Klyne Snodgrass: "Jews believed Samaritans to be people of doubtful descent and inadequate theology."[12] That sounds like what I hear today from too many religious leaders about the people they don't like. Clearly, this was a tense relationship. Jesus once completely surprised the Samaritan woman at the well by even talking to her and asking for a drink of water. So who was this Samaritan, and what did he do that Jesus commended in his parable?

First, the Samaritan would not have been from the immediate area, so the injured man would not easily qualify as his "neighbor." Second, Samaritans were not Gentiles and were bound by the same purity laws as the Jews; yet this one seems to ignore these laws when he stops and

10. Ibid.
11. Luke 10:37.
12. Snodgrass, *Stories with Intent*, 345.

approaches an unidentified stranger—risking his own defilement. And when he sees the man is not dead but severely hurt, he begins to treat the wounds with his own oil and wine and to bandage him as best he can. Then he places the man on his own donkey and takes him to a nearby inn where he can get him the help and rest he needs.

Now the robbery victim, of course, has no money; so the Samaritan pulls out of his own pocket two denarii, or about two days' wages, which will pay for about two weeks at the inn. After he spends the night getting the injured man settled and taken care of, he goes on his way again the next day. But he promises the innkeeper that he will come back to pay whatever else is owed to meet the recovery needs of this man, a total stranger to him. There is no way to ensure that his money will be returned, and it is clear that the Samaritan doesn't expect anything in return.

In offering to pay more for the injured man, the Samaritan obviously has to identify himself to the innkeeper, and here is why that is important. The motivation for the attack on this man, which the parable does not describe or explain, could well have been the violence of "blood revenge," with one group or clan taking out its grievances on a member of another. Being quite familiar with gang violence in our urban communities, I can easily understand that reality and pattern. If you assist a victim of such gang violence, you can easily become the gang's next victim. So the Samaritan was again putting himself at risk for this man.

The Good Samaritan shows the difference between what New Testament theologian Sharon Ringe calls "having" a neighbor and "being" a neighbor: "No one can simply *have* a neighbor; one must also *be* a neighbor. Neighboring is a two-way street. The parable changes in a fundamental way how the question about neighbors is usually framed. The Gospel records no one's response to this story—neither the lawyer's nor the onlookers'. The story simply stands as yet another challenge to the transformation of daily life and business as usual which lies at the heart of the practice of discipleship."[13]

13. Sharon Ringe, *Luke* (Louisville: Westminster John Knox, 1995), 160.

We all *have* neighbors, but the gospel requires us to *be* a neighbor. The Good Samaritan shows us how, and Jesus says this is the example we are to follow. Snodgrass summarizes: "The parable is most often interpreted as an example story intended to show that love does not allow limits on the definition of the neighbor. . . . It is about a compassionate Samaritan and is intended to teach about the love command."[14] Jesus is clearly saying he doesn't want us to place limits on who our neighbor is and who is therefore worthy of the love God asks of us. He answers the question that keeps getting asked in our public life. We are indeed our brothers' and sisters' keeper.

Crossing All the Boundaries

The Good Samaritan is, therefore, crossing all kinds of boundaries and taking all sorts of risks by helping somebody in need. And that is the point Jesus is making, and it's the answer to the question, who is my neighbor? Humanity wants to put up boundaries, walls, and restrictive definitions around the concept of our neighbor. Those whom we can't fully identify, who are outside our group, who are different from us, or who might even place us in new, uncomfortable, or even dangerous situations—we want to prevent these people from being defined as our neighbors. But, says Jesus, they are our neighbors in the eyes of God. This Samaritan, on his way down the Jericho road, sees another person in trouble and breaks all the rules and boundaries to help him. Most of all, he shows that compassion and love require action and are not just ideals or feelings.

Every society creates boundaries—barriers between itself and "others"—and Jesus is telling us to cross those cultural, racial, religious, regional, and tribal boundaries to find our "neighbors." The fact that Martin Luther King Jr. would conclude that this passage was central to the struggle against racism is not surprising. We naturally seek and hide behind our created boundaries to excuse ourselves from loving those who are different or removed from us, but this parable stands

14. Snodgrass, *Stories with Intent*, 348, 352.

right in the way of that. Jesus obliterates all our notions of acceptable boundaries between neighbors. If our boundaries are drawn narrowly enough, we can avoid the costs of loving the "neighbors" who stand outside of them. But again, Jesus says no to that because there are no "nonneighbors" in this world. All of God's children are our neighbors, and that radical concept is absolutely essential to the idea of the common good. Indeed, it is a spiritual foundation for the common good.

This basic ethic from the Good Samaritan parable—that there are no boundaries for our definitions of "neighbor"—needs to be the moral guide and compass for us now in an increasingly globalized world. And the good news is that it is being adopted and enacted by many of the brightest and most committed members of the next generation. To think of their neighbors across the world as easily as right next door is coming naturally to younger people, who have a far more global perspective of life than their parents do.

That is a very important thing, because the problems and threats that now face us are truly global in nature and don't know any boundaries. Global pandemic diseases aren't stopped by the walls that we erect. Natural disasters, such as tsunamis and earthquakes, respect none of our national borders. The threats posed by rapid climate change could affect all of our children and grandchildren, wherever they live. Massive migration caused by poverty, conflict, or environmental pressures creates brand-new tensions and upheavals for new immigrants and for the people who live in places where those immigrants end up. And the impact of war and violence in one part of the world has shown a deadly capacity to spread its costs in both financial and human terms to many other places.

The reality of our global village speaks very directly to the ethic of Jesus's parable: we are all neighbors now, whether we like it or not. Both that global reality and new international perceptions regarding the true identity of our neighbors are causing a great expansion of global travel, connection, and responsibility. Students I've taught have gone on to medical school and ended up working in places with intense health care needs with groups like Doctors Without Borders, whose name itself speaks directly to the ethic of the Good Samaritan. Some exemplary journalists regularly place themselves in great danger, not just to cover situations of terrible conflict but to actually be among the victims of violence in order to tell their story. As I wrote this book, two of those heroic reporters were killed in Syria, the American war correspondent Marie Colvin and young French photographer Rémi Ochlik.[15]

Young couples from our own Sojourners community have ventured into some of the poorest and most conflict-ridden places around the world, such as Palestine, the Philippines, Central America, and Kenya, to serve with groups like the Mennonite Central Committee or World Vision. Even Christian musical groups have contributed, such as when Jars of Clay created the new "Blood:Water Mission" project, which pours time and money into building wells in southern Africa and addressing HIV/AIDS. Groups like Amnesty International have gained credibility by holding all governments, regardless of their ideologies, accountable for protecting the human rights and dignity of their peoples—again affirming their status as our neighbors.

And no cause has attracted more of the younger generation than the "new abolitionist" movement being directed against the sex trafficking of women and children in both poor and affluent countries—with more slaves today than there were when William Wilberforce ended the slave trade two hundred years ago. My friend David Batstone, who leads the Not for Sale campaign against human trafficking and slavery,[16] tells me moving stories about his students and even his own children going to engage those campaigns in Thailand, India, Peru, and around the world. In every case, the moral and spiritual foundation of that involvement comes right out of this Good Samaritan parable, in which Jesus is telling us to bring down all the boundaries and walls that separate us from responding to our neighbor.

15. Rod Norland and Alan Cowell, "Two Western Journalists Killed in Syria Shelling," *New York Times*, February 22, 2012, http://www.nytimes.com/2012/02/23/world/middleeast/marie-colvin-and-remi-ochlik-journalists-killed-in-syria.html?pagewanted=all.

16. See http://www.notforsalecampaign.org.

An Ethic for Our Global Neighbor

An ethic for our global neighbor is emerging now. And it comes right out of Jesus's parable. People are learning the lessons of the Good Samaritan and have chosen to live out that ethic on a global scale. In reaching out to those they now define as their neighbors, young people are making new connections and commitments, forging alliances, seeking to resolve conflicts, and giving their time and energy to actually solving problems instead of just talking and complaining about them. It's a wonderful thing, for example, to sit in on an intense discussion among young social entrepreneurs—from both the private and nonprofit sectors at places like the World Economic Forum—about how to solve the problem of water management and conservation in the world today, which is likely one of the greatest problems we will ever face. Just watching and listening to their conversation is a great encouragement to me because it is clear that the global identity and ethic of the neighbor is now being applied across all boundaries and around the world. I think Jesus might be smiling too.

This ethic that reminds us to love our neighbors as ourselves now even extends to defining those who make the products we use as neighbors. That extension is especially occurring among many young people who don't want to mindlessly consume products that are made by exploited children who are the same age as they are. Yes, the ethic of the Good Samaritan is even extending to our shopping habits.

I was invited to speak to a conference at the Brookings Institution in Washington, DC, about the terrible violence in the Congo, fueled by brutal militias who rain down terror on helpless civilian populations. The discussion was focused on how the money that supports these militias and buys their weapons comes from the "dirty minerals" they control and sell—minerals that are essential in making our cell phones.

I was the lunchtime speaker, whose role is always to try to be inspirational as people eat their meal. I started by reciting the Good Samaritan passage to a very diverse (and mostly secular) audience; reading the Bible got their attention. I asked how the discussion Jesus had with his legal questioner in the Gospel story might apply to our globalized world and even to the problem of dirty minerals. Are the individuals involved in making our lives work now (and most of us would say that we can't function without a cell phone!) really our neighbors, left on the side of the global road—alone, fearful, and vulnerable?

Jesus taught his disciples the Golden Rule: "Do to others as you would have them do to you" (Luke 6:31). This is the ethical commandment that is held in common with all the world's major religious traditions. It is both our common ground and our higher ground. In the same way, Jesus affirmed that the way to eternal life is to obey these commands: "'Love the Lord your God with all your heart and with all your soul and with all your strength and with all your mind'; and 'Love your neighbor as yourself'" (Luke 10:27 NIV; see Mark 12:29–31).

I explained how somebody in Jesus's audience got the bright idea to ask him the question, "And just who is my neighbor?" and how he responded with this famous story. I suggested that when we hear the story it is easy to condemn the priest and the Levite for leaving somebody by the side of the road. But they were technically just obeying the law. They were fulfilling, as they saw it, their responsibilities to their pre-scribed roles. They were both supposed to stay "clean" in order to fulfill their duties. Touching the bloody body would make them "unclean" and cause problems for them once they got to Jericho. Responding to the injured man could also take too much of their time or put them in a risky or dangerous situation. My job, they said, is at the end of the road. I can't get involved in the mess by the side of the road. It would only slow me down on the way to my responsibilities in Jericho.

Then I asked, what if someone in Jesus's audience today had the same bright idea to ask him the same question—now? "And who is my neighbor?" What might be his parable today? In that room filled with activists and policy makers, CEOs and heads of nonprofit organizations, I asked them to all hold up their cell phones. I said, let's be honest, cell phones have become the "significant other" for lots of people today. Many spend more time with them each day—thumbing away on the keyboards or having long conversations from anywhere and everywhere—than with any person in their lives. But what was the road that brought our cell phones to us? It is worrying to think that it may be a far more dangerous one than the Jericho road.

Do we know or really understand, for example, that many of the key materials in our cell phones come from minerals that are at the heart of violent conflicts in places like the Congo? Brutal militias are selling those "dirty minerals" to buy the weapons they use to kill and destroy thousands of people in Africa. What are we going to do about that? What about the revelation that some of our favorite gadgets, such as the iPhone and iPad, are made in China by people working under horrendous conditions that cause some to lose the use of their hands?[17] The stories go on and on: on the side of the road that brings us all our technical devices, clothing, delectable chocolates, and more are the many victims who have literally been beaten, robbed, and left to die. Whoever is involved in making your cell phone, I told the conferees, who were all now holding their smart phones in the air, is your neighbor! Does the meaning of the parable of the Good Samaritan today, I asked them, suggest that *economic supply chains should also become value chains*?

People stopped eating their lunch and you could have heard a pin drop. Imagine Jesus holding up our cell phones, I suggested. Your neighbor, he might say, is every man, woman, and child who touched the supply chain used to make your phone, or the clothes you wear, the computers you type on, the food you eat, and the cars you drive. Your global neighbors in these supply chains are all God's children. The theological reality that people of faith must try to live out is that our neighbor is not defined by geographical proximity. Our neighbor is the person in need. So it's time to look at what is happening along the bloody road of our consumer supply chains.

Turning Supply Chains into Value Chains

Sometimes, caring for our global neighbor might mean a change of plans or maybe a change in products. Sometimes, caring for our neighbor

17. "In China, Human Costs Are Built into an iPad," *New York Times*, January 25, 2012, http://www.nytimes.com/2012/01/26/business/ieconomy-apples-ipad-and-the-human-costs-for-workers-in-china.html?pagewanted=all.

means we have to slow down a little bit and think about what we are doing and buying. Sometimes, caring for our neighbor might cost us some time and even some money. There are many people who haven't wanted to get involved in the mess by the side of the road. They walk by it and say that it's somebody else's responsibility. My job, they say, is at the end of the road in Jericho. I'm just being faithful to my shareholders by maximizing profit. My job is just getting the products people want into the hands of those that want them. I can't be worried about those who get left by the side of the road of my supply chain. If I stop to help clean up the mess along the way, it might cost too much time and money.

It's not my job; I'm just responsible to the consumer. It's not my job; I am just a consumer. It's not my job; I'm not breaking any laws or rules. It's not my job; that's why they have boards of directors. It's not my job; it would be too inconvenient or expensive to stop and help. And hey, if a few people do get hurt along the way, are there not some Good Samaritans around who will take care of them? Isn't that why we have faith-based and charity organizations?

Jesus said that we are *all* responsible. It doesn't matter if we think we have a good excuse to just keep on walking by and ignore all the injustice along the road of our supply chains. And since we are already responsible, the fact that we also benefit at the end of these supply chains makes us even more responsible. There might be an excuse to give your supervisor about why you just walked on by; there might be an excuse to give your shareholders to just walk on by; there might be an excuse to give your customers to just walk on by; but there is no moral excuse for how we are now treating our neighbors who are falling along the side of the road of the global supply chains, which are now the world's main roads. And if we are part of the faith community, there are no excuses at all.

But the very good news is that there are many Good Samaritans walking along the road now—especially from a younger generation—and they are stopping to help those who have been beaten, robbed, and left for dead. Some are religious believers and some are not, but they all tend to believe that their neighbor is not defined by color, creed, religion, or borders and that we are all God's children and need to be treated fairly. Whether they are high school students in America who text each other or the young people working in dangerous conditions in the mines of eastern Congo, they are getting connected.

The movement is aiming toward new relationships and new rules. Building relationships is usually the beginning of establishing some new rules. Of course, no rules are going to fix every problem. It takes work, vigilance, monitoring, and a continuing effort to transform the conditions and contexts in which people participate in supply chains. But we continue to hear that fairer rules really do help the people caught in dangerous working conditions or in bloody and violent conflicts. Fairer rules and better protective standards are the best step to make sure that we—whether manufacturers, investors, or consumers—don't just walk on by.

A key to the Congo's peace and prosperity, for example, will be to ensure that we aren't putting money into the hands of violent militias and that the country's natural wealth benefits the people who live there. We have a responsibility. We have a job. We can't just walk on by with our excuses, because the people of the Congo are our neighbors.

The good news is that there are growing campaigns to hold businesses accountable for their supply chains. These campaigns incorporate language about transparency, monitoring, and protection, all aimed at the defense of our global neighbors along the dangerous road of supply chains. They are focused on changing business practices at all points on supply chains. This is a change of major proportions, and it will take many years to implement. But it is now under way and growing each day. At Georgetown University, where I teach, a campus-wide assumption now exists that no Georgetown T-shirt, sweatshirt, or school apparel will be sold that doesn't pass the muster of rigorous tests about how the workers are treated—because the Georgetown students care about that.

Our leading companies now face growing pressures—from consumers, investors, boards of directors, and the media—and their supply chains are being scrutinized under an ethical microscope. Many people in business I talk to now actually believe that such rigorous pressure will benefit not only factory workers but also the environment. Getting caught under the spotlight of ethical inquiry makes companies very uncomfortable but may ultimately be in their best interest if such scrutiny spurs them to produce stronger, more responsible, and more forward-looking businesses. Even in the nation's business schools, vibrant conversation is going on about how the practice of turning supply chains into sustainable value chains will help build business credibility while creating loyalty among customers and among ever more discerning stakeholders of all kinds.

Listen to what some of these companies who have been under scrutiny are now saying, obviously in large part because of the supply chain campaigns that have been directed at them.

Nokia, the world's largest vendor of mobile phones during the first decade of this millennium, assures us: "We take continuous action to ensure that metals from conflict areas do not enter our supply chain. We require our suppliers to confirm that our ban of conflict metals is respected and our requirements fulfilled. . . . We are actively working on industry initiatives to improve traceability of minerals."[18]

Nike, which was once the focus of every antisweatshop activist's most passionate energy, now has statements like these. Its "ambition" statement is "to help Nike, Inc., and its consumers thrive in a sustainable economy where people, profit and planet are in balance."[19] On their website, they continue:

> That's how Nike approaches corporate responsibility. It's not just about getting better at what we do—addressing impacts throughout our supply chain—it's about striving for the best, creating value for the business and innovating for a better world. . . . As environmental, social and economic challenges in our world proliferate, they demand our best performance. We're using the power of our brand, the energy and passion of our people and the scale of our business to create meaningful change. The opportunity is greater than ever for our sustainability strategy to drive

18. "Human Rights and the Supply Chain," Nokia website, http://www.nokia.com/global /about-nokia/people-and-planet/impact/supply-chain/human-rights-and-the-supply-chain.
19. Umair Haque, *Betterness* (Boston: Harvard Business Review Press, 2011), Kindle edition, locations 689–90.

business growth, build deeper consumer and community connections, and create positive social and environmental change.[20]

While Nike is far from having improved everything it can, it has realized that to maintain its credibility and its customers, it has to dramatically change how it does business.

Obviously, *saying* and *doing* are very different things, but without these global campaigns pressuring companies, such large corporations would not be talking like this. These are just two examples from industries in which supply chains are most often exploited. But they are part of a bigger story that is being told across the world of business. Implementation and monitoring are the keys now. The fair trade movement, especially strong in the United Kingdom, has found its way into every major food and department store there; and I am amazed at the breadth of the products involved that I see on visits to my wife Joy's family in England. The UK-based Fairtrade Foundation, for example, regularly tracks cocoa to source farms and has taken strong actions against farms that fail to live up to the standards and requirements of a "fairtrade farm."[21] And that information is made available to consumers, so that they can make choices based on their values and not just on the price of products. In 2009, the Deloitte company, along with the World Economic Forum, produced a report called *Sustainability for Tomorrow's Consumer: The Business Case for Sustainability*. It reported that the business world is responding to "more public and investor scrutiny of the traditional supply chain."[22]

The ethics of who my neighbor is are changing—for the better. The moral compass for that change is derived from our most ancient religious traditions but is now being picked up by the youngest members of our globalized world. We are called to play the Good Samaritan on life's roadside, wherever we directly encounter people in need; but

20. "Responsibility at Nike, Inc.," http://nikeinc.com/pages/responsibility.
21. BBC News, "Tracing the Bitter Truth of Chocolate and Child Labour," March 24, 2010, http://news.bbc.co.uk/panorama/hi/front_page/newsid_8583000/8583499.stm.
22. World Economic Forum and Deloitte Touche Tohmatsu, *Sustainability for Tomorrow's Consumer: The Business Case for Sustainability* (Geneva: World Economic Forum, 2009), 8, http://www.deloitte.com/assets/Dcom-Global/Local%20Assets/Documents/Bus-Sustainability-print_OK.pdf.

that will be only an initial act. One day we must come to see that in order to protect men, women, and children from being constantly beaten and robbed as they make their journey on life's highway, the Jericho road must be transformed! And that commitment is all about the common good.

···6···

The Beloved Community
Welcomes All Tribes

Our goal is to create a beloved community and this will require a qualitative change in our souls as well as a quantitative change in our lives.

—Rev. Dr. Martin Luther King Jr.[1]

As a nation and as a people, as a home, as a family, we've made a lot of progress—we've come a distance. But we're still not there. We have not yet created the beloved community. We have not come to that point where we recognize the dignity and the worth of every human being. It is still a struggle. . . . We still have a distance to go before we create one family, one house—the American house.

—Representative John Lewis, Georgia[2]

1. Martin Luther King Jr., "The Only Road to Freedom," in *A Testament of Hope: The Essential Writings and Speeches of Martin Luther King, Jr.*, ed. James M. Washington (New York: HarperCollins, 1991), 58.
2. John Lewis, "We Haven't Built the Beloved Community," *GRITtv with Laura Flanders*, October 8, 2010, http://www.youtube.com/watch?v=CsTE8rtC1Gc.

The beloved community welcomes all tribes—all the families, groups, races, clans, and nations that make up our very diverse human mosaic. This vision of community is embedded in the experience of the early church, which crossed all human boundaries; it was the underlying foundation for the civil rights movement, as Dr. Martin Luther King Jr. and Congressman John Lewis testify above; and it has its more limited secular manifestation in the vision of a pluralistic democracy that is intended to serve the common good.

So let's look at some relevant Scriptures and see how they might guide us in the context of a nation and world whose demographics are changing fundamentally. Our rapidly changing world depends on leadership that can help us navigate the turbulent waters of our tribal and common identities.

All Are Welcome

There can be no division into Jew and non-Jew, slave and free, male and female. Among us you are all equal. That is, we are all in a common relationship with Jesus Christ. (Gal. 3:28 Message)

Don't become so well-adjusted to your culture that you fit into it without even thinking. Instead, fix your attention on God. You'll be changed from the inside out. (Rom. 12:2 Message)

God welcomes all our human tribes and asks us to welcome the outsiders. Throughout the Scriptures, we see God actively affirming diverse cultures rather than trying to make them into one. There are biblical imperatives for breaking down the cultural barriers that divide humanity, especially in the new community that forms around Jesus. And a very dramatic description of the end of history in the book of Revelation shows the preservation of multiple cultures who *together* offer praise and worship of God, with their diverse cultural expressions as a means of their worship in the kingdom of God (Rev. 7:9–10).

Near the beginning of biblical history, from the tower of Babel onward, we see geographical dispersal and linguistic diversity as a means to execute God's cultural mandate given in Genesis 1:28 to go and fill all the earth. Even as God calls out Abraham as a "blessing" to all nations and forms his covenant with Israel (Gen. 12:2), God demands inclusivity among the people of God and encourages foreigners and faithful Gentiles to worship at his temple. How God's people treat both strangers and the poor, he says, will be a sign of how they will be judged—either blessed or cursed. The children of Israel needed to be constantly reminded that they were chosen not for their own superiority, strength, and power but rather for their ordinariness, smallness, and limitations, attributes that required them to trust in God. They were chosen not as a special blessing for themselves but to be a blessing to others—and to the world. And their temple is described by the prophet Isaiah as "a house of prayer for all peoples" (Isa. 56:7).

The story continues as God miraculously enters the realm of humanity with his Son, Jesus Christ, as the fulfillment of God's purposes and the inauguration of his kingdom. Instead of taking up the long-awaited messianic mission of leading Israel in military victory over its oppressors, Jesus shatters all nationalistic expectations and proclaims that "God so loved the world that he gave his only son" (John 3:16). He fulfills Isaiah's prophecies of a "suffering servant" to save humanity rather than being the warrior king that nations always prefer (Isa. 52:13–53:12).

Not only does Jesus affirm all nations' access to God's salvation, but as we have just seen in his parable of the Good Samaritan, he had the audacity (at least that is what some of the listeners would have thought) to depict Israel's ethnic enemy as the moral protagonist in the story. After Christ's ascent to heaven, we see the coming of the Holy Spirit, which creates a glorious display of cultural diversity at Pentecost (Acts 2); and the gospel spreads throughout the Middle East and far beyond the Jewish community. The apostle Paul, in his letter to the Ephesians, highlights the cross of Christ, which breaks down the barriers between God and human beings and also mends great human cultural rifts—like the one between Jews and Gentiles.

In Galatians, 1 and 2 Corinthians, and Colossians, Paul proclaims a unity in Christ among Jew and Greek, male and female, slave and free.

All are now one in Christ Jesus. The Galatians 3 text quoted above was used as a baptismal formula in the early church and taught directly to converts in order to change their cultural sense of themselves. *The three barriers named correspond to the most historic divisions between human beings: race, class, and gender.* That all of those divisions are healed in Jesus Christ is the claim of the early church. Jews and Gentiles now lived and worshiped together, slaves were treated with the same respect as masters, and women found a freedom of expression unheard of in the patriarchal ancient world. The New Testament indicates how radically different and diverse the welcoming culture of the early church was in its own context, which other historical accounts confirm. Its egalitarian living and sharing, as described in the first chapters of Acts, provoked great cultural attention and lent a powerful impulse to the evangelism of the early Christian community. Freedom, welcome, affirmation, and equality were as attractive then as they are now, and the first Christians exemplified these qualities (unlike some of our churches today).

Finally, as foretold by the apostle John in Revelation, even in the future of God's reign human culture is not abolished and replaced with a new, otherworldly, heavenly culture—not at all. Rather, human cultures in all their diverse manifestations of language, ethnicity, and nationality are *preserved* in holy unity. Indeed, their collective but distinct expressions become the *means* to express the heart of human vocation: to worship and glorify God. Revelation 7:9–10 says, "After this I looked, and there was a great multitude that no one could count, from every nation, from all tribes and peoples and languages, standing before the throne and before the Lamb, robed in white, with palm branches in their hands. They cried out in a loud voice, saying, 'Salvation belongs to our God who is seated on the throne, and to the Lamb!'"

Thus we have a hopeful and radical vision of diversity throughout biblical history with the purpose of bringing a divided humanity into reconciliation with God and one another. And there is a clear and consistent theme that "outsiders" have an important place and role in that community of faith and should be embraced and included rather than condemned and banished. Indeed, those relationships with the outsider can even become instruments for our salvation.

God Bless America?

I got lucky and married Joy Carroll, a wonderful woman who was born in London, England. She's a Brit, and my two boys are bilingual—or as they say, "half" American and "haaf" English. Joy was one of the first women ordained in the Church of England as a priest, is from an evangelical family, and knows her Bible well. Soon after we met, she was here for a visit and kept hearing the phrase "God bless America" everywhere she went. She even saw the slogan on some bumper stickers. She was puzzled, and asked me, "Don't they know that's not found in the Bible?" Now Joy actually loves her new country and has become a US citizen (we have the picture from the ceremony at the Library of Congress, with the whole family waving American flags!), and she thinks it's great to ask God to bless your country—"God bless the UK" too—as long as you don't think that God has *especially* blessed America. Or, as my boys like to say, "God bless the world." Where do we find our identity: in nation, culture, class, race, gender—or first and foremost in God and a new and international community of God's people? There is a long tradition in this country of attributing divine purposes to the founding of the United States and even of invoking a religious mandate for "American exceptionalism."

But what does the Bible say about nations? For the most part, they don't come out very well in the Scriptures, and while God uses both good and bad nations for his purposes, they are not often seen as central to God's plan. There are some very tough words in the Bible about "the nations." The psalmist puts them in their place: "The nations are in an uproar, the kingdoms totter; he utters his voice, the earth melts. . . . Be still, and know that I am God! I am exalted among the nations, I am exalted in the earth" (Ps. 46:6, 10). God's transcendence over every nation and their false exaltation of themselves are clearly set forth in many biblical texts. Psalm 59 calls out to Yahweh: "Awake to punish all the nations; spare none of those who treacherously plot evil. Each evening they come back, howling like dogs and prowling about the city. There they are, bellowing with their mouths, with sharp words on their lips. . . . But you laugh at them, O Lord; you hold all the nations in

113

derision" (Ps. 59:5–8). Isaiah describes the nations' lack of importance, despite their own sense of self-importance: "Even the nations are like a drop from a bucket, and are accounted as dust on the scales. . . . All the nations are as nothing before him; they are accounted by him as less than nothing and emptiness" (Isa. 40:15, 17). There are not many words of exception in the Bible to the follies and illusions of nations and God's power over them.

What's Right and Wrong with American Exceptionalism

The Bible clearly does not affirm or predict America as Israel's exceptional replacement as the chosen people of God. The idea of the "new Israel," as some have called America, ignores that fact and forgets that there is still an old Israel in the world whose covenant with God has not expired. But the primary Christian focus is now on a universal and international community centered in Jesus Christ, who breaks down the principal human barriers and divisions—race, class, and gender; there is no longer Jew or Gentile, slave or free, male or female. So for Christians, any conversation about the future of the world and the exceptional vocation of humanity does not start with a nation-state. It must start with the new multinational community of the church. We can say it even more clearly in regard to American exceptionalism. Jesus's followers in the United States are called to be Christians first and Americans second. As simple and basic as that affirmation is, it remains a radical statement of interest, identity, loyalty, and priority.

So there is *no* divine mandate for American exceptionalism in the sense of a unique, special, and exceptional relationship between God and the American nation, regarded as unlike all other nations. Of course, God uses and works through all nations—both the righteous and the unrighteous. But when politicians say that God has granted the United States or any other country a special role in human history, they are theologically wrong and politically dangerous.

Robert P. Jones, CEO of the Public Religion Research Institute, has studied the polling on American exceptionalism and reports:

Americans who affirm the idea of "American exceptionalism," a belief that God has given the U.S. a special role in human history, have a distinctly more militaristic approach to foreign policy than those who do not affirm this idea. Those who believe in American exceptionalism are more likely to favor military strength over diplomacy as the best way to ensure peace, and they are also more likely to say torture can be justified than those who do not believe God has given the U.S. a special role.[3]

Cal Thomas, a conservative Christian columnist, asserts "a huge difference between affirming American exceptionalism and the claim by some that God favors America more than other nations. That is idolatry. Jesus didn't die and rise for Americans, who did not exist in His time, but for everyone from every land and for all time."[4] Or as *Politico* columnist Michael Kinsley says, exceptionalism easily becomes "the theory that Americans are better than everybody else."[5]

Perhaps most important, the danger of American exceptionalism comes in making "exceptions" for America's actions when we violate our best values or accepted international rules of behavior. That's what creates disasters and the kind of blatant hypocrisy that is seen by others around the world. Ignoring human rights is wrong, and America is no exception. Supporting brutal regimes is wrong, and America is no exception. Fighting unjust wars is wrong, and America is no exception. Torture is wrong, and America is no exception. Making and using weapons of mass destruction is wrong, and America is no exception. There can be no exceptions for breaking basic principles and values. When that happens, everyone loses.

American history has much that is unique. But we often make the mistake of thinking that "different" means "better." Theologian Brian McLaren says it well:

3. Public Religion Research Institute, *Old Alignments, Emerging Fault Lines: Religion in the 2010 Election and Beyond* (Washington, DC: Public Religion Research Institute), 19, http://publicreligion.org/site/wp-content/uploads/2011/06/2010-Post-election-American-Values-Survey-Report.pdf.

4. Cal Thomas, "Of Course America Is Exceptional," *Washington Post*, November 29, 2010, http://onfaith.washingtonpost.com/onfaith/panelists/cal_thomas/2010/11/of_course_america_is_exceptional.html.

5. Michael Kinsley, "U.S. Is Not Greatest Country Ever," *Politico*, November 2, 2010, http://www.politico.com/news/stories/1110/44500.html.

When exceptionalism degenerates into a sense of national superiority, entitlement, smugness, and inflated self-importance, it simply becomes a camouflage for pride, an attractive quality in neither politics nor ethics. Such dangerous pride, the Bible says, goes before a dangerous slide. . . . In whatever ways America has been uniquely blessed, with that blessing comes not exceptional geo-political privilege but exceptional moral responsibility. It doesn't give us additional moral "exceptions," but rather intensifies our moral obligations to our neighbors. As Jesus said, from those who have been given much, much will be expected. Exceptional blessing means exceptional responsibility.[6]

Why I Love My Country

Of course you can love your country. I love mine. But patriotism, loving your country, is different from nationalism, which can make an idol of a nation and put its interests above all others. When I watch *The Sound of Music* with my kids, I must confess I always get teary-eyed when Captain von Trapp sings "Edelweiss," a love song to his native Austria. But he simply loves his country; he is not practicing Austrian exceptionalism.

What do I love about America? I love the land, one of the most spectacularly beautiful countries in the world (and I've visited many of them). I love walking our long stretches of beaches, hiking our majestic mountains, seeing the desert skies, walking beside the rivers, sailing along the coasts, and visiting hundreds of lakes in my home state of Michigan, where I camped as a kid. I even love some of our big cities! "O beautiful for spacious skies, for amber waves of grain, for purple mountain majesties, above the fruited plains."[7] I love our many diverse cultures, including their music, their food, their art, their sports, and their particular stories and histories.

And I do love baseball. My wife, the Brit, is a Little League baseball commissioner, and I've coached both of my sons' teams. Baseball is a

6. Brian McLaren, "American 'Exceptionalism' Can Degenerate into Superiority," *God's Politics* (blog), December 3, 2010, http://sojo.net/blogs/2010/12/03/american-exceptionalism-can-degenerate-superiority.

7. Katharine Lee Bates, "America the Beautiful," originally published as "Pikes Peak" (1895).

wonderful American game, unlike any other in the world. A night at any ballpark in America is a great night for me. And so is walking over to the baseball field right next door to watch a Little League game after dinner with everybody sitting on the hill.

I especially love our best national values: freedom, opportunity, community, justice, human rights, and equality under the law for all of our citizens of every race, creed, culture, and gender, not just for the rich and powerful. In particular, I love our tradition and history of democracy, its steady expansion here, and how it has inspired the same all over the world. We take legitimate pride in seeing how our founding documents have been the models for many new nations.

For me, a very vivid personal experience of that history comes from South Africa, ten years before their first free elections, which put Nelson Mandela in office. I had literally been sneaked into the country to support their persecuted faith leaders and help develop new strategies and partnerships between the South African and American churches. One night, I was staying in the Soweto Township home of Frank Chicane, the head of the South African Council of Churches. Late that evening, Frank wanted to show me something and spread some papers out on his kitchen table. He confided in me that Nelson Mandela, even while still in prison, had asked a few people to begin the drafting of a new South African constitution. And Frank was one of them.

As he began to show me the work, I noticed two other documents on the table: the American Declaration of Independence and the Constitution of the United States. Ironically, at that very moment there were two South African military vehicles outside Frank's house: the one that always parked there to monitor Frank and one to monitor me, because the government had discovered I was in the country. The South African regime of apartheid was being supported at the time by the American government's "constructive engagement" policy, but inside a little house in a black township, a dissident clergyman was drafting a new constitution based on the documents that announced American freedom. Despite the contradictions in all that, I loved that exceptional contribution from my country.

What I don't love is when my country violates its values and ideals and behaves badly, as when we supported the white South African government for far too long, as well as too many other terrible dictatorships around the world. I don't love when my country acts out of greed and only for power, or with blatant hypocrisy, or like an empire. The gospel has never lived easily with empire. Christians have a prophetic vocation, in whatever nation they live, to lift up the values of the kingdom of God and call nations to honor their best values in light of those principles.

Martin Luther King Jr. did that the best. America was wrong about race—just wrong. My little church in Michigan was wrong about race. King held his Bible in one hand and the Constitution in the other. And he challenged the nation to change. King's critique was based on the American values we were violating as well as the biblical values we were betraying as Christians and Jews. Likewise, the Arab Spring of 2011 saw youthful protesters force the United States to remember and restate its democratic values, which it had ignored for decades throughout the region of the Middle East. Why? Because of oil. We forgot our values, and a new generation of Middle Eastern activists is making us remember them again.

I also love our American social movements: abolitionists who fought to end slavery, civil rights activists, suffragettes, labor organizers, human rights campaigners—these are my heroes. But ultimately, I love the Jesus movement: the kingdom of God, which knows no nation-state and is God's plan for the world.

God and America

In American history, we've seen two ways to lift up faith in public life. One is by invoking the language of faith to hold the nation accountable to God's intentions, calling us to justice, compassion, humility, and even repentance, as Abraham Lincoln so eloquently did. The other is to invoke God's blessing on ourselves and on our nation's activities, agendas, purposes, and wars. We've seen both. Patriotism, as Michael Dyson says, is the "critical affirmation of one's country in the light of its best values, including the attempt to correct it when it is in error."[8]

Again, if we're Christians, we critique America by our Christian principles—not the other way around. There's no disputing that fellow believers in the body of Christ around the world do not share our belief in American exceptionalism. And the body of Christ internationally often disagrees with much of American foreign policy, such as the war in Iraq. Even conservative evangelicals in Great Britain disagreed fundamentally with our invasion of Iraq.

N. T. Wright is a New Testament theologian and also a Brit who says he loves the United States and likes to visit. He writes this:

> I want to say, Yes, God has called America to a special place in the world at this moment in history. In the Bible God calls many nations and peoples to particular roles and purposes. . . . However, it is clear throughout scripture that God calls wicked and violent nations as well as righteous and peace-loving ones—and that, when the former have accomplished his purpose, God will judge them according to what they have done and the spirit (e.g. of arrogance, carelessness of life, etc.) in which they have done it. . . . So just as I believe God has granted America a special role in human history, I believe that God has granted e.g. Norway, Nigeria, New Zealand, Nicaragua, etc. a special role as well. And what God calls in one generation may move and shift over time; the great Old Testament prophets saw God's hand in the rise of Assyria, Babylon, Persia, Greece, Syria, Egypt and Rome—and also God's judgment on all of them for the ways in which they carried out their commission inappropriately.[9]

The problem with American exceptionalism is that it sometimes has a very low view of sin. America, like any other nation, is a nation full of many sins. We underestimate the power of sin when we put too much stock in American virtue and let America off the hook, even for violating

---

8. Michael Eric Dyson, "A 'True Revolution of Values,'" excerpt from *Pride* (Oxford: Oxford University Press, 2006), Beliefnet, January 2006, http://www.beliefnet.com/Faiths /Christianity/2006/01/A-True-Revolution-Of-Values.aspx.

9. N. T. Wright, "God Calls Nations to Special Roles," *Washington Post*, November 30, 2010, http://onfaith.washingtonpost.com/onfaith/panelists/nicholas_t_wright/2010/11 /god_calls_nations_to_special_roles.html.

our own best values. Do we love America enough to tell the truth about its bad behaviors? That is what prophetic faith does. Christians believe they are part of a global community, and our first loyalty—ahead of any loyalty to a nation-state—is to the global body of Christ. And that should be true for every Christian, no matter what country he or she lives in.

Brian McLaren describes the only kind of exceptionalism that is theologically justified: "What we want is to be a good and distinct people, the best possible version of ourselves, not merely fulfilling (and exploiting) some national myth of manifest destiny, but instead creating a national legacy for our children and grandchildren, a great nation among other great nations, through wisdom, justice, freedom, compassion, and action."[10]

A Microcosm of the World's Future

Martin Luther King Jr. spoke of "the beloved community," a vision that appears throughout his speeches and writings. But his concept was always more theological than political.

In an article adapted from their book *Search for the Beloved Community: The Thinking of Martin Luther King Jr.*, authors Kenneth Smith and Ira Zepp describe how central the concept was for King.[11] We sometimes forget that Dr. King was also Rev. King, a Baptist preacher as well as a civil rights movement leader. On many occasions, King said the purpose of the Montgomery bus boycott wasn't just equal access for both blacks and whites to all the seats on the bus but also "reconciliation" and "redemption, the creation of the beloved community."[12] And when it came to a mission statement for his own organization, the Southern Christian Leadership Conference, King boldly asserted, "The ultimate aim of SCLC is to foster and create the 'beloved community' in America where brotherhood is a reality. . . . SCLC works for

10. Brian McLaren, "America the Exceptional," *Sojourners*, January 2012, http://sojo.net /magazine/2012/01/america-exceptional.

11. Kenneth L. Smith and Ira G. Zepp Jr., "Martin Luther King's Vision of the Beloved Community," *Religion Online* (originally published in *The Christian Century* [April 3, 1974]: 361–63), http://www.religion-online.org/showarticle.asp?title=1603.

12. Ibid.

integration. Our ultimate goal is genuine intergroup and interpersonal living—integration."[13] And in a sermon delivered on the last Christmas Eve of his life, King declared: "Our loyalties must transcend our race, our tribe, our class, and our nation."[14] Smith and Zepp say that King held a powerful vision of a "completely integrated society, a community of love and justice wherein brotherhood would be an actuality in all of social life. In his mind, such a community would be the ideal corporate expression of the Christian faith."[15]

King certainly fought for desegregation and equal access to all public facilities and services, but that was a battle against the negative and brutal force of segregation. Integration was a positive force, he felt, for the kind of new community he wanted to see for America. You can legislate against injustice, and King knew the nation needed to. He said the law could not make white men love him but could keep them from lynching him.[16] But King knew you could not legislate reconciliation and love; yet that was the basis for the beloved community. For King, both the civil rights movement and the true church—the church as it was meant to be—were really a *microcosm* of what society was supposed to be and what history would ultimately be. The campaigns of the movement were always around specific and concrete demands—like civil rights and voting rights—but the spiritual and philosophical vision that both inspired and drove King was that of the beloved community.

Historian Charles Marsh sums up the relationship between the civil rights movement and the mission of the church in King's mind: "The fading of the 'old order' and the emergence of a 'new age' is not written into the genetic code of American history as its manifest destiny."[17] In other words, the progress from the civil rights movement was not

13. Ibid.

14. Martin Luther King Jr., "Christmas Sermon on Peace" (Ebenezer Baptist Church, Atlanta, Georgia, December 24, 1967), http://www.thekingcenter.org/archive/document/christmas-sermon.

15. Smith and Zepp, "Martin Luther King's Vision."

16. Martin Luther King Jr., in *The Wall Street Journal*, November 13, 1962.

17. Charles Marsh, *The Beloved Community: How Faith Shapes Social Justice from the Civil Rights Movement to Today* (New York: Basic Books, 2004), 50.

destined or ordained by the American nation. Those gains were not inevitable. Rather, claims Marsh, the "beloved community depends on a theological, one might say ecclesiological, *event* of the cross. In other words, the brotherhood and sisterhood of humankind radiated out from the fellowship of the faithful."[18] Those historic achievements of the civil rights movement radiated from the community of faith into the wider society. That is because the cause of the movement was, in fact, deeply moral and theological and not just political. Marsh says, "If 'segregation is a blatant denial of the unity which we all have in Jesus Christ,' as King said, then reconciliation demonstrates to the world the truth that 'in Christ there is neither Jew nor Gentile (Negro nor white) and that out of one blood God made all men to dwell upon the face of the earth.'"[19]

King was, in fact, making a democratic argument that was based in the theological meaning of Galatians 3:28, which we have been discussing. And King believed that the christological facts of what occurred at the cross had now created new *social space* in American society. Marsh concludes with how Dr. King's theology changed sociology:

> Thus, the beloved community is the new social space of reconciliation introduced into history by the Church, empowered by the "triumph and beat of the drums of Easter." . . . The beloved community is established by the "great event on Calvary" . . . "the great event that stands at the center of our faith which reveals to us that God is on the side of truth and love and justice," as King explained in his Dexter sermon, "Paul's Letter to American Christians."[20]

Therefore, Martin Luther King Jr. is valuable to us not only as a civil rights leader and a Christian minister but also as a prophet for what we are visioning as the common good. He was both a theoretician and a practitioner of how we are supposed to relate to one another in a society. What are the obligations we owe each other? How are things supposed to work, and why? Why can't we just live as individuals,

18. Ibid.
19. Ibid.
20. Ibid.

and why are we so caught up in these nets of social relationships? In one of King's most profound reflections about our personal and social relationships, and about the basis for them, he tells us about the "structure of reality":

> All I'm saying is simply this; that all life is interrelated, that somehow we're caught in an inescapable network of mutuality tied in a single garment of destiny. Whatever affects one directly affects all indirectly. For some strange reason, I can never be what I ought to be until you are what you ought to be. You can never be what you ought to be until I am what I ought to be. This is the interrelated structure of reality.[21]

The Children of God

My own pastor, Dr. Jeffrey Haggray of First Baptist Church in Washington, DC, speaks more and more about "the beloved community." The inspiration for him comes from the apostolic expression of that kind of community in Acts 2:42–47 and from the visions in the book of Revelation of that diverse community's worship, which we have already discussed. But the heart of it for Jeff Haggray is found in the fourth chapter of John's first epistle, which describes how "perfect love casts out fear."

> So we have known and believe the love that God has for us. God is love, and those who abide in love abide in God, and God abides in them. Love has been perfected among us in this: that we may have boldness on the day of judgment, because as he is, so are we in this world. There is no fear in love, but perfect love casts out fear; for fear has to do with punishment, and whoever fears has not reached perfection in love. We love because he first loved us. Those who say, "I love God," and hate their brothers or sisters, are liars; for those who do not love a brother or sister whom they have seen, cannot love God whom they have not seen. The commandment we have from him is this: those who love God must love their brothers and sisters also. (1 John 4:16–21)

21. Martin Luther King Jr., "social justice" speech (Kalamazoo: Western Michigan University, December 18, 1963), http://www.wmich.edu/library/archives/mlk/transcription .html.

This is a demanding concept of love—that those who say they love God but do not love their brothers and sisters are "liars." We can't see God, but we say we love him; yet we can see our brothers and sisters and don't love them! This is the Bible's "fullest teaching on love," says Rev. Haggray, and that love is at the heart of the beloved community. John's epistle answers all the arguments about who we are supposed to love—it is all of God's children and not just those who are baptized into our faith community.

All people are God's children. Whatever race, tribe, culture, class, nation, gender, or sexual orientation we are from or identify with, we are all God's children. All people are created in the image of God; all people are part of the family of God. There are no "outsiders" to the kingdom of God because all are welcome. And the believing community is supposed to live that out and teach that truth to the rest of the world. The faith community is to extend hospitality and welcome to the stranger and the outsider as a testimony to them that they are part of God's family. These are theological commitments that, as in the case of King and the civil rights movement, can have social and political consequences.

Pastor Haggray takes what he calls "prayer walks" around Washington, DC, and has become especially conscious of the changing demographics of our nation's capital. He passionately describes what he has seen on those long walks and how the city is such a diverse place of cultures, tribes, and nations. And the human pictures of that community have given him a vision for the mission of our church—to be a place where all the tribes are welcomed into a beloved community that wants to follow Jesus. The parish around our church evidences that international community, thriving along Massachusetts Avenue and Embassy Row, Dupont Circle, 16th Street, Pennsylvania Avenue, and Connecticut Avenue, all with diverse cultures on display. And as Jeff watches all those people, he is imagining what it would take for us to welcome them and how our church could be transformed to be that welcoming place.

We have already discussed that famous text from John 3:16, "For God so loved the world that he gave his only Son, so that everyone who believes in him may not perish but may have eternal life." That's a very familiar passage for evangelical Christians. But the next verse, verse 17, says, "Indeed, God did not send the Son into the world to condemn the world, but in order that the world might be saved through him." Somehow the churches have focused more on the condemnation than the love. And our condemnation of others is usually manifest in a return to our tribal identities.

"Who is this Jesus?" a new world wants to know. "What is this gospel?" and "What does it mean for me?" the people from many tribes are asking. In answer, Jeff Haggray says we have to "peel back as many layers of 'cultural religion' or 'cultural Christianity' as possible, including traditions and cultural influences that conceal the basic claims of our faith; for a complex world will not be persuaded to follow Jesus by a culturally bound message that is shrouded in parochial influences and preferences."[22]

Paul says in his Epistle to the Romans that our cultural conformity is an obstacle to our true worship of God:

> Therefore, I urge you, brothers and sisters, in view of God's mercy, to offer your bodies as living sacrifices, holy and pleasing to God—this is your true and proper worship. Do not conform to the pattern of this world, but be transformed by the renewing of your mind. Then you will be able to test and approve what God's will is—his good, pleasing and perfect will. (Rom. 12:1–2 NIV)

There is a clear and negative connection between worship and cultural conformity. Not conforming to the "pattern of this world" is related to our "true and proper worship." This text jumped out at us as young seminarians nearly four decades ago as we viewed what we called "the American captivity of the churches." Christians are often drawn to their natural groups and their cultural preferences, and they "condemn" those who don't fit those preferences and even discriminate against other tribes who are not their own—as white Christians did to their black fellow Christians. J. B. Phillips has my favorite paraphrase of that text:

22. Jeffrey Haggray, "Our Mission, Our Message" (sermon, First Baptist Church, Washington, DC, March 18, 2012), http://www.firstbaptistdc.org/multimedia/listen-to-weekly -sermons.

"Don't let the world around you squeeze you into its own mold."[23] And that is always the danger—staying inside our tribe and defining that as true worship while relegating all others to the status of outsiders. As we have seen, the biblical narrative strongly advances a gospel that breaks down our human barriers and especially welcomes the outsider, who could, if allowed, be a messenger of salvation for us.

And the way we express that faith is through our life together as a beloved community in the world—by the ways we live together, treat each other, worship together, pray together, serve one another, and serve our community to embody and model God's love for the whole world.

What My Mom Taught Me

My mother used to give us kids two instructions: first, if there is a kid on the playground that nobody else is playing with—you play with that kid. And second, if there is a bully picking on other kids—you be the one to stand up to him or her. Those two principles have served me well. And I can almost hear my mother's voice sometimes.

On one occasion, I wore purple while speaking at an evangelical Christian college, and I was pleased to see people passing out purple ribbons just before chapel and announcing why. We were joining others across the country who believed that bullying should never be tolerated at any time, at any place, or for any reason. The purple was to commemorate "Spirit Day," in memory of young people who had taken their own lives as a result of harassment and bullying inflicted on them because of their sexuality. We all wore purple because we were followers of Christ.

A bully is a person who habitually intimidates, harasses, or commits violence against those who are smaller, weaker, or more vulnerable because of their "outsider" status. A bully stands in opposition to all of what Christ taught and lived. This sort of harassment is indefensible. And the stories of young kids being so bullied that they take their own lives have been heartbreaking to hear.

23. Rom. 12:2 (Phillips New Testament in Modern English).

That bullies target gay and lesbian people should mean that Christians give extra attention to protecting and standing up for them. That any community or group of people is regularly the target of harassment and hate means Christians should be on the front line of defense against any who would attack.

But many bullies don't know they are bullies. A bully might think that his or her words don't matter that much or affect others that greatly. A bully might think that he or she is being funny or just kidding around. A bully might think that he or she is just saying what everyone is thinking.

There is disagreement within the Christian community when it comes to issues of human sexuality. And there will be theological differences and biblical work going on for some time around issues like gay marriage. Probably, people who are young now will find the way forward because their generation has made this an issue through the relationships they have with people who are gay. They believe in equal protection under the law for everybody. And they believe that all God's children should be welcomed with the gifts, talents, ministries, and relationships they bring that have authenticity and integrity. I agree with them. But even before we find all our answers, there should be a united front against all who would disrespect, disparage, or denigrate anyone created in the image of God.

Here is what I have learned about "outsiders." My tribe taught me to be afraid of them and to stay away from them because they were dangerous. But I didn't. So I broke the rules by going to where they were. I have often said that I've learned the most about this world from being in places where I wasn't supposed to be. The outsiders have taught me more about the real world than the insiders ever have. And the outsiders were a vehicle for my learning the true meaning of the gospel. I think that's why God is always telling his people to welcome the strangers, the foreigners, the poor—the outsiders.

For many young believers today that means welcoming undocumented workers and fixing a broken immigration system. It means collaborating with young Muslims to build better communities and a cooperative future. It means trying to free those being trafficked or exploited. It means making the poor, more than the rich, the measure of their vocational choices. And it means treating gay and lesbian friends as their brothers and sisters. It means always listening to the outsiders.

The evangelical college students that day joined in prayer for the family and friends of every young person who had taken his or her own life because of bullying. They wanted to send a message of hope to any person who has been teased, harassed, or bullied by another because of his or her sexual orientation. And even if they were not clear about their own views of homosexuality or gay marriage, they were standing in the way between bullies and their victims.

At an evangelical Christian college in the Midwest, there was a lot of purple. And the airline security official who checked my boarding pass before my flight home saw my purple ribbon and said, "I see you're wearing purple today; that's a good thing."

Days later I was taking my boys to school and raised the issue of bullying and gay teen suicides to see what they had heard about it. My twelve-year-old, Luke, of course knew all about it, while seven-year-old Jack hadn't heard yet. But Jack spoke of a boy on the playground of his school who was sometimes a bully to others. Before I could say a word, Luke said to his little brother, "Now Jack, you need to talk to him. He will respect and listen to you because you are an athlete, a good student, and very popular. Kids who are strong need to be the ones who stand up for those who get bullied. Jack, part of our job is to make sure nobody gets bullied at our schools. Understand?" Jack said, "Yes," and I could just feel his grandmother smiling. It will be commitments like Luke's and Jack's that help create a beloved community and make a way for the common good.

··· 7 ···

Surprising Our Enemies

If we have no peace, it is because we have forgotten that we belong to each other.

—Mother Teresa

The followers of Jesus have been called to peace. When he called them they found their peace, for he is their peace. But now they are told that they must not only have peace but make it. And to that end they renounce all violence and tumult. In the cause of Christ, nothing is to be gained by such methods. His kingdom is one of peace, and the mutual greeting of his flock is a greeting of peace. His disciples keep the peace by choosing to endure suffering themselves rather than inflict it on others. They maintain fellowship where others would break it off. They renounce all self-assertion, and quietly suffer in the face of hatred and wrong. In doing so they overcome evil with good, and establish the peace of God in the midst of a world of war and hate.

—Dietrich Bonhoeffer[1]

1. Dietrich Bonhoeffer, *The Cost of Discipleship* (New York: Touchstone, 1959), 112–13.

Loving our neighbors is hardest when they are also our enemies. But Jesus tells us to love them anyway. Loving our enemies is the most difficult gospel command of all. Loving our neighbors is hard enough, but loving our enemies seems impossible. Those whom we define as "the other" fall outside our boundaries of "the neighbor," and we feel justified in treating them very differently. But in a world full of conflict and enemies, we need to learn how to do better. What might it mean to *surprise* our enemies?

Conflict Resolution

> If your enemies are hungry, feed them; if they are thirsty, give them something to drink; for by doing this you will heap burning coals on their heads. Do not be overcome by evil, but overcome evil with good. (Rom. 12:20–21)

> But I say to you that listen, Love your enemies, do good to those who hate you. (Luke 6:27)

> Blessed are the peacemakers, for they will be called children of God. (Matt. 5:9)

How many sermons have we heard in our churches about loving our enemies since September 11, 2001? We now seem to be in a perpetual state of war with "enemies" who are very hard to find or completely defeat. The "war on terror" is unlike any we have ever fought, and it is harder still to tell when or how it will ever end. The primary strategy with which the United States and those nations it persuaded to join it chose to deal with the threats of terrorism was wars of occupation. But the effectiveness, sustainability, and morality of such wars have come under great doubt. Many folks are suffering from "war exhaustion." Is there a better way to deal with our enemies, both perceived and real?

Nations tend to turn their enemies into "the other" and attribute all manner of malevolent motivations and frightening capacities to them. Much of that is often overstated, and in view of the actual facts, some of it is completely false. We fought the whole war in Iraq—at an enormous human and financial cost—over facts and justifications that were patently untrue, making the horrible numbers of deaths, injuries, and permanently damaged lives all the more painful to bear. The war in Afghanistan, begun to pursue those who had attacked the United States on 9/11, has turned into the longest war in American history, with no near end in sight and a multitude of problems that just seem to get worse.

Although much of any nation's propaganda (which all nations use) about its enemies is not truthful and needs to be vigorously challenged, it is also true *that we will have real enemies in this world*, as persons, groups, and nations; even our faith communities will encounter them. Jesus's teaching does *not* assume that we won't have any enemies; rather, he instructs us on how to act when we encounter them. What Jesus and Paul are saying in the passages above is actually guidance for *better* and even *more effective* ways of dealing with our enemies. It may well be that our continual habit of going to war to deal with our enemies is running out of any real effectiveness or moral support.

Another and perhaps better way to discuss the problem of enemies, conflict, violence, and war is to turn to the language of *conflict resolution*—a concept and course of action used on the field of battle that is growing around the world. More people, especially young people, are turning to conflict resolution skills with fresh and creative energy, and a whole new discipline and experimental practice is emerging. What actually works in solving conflicts is being examined in new and creative ways.

It starts with the recognition that *human conflict is inevitable* between persons and families; between groups, clans, and tribes; between different cultures; and certainly between nation-states. To assume otherwise is foolish, from the perspective of history, certainly, but also in light of our best theology about the nature of the human condition. Yet it is also true that *most* human conflicts are resolved without recourse to violence. Most of our very human battles end without killing or wounding each other. So the obvious task before us, in a world engulfed in so much conflict, is to *increase* the use of more peaceful means of resolving those human conflicts. Given the terrible costs and consequences of the world's dreadful level of current conflicts, learning the art and science of conflict resolution is absolutely essential for the common good.

Here is where our religious traditions should help us, rather than merely providing more ammunition for the conflicts, as religion at its worst often does. What can religion, at its best, teach us about being peacemakers, who Jesus says are the children of God?

Jesus's instruction to love our enemies does not mean we simply submit to their demands and domination over us. In fact, what he means by loving them, in light of the courses of action he suggests, actually implies a strategy more like nonviolent resistance than weak submission. When Jesus instructs his followers to turn the other cheek, go the extra mile, or give their adversary their cloak, he is suggesting that these can be effective tactics to shame and confront the Roman soldiers who are the occupiers of the Jewish people. When you can't defeat your enemy militarily, there are other ways to embarrass him, reveal his hypocrisy, and even force him to think about what he is doing. Theologians Walter Wink, in *Engaging the Powers*,[2] and Glen Stassen, in *Just Peacemaking*,[3] have eloquently described this in their exegesis of the Sermon on the Mount.

Paul's words are fascinating when he suggests we "heap burning coals of shame on their heads" (Rom. 12:20). What? Is that kind of talk consistent with loving our enemies? Yes indeed; it means to *surprise* them with our love in ways that could even make our enemies reconsider what they are doing to us and others. If our enemies are hungry, feed them rather than acting to make them hungrier and angrier. If they are thirsty, give them something to drink instead of policies that cause their loved ones to die of thirst and that further turn them against us. Paul's approach here is not some naive pacifism but rather a shrewd way to change the situation, turn the tables, and change the outcome of conflicts.

The leaders of international relief and development agencies, on the ground in situations of conflict, sometimes suggest that if the

2. Walter Wink, *Engaging the Powers: Discernment and Resistance in a World of Domination* (Minneapolis: Fortress, 1992).
3. Glen H. Stassen, *Just Peacemaking: Transforming Initiatives for Justice and Peace* (Louisville: Westminster John Knox, 1992).

United States were to drop massive amounts of food and medicine into enemy territories, it could have a far greater effect than our bombs do. Bombing an enemy population usually unites them against us and can even pull them together around the terrible governments and dictators who are often the real targets of our attacks. People working every day in those places suggest that filling those countries with the things they desperately need (food, medicine, etc.) could change their attitudes toward us and even toward their governments, who are often failing to meet their needs. And ultimately, food is cheaper than bombs.

Many have learned—on a personal, familial, and communal level—how a surprising warm or understanding word or "soft answer"[4] can sometimes dispel anger, when a different kind of response might just create another confrontation. Serious listening and even absorbing some of the anger behind the understandable and even legitimate grievances that people have will often ultimately defuse anger and conflict, whereas fueling it more with a hostile response will escalate it. How to de-escalate conflict is something we have learned in community and pastoral situations, and it may be time to apply those same concepts to the political and international arena. The field of conflict resolution is doing this all over the world.

The Day That Changed Everything

On the morning of September 11, 2001, I was at home in Washington, DC, getting ready to go to the Sojourners office. I was upstairs listening to the news on NPR (National Public Radio) when I heard the first confusing report of a plane crashing into the south tower of the World Trade Center. I called downstairs to Joy and asked her to turn on the television to see what was going on. Moments later, as we ate breakfast together with our three-year-old son, Luke, we watched the second plane strike the north tower. I still remember my first words to Joy: "This is going to be bad, very bad."

4. Prov. 15:1.

133

Of course, I meant more than just the damage to the Twin Towers and the lives lost, which became far greater than any of us imagined at first. Rather, my first and deepest concern was what something like this could do to our nation's soul. I was afraid of how the United States would respond to a terrorist attack of this scope.

But as the towers collapsed, and the suffering from this horrible event became increasingly clear in the hours and days that followed, other parts of the American soul revealed themselves: the heroic responses of the first responders and a city and nation of people taking care of each other. As ordinary citizens gave their lives for strangers, they became their brothers' and sisters' keepers. In the days following the 9/11 attacks, the stories of pain, loss, and self-sacrifice brought Joy and me to tears several times. The suffering of many led to acts of service from many more.

For a moment, the world's last remaining superpower was vulnerable, and we all felt it. In Washington, people fled from downtown DC, literally running out of the city; and many gathered to pray at places like the Sojourners office. Joy helped Luke set up a little water station as people frantically rushed by our house.

With our sudden sense of vulnerability, we were, perhaps for the first time, like most of the world, where vulnerability is an accepted part of being human. In those first days following 9/11, the United States, and not the terrorists, had the high ground. The world did not identify with those who cruelly decided to murder innocent people in response to their grievances, either real or imagined. Instead, the world identified with a suffering United States. Even the front cover of the French newspaper *Le Monde* ran the headline, "We are all Americans."[5]

But I was most worried about how the US government would respond. Within a short time, the official reaction would simply be defined as *the war on terror*—a decade of it—resulting in many more innocent casualties, more even than on September 11, 2001. As a result of America's own suffering, many others in Afghanistan, Iraq, and around the world now also suffer, all in the name of our war on

5. "Nous sommes tous Américains," *Le Monde*, September 12, 2001, http://www.free republic.com/focus/f-news/523345/posts.

terror. The opportunity for deeper understanding, reflection, and redirection eluded us as we sought to *erase our vulnerability* with the need to demonstrate our superior force and power. This was done quite easily in the early days of both our new wars. But now we see that the longest series of wars in American history has failed to resolve or reverse the causes of the violence that struck us on 9/11 or to ensure our safety. In fact, the wars of occupation have made many things worse.

The world expected and would have supported a focused and sustained effort to pursue and bring the murderous band of criminals to justice. But ten years of manipulated and corrupted intelligence, continual war, practices and policies of torture, secret armies of assassins, global violations of human rights, indiscriminate violence with countless civilian casualties, and trillions of dollars spent have caused our nation to lose the high ground.

A Better Response

Fortunately, the official and failed responses of Washington, DC, to the tragedy of 9/11 have not been the only ones. A new generation of Christians is asking how Jesus would respond to events like these. Many of them would agree with what former United Methodist bishop Will Willimon said in the evangelical magazine *Christianity Today* on the tenth anniversary of the terrorist attacks: "American Christians may look back upon our response to 9/11 as our greatest Christological defeat. . . . When our people felt very vulnerable, they reached for the flag, not the Cross."[6] As many of those who grew up in the decade since 9/11 confront the conflicts of their world, they are reaching for goals different from those their government has reached for. They are forging alternative and more creative responses to issues of injustice and violence and rejecting the cycle of terrorism and war that marks Washington's failed strategy and failed moral logic.

6. Will Willimon, "How Christian Leaders Have Changed Since 9/11," *Christianity Today*, September 7, 2011, http://www.christianitytoday.com/ct/2011/september/howleaderschanged .html?start=5.

Despite the hateful diatribes of fundamentalist leaders across all religious traditions, many pastors have decided to love their neighbors, and even their enemies, in response to Jesus's call. Their stories are slowly being told, from American neighborhoods where Muslims have moved in, to conflict areas around the world where faith is being used for bridge building and healing rather than for revenge killings. Christian leaders are sharing meals, fasting, and praying with Muslim leaders. Some have defended each other's congregations and homes in the face of heated threats and rhetoric. While differences between faith traditions are not being glossed over, the nature of a loving and reconciling God is being courageously affirmed across religious lines. In all of this, they are saying that their governments' responses need not define their own.

It has become a school and household conversation. My sons, Luke and Jack, both understand what Christianity and Islam are and are not. In their classrooms, they have friends who are Muslim. One day Jack, who missed the events of 9/11, heard a disparaging remark on television about Islam and quickly retorted, "That's not true, there is a Muslim boy in my class, and he is not like that at all." Luke and I watched the National Geographic special on the tenth anniversary of 9/11, which described the horrible and extraordinary events of the day that we remember. It helped him to put the pieces in place from his memories of 9/11, when he was a three-year-old. I was struck with how he looks at the world with more sympathy than fear and how strongly he feels about war's inability to solve the problems and conflicts between people.

Each year, the actions of extremists can mar the commemoration of the 9/11 terrorist attacks and even ignite more violence. But many interfaith services also mark the anniversary events. At Ground Zero in New York City on the tenth anniversary, evangelical leaders from around the globe called for peace and unity. We said that while religion has too often been the cause of conflict, it can also heal. We lifted up examples of Christians and Muslims living together peacefully, even in the most conflicted parts of the world, and called for Christians to be good neighbors to the Muslim community. When we gather in our houses of worship during those anniversary weeks, many pastors remind their parishioners of two fundamental truths: we must not be overcome by evil but rather overcome evil with good, and, in the words of the hymn, "they will know we are Christians by our love" (see John 13:35).

But that morning of September 11, 2001, changed everything about the United States and the world and has set the framework for most questions about our enemies, about how to respond to the real threats of violence in the world today, and about the efficacy and morality of wars of occupation in protecting our national security. An absolutely criminal, cowardly, and vicious attack on so many innocent people was made even worse by the distorted invocation of religion to justify the premeditated murder of thousands. That utter religious hypocrisy by a criminal few has led to the suspicion of an entire religious community of one billion Muslim people.

In the first decades of the twenty-first century, it is Muslims who often find themselves named as "the other," and that is one of the greatest challenges before us. Political tirades against "Islamic radicalism" are common now, as are highly symbolic state legislations against "sharia law" (as if it were a real threat in Tennessee). Mosques and Islamic centers have been victims of verbal attacks and acts of vandalism, from Manhattan, near Ground Zero, to every region of the United States. We've heard Islam sadly called "an evil religion" by a few prominent evangelists and even seen accusations by Barack Obama's opponents that the professing Christian president is secretly a Muslim.

Changing the Story

It is easy to believe that hostility toward Muslims is on the rise in our country. But this narrative of constant conflict doesn't tell the whole story. In my work with religious communities across the country, I have seen interfaith relationships strengthened in recent years, not in spite of 9/11 but because of it.

In the run-up to the ninth anniversary of 9/11, the battle over a proposed Islamic community center in New York City and the hateful rants of Florida pastor Terry Jones, who threatened to burn Qur'ans on September 11, were both painting a picture of great tension between faiths.

But that story was changing at the Heartsong Church in a suburb of Memphis, Tennessee. What happened there gives us clues about how to surprise those called "the other" or even "our enemies," and about what most changes people's attitudes. In a rare departure from the cable networks' steady drumbeat of religious conflict, this alternative story was featured on CNN and was broadcast around the world.[7]

The year before, Heartsong's pastor, Steve Stone, learned that the Memphis Islamic Center had bought land adjacent to his church, in the suburban town of Cordova. Did he protest the plans for an Islamic center next door? No. He put up a large red sign right out in front of his church saying: "Heartsong Church Welcomes Memphis Islamic Center to the Neighborhood."

The Muslim leaders were astonished. They had dared to hope only that their arrival would be ignored. It had not occurred to them that they might be welcomed. They asked for a meeting with Pastor Stone, and new relationships formed. Before long, Christian and Muslim children were playing together, and their parents began to talk and share meals. Believers who knew almost nothing about each other's faith began to have conversations.

The Islamic Center's new building was still under construction, so its members were offered Heartsong Church for their Ramadan prayer services the following year. Heartsong's community barbecues were now serving halal meat, and the two congregations were planning joint efforts to feed the homeless and tutor local children. CNN's story was a dramatic alternative to most of the media coverage around the controversy over the "Ground Zero mosque" and the threatened Qur'an burnings. The picture of a Christian pastor and the leader of a Muslim congregation talking together as friends showed mutual respect and even affection, and it was a very sharp contrast to all that we had been seeing in the American and global media.

7. "Tennessee Church Welcomes Muslim Neighbors," CNN *Belief Blog*, September 10, 2010, http://religion.blogs.cnn.com/2010/09/10/tennessee-church-welcomes-muslim-neighbors.

When I spoke to Steve Stone, he told me about a phone call he had just received late at night from a group of Muslim men in Kashmir, Pakistan. They told him they had been watching CNN when the segment on Heartsong Church aired. Afterward, they said, "We were all very silent." Then, they reported, one of the community's leaders said to those who were gathered: "I think God is speaking to us through this man." Another said: "How can we kill these people?" A third man went straight to the little local Christian church near their mosque and proceeded to clean it, inside and out, with his own Muslim hands.[8]

In America, we had been hearing a lot about hostility toward Muslims in our country. We heard a lot about Jones's threats and about arson at the site of another Tennessee mosque project, in Murfreesboro. But we had heard little about people like Stone and his new admirers in Pakistan. And that was everyone's loss. Stone said he was just trying to love his neighbors, as he believes Jesus instructs Christians to do—even including those they might consider to be their enemies. Those are the words of Jesus, he said. A few critics called Stone a heretic for letting Muslims worship in his church and asked how he was witnessing to Christ. Stone responded, "By loving them as our neighbors—because they actually are our neighbors—just like Jesus asks us to."[9]

But at 1:30 one morning during a remarkable phone call, the residents of a small town in Kashmir told Stone: "We are now trying to be good neighbors, too. Pastor Stone, tell your congregation we do not hate them, we love them, and for the rest of our lives we are going to take care of that little church."

Bob Smietana, religion writer for the *Tennessean* (Nashville), reported on the Heartsong story. He had been covering the vandalism and hatred expressed at other locations in Tennessee against Muslims. But, he reported,

> in Cordova, things have been peaceful. There have been no marches against the mosque or other public opposition. Aside from some angry emails, the two congregations have gotten mostly positive feedback about

8. Jim Wallis, "A Test of Character," *Sojourners*, December 2010, http://sojo.net/magazine /2010/12/test-character.
9. Ibid.

their relationship. They've been featured on local and national news. A film crew from Bahrain came to town to film a story on the congregations. . . . That small act of kindness was the start of an unlikely friendship between the two congregations, one that made headlines around the world.[10]

What are the implications of all this? What best changes hearts and minds in dangerous places like Pakistan: an example of Christians loving their neighbors or our aggressive military strategy?

Trusting Relationships

The connections between faith leaders also helped avert a tragic conclusion to the Terry Jones Qur'an-burning saga, which was occurring at the same time. Religious leaders from many traditions condemned Jones's threats, while, behind the scenes, a number of Christians reached out to support Feisal Abdul Rauf, the imam behind the proposed Islamic community center in New York.

I had been in close dialogue for several weeks with the imam and his wife, Daisy Khan. We had been friends since a few months after the 2001 attacks, when we participated together in a forum on religious fundamentalism at the Cathedral Church of Saint John the Divine in New York. From their words that day, I trusted Rauf and Khan and knew that we would be able to work together as peacemakers between faiths.

The storm around the imam and his wife about their proposed community center was already bad enough; but on Thursday, September 9, 2010, it threatened to get a lot worse. That afternoon, Jones announced that he would be heading up to New York to talk with the imam on the anniversary of 9/11. He seemed to think that he could leverage his Qur'an-burning threat to pressure Rauf to move his center and, in the process, get even more attention. The idea was offensive. It suggested a moral equivalence between burning the holy book of a billion people and building a community center, and it presumed that an important

10. Bob Smietana, "Peace Be upon Them," *Sojourners*, September/October 2011, 16–18.

and respected Muslim leader should bargain with the irresponsible pastor of a tiny church.

How, I wondered on September 10, could evangelicals—members of the faith tradition that Jones claimed—run interference? I felt strongly that we were the ones who should deal with Jones, rather than the beleaguered imam whose faith he had demonized. And I promised Daisy Khan we would do it—even though I wasn't sure how.

An hour later, I got a call from a good friend, Geoff Tunnicliffe, the international director of the World Evangelical Alliance. He was in New York and wanted to know what he could do to help "your friend the imam." He explained that he had Jones's cell phone number and had spoken to him earlier in the week. In an effort to talk Jones out of his original plan, he had asked him, "Will you be willing to be with me when I have to talk to the widow of an evangelical pastor in the Middle East who is killed because of what you are about to do, or to a congregation whose church is burned to the ground as a result of your Qur'an burning? Will you help me explain to them why you had to do this?"

Tunnicliffe was the right person in the right place at the right time, and he pulled together many of New York's evangelical leaders to talk with Jones. On the conference call in New York that ensued, Geoff said the Florida pastor seemed "lost." Others described the exchange as "powerful," "productive," and "reflective." During the conversation, Jones vowed not to burn a Qur'an on the 9/11 anniversary and even asked what an apology might look like. He did not seek out a confrontation with Rauf the next day but instead went home. Jones eventually returned to his old anti-Muslim rhetoric. But trusting relationships between Christians and Muslims helped to prevent the threatened burning of the Qur'ans on that anniversary of 9/11.

Interfaith Cooperation as a New Movement

Similarly powerful, productive, and reflective exchanges have occurred in churches all over the country after 9/11, when hundreds of Christians have turned out to hear a visiting Muslim scholar or imam speak to their congregation. We saw it in Jones's hometown of Gainesville, where Trinity United Methodist Church, literally next door to Jones's congregation, brought together an estimated two thousand people for a "Gathering for Peace, Understanding and Hope," but it failed to spark media attention.[11]

Most hopefully, I have seen the story changing with a new generation. Several years ago, I came home from work one night to find a young man sitting on my doorstep. He said he had come across the country to see me and asked if he could have just fifteen minutes. He got that, and more, and we have been talking ever since. His name is Eboo Patel, and he has written, "If religious extremism is a movement of young people acting, and interfaith cooperation is a movement of senior theologians talking—then we lose. . . . The noise about religion and religious diversity is dominated by the voices of aggressive atheists who hate religion, religious extremists who hate people, and religious bigots who hate Islam."[12] Eboo created the Interfaith Youth Core, based in Chicago, an exciting organization that brings young people from different religions together on college campuses and in cities around the nation, not just for discussion but for action in community service, which makes for even better conversations. Says Patel, "We are creating a new category in American and global life, which is the category of interfaith cooperation. Right now, people need to see a progressive Muslim."[13] Eboo gives me a lot of hope.

When we see a disturbing rise in religious intolerance in the United States and waves of a new Islamophobia sweeping the country, how should Christians respond? This question raises other questions that get to the heart of the issue, and our answers to them will demonstrate important things about ourselves, our faiths, and the character of our country.

The first question is, does our judgment of our neighbors come from their religious labels or the content of their character? I don't advocate a bland interfaith pluralism that blurs the significant differences between

11. Jim Wallis, "Jim Wallis on the Story behind Pastor Terry Jones's Change of Heart," *Washington Post*, September 19, 2010, http://www.washingtonpost.com/wp-dyn/content/article/2010/09/17/AR2010091702398.html.

12. Eboo Patel and Rose Marie Berger, "Radical Possibility," *Sojourners*, February 2009, 14.

13. Ibid.

religions, but I believe my religious tradition calls me to be a peacemaker and to love my neighbors, especially when I do not agree with them. When Muslim leaders step up to lead initiatives to reduce tensions and promote understanding, do we judge them by the actions of terrorists (whom these leaders have condemned) or by their own integrity and character? This does not mean that we have to agree on everything but rather that we're called to love and respect each other.

The second question is, do I believe in freedom for my religion or freedom of religion? The "establishment" and "free exercise" clauses of the First Amendment were revolutionary statements. They represent ideals we aspire to but have not always lived up to. Anti-Semitism, anti-Catholicism, and other forms of religious bigotry have reared their ugly heads over and over in our history. But ultimately, minority groups have flourished here because of our strong history of religious liberty. Whether we allow religious freedom for Americans of the Muslim faith—near Ground Zero or anywhere else—will give evidence of our own character, of the integrity of our faith, and of our real commitment to the ideals that have distinguished our nation.

Daisy Khan is demonstrating that women in her Muslim tradition will play a key role in changing attitudes. She says:

> Islam is becoming an American religion, and this represents a victory for all Americans who cherish our nation as a beacon of tolerance and acceptance of all traditions. . . . Now as Muslims continue to find our way in American public life, we ask Christians to respect and support us. We ask them to consider us citizens, allies, and brothers and sisters in faith, rather than strangers, enemies, or competitors for devotees. Hear us and help us tell our story. I firmly believe that the core values of Islam—faith in and obedience to the Divine, reverence for individual rights and communal well-being, compassion and justice, respect for pluralism and diversity—are entirely resonant with American values.[14]

Finally, we must ask a third question: In the face of global terrorism, who wins when the United States restricts religious freedom? Religious sensitivities, especially around Ground Zero, are understandable.

14. Daisy Khan, "Balancing Tradition and Pluralism," *Sojourners*, February 2009, 15.

September 11 was a crime against humanity, and, tragically, it was the first significant encounter many Americans had with radical Islam or Islam of any sort. But this is why the mission of interfaith cooperation is very important for reducing tensions and building better understanding. In order for our country to continue healing, more of us need to build trust with those who are religiously different from us, especially with the many Muslims who love this country. There are thousands of interfaith conversations, service projects, and relationships that have been built since 9/11 that should be lifted up and encouraged. This tension is really about the role that faith will play in America and around the world. It is about whether we will accept Muslim citizens as true citizens or as second-class citizens. It is about whether we will blame one billion Muslims worldwide for the actions of a small number of Muslims who tried to use their brand of faith to murder innocent people. It is a test of both our character and our faith, and we dare not fail it.

How to Overcome Religious Extremism in the Middle East and the United States

Most of our discussions of US foreign policy and the Middle East say more about politics than they do about the fundamental issues we must confront if we want to see substantial change. So let's look at the basic issues and fundamental choices we need to make.

Today the Middle East—where about 60 percent of the population is under the age of twenty-five—is a region dominated by humiliation and anger. Failure plus rage plus the folly of youth equals an incendiary mix.

The roots of anti-American hostilities in the Middle East run deep (literally and figuratively). We can start with the fact that *our* oil (we seem to think it must be ours to sustain our oil economy) lies beneath *their* sands. Couple that with US support of repressive and backward regimes, the continual presence of foreign troops on their land and in their holy places, and the endless wars waged there, ultimately fueled by the geopolitics of energy. Add to that explosive cocktail the unresolved Israeli-Palestinian conflict, which continues to drive the deepest emotions of mutual frustration, fear, and retaliation throughout the Middle East and the rest of the world.

Injustices and violence caused by the oil economy have sparked a reaction from dangerous religious fundamentalists in the Muslim world. Fundamentalism—in all our faith traditions—is both volatile and hard to contain once it has been unleashed, and it is hard to reverse its essentially reactive and predictably downward cycle.

Here are three principles that may help us navigate a path out of this mess. First, *religious extremism will not be defeated by a primarily military response to it.* Ample evidence proves that such a strategy does not work and often makes things worse. Religious and political zealots prefer huge military responses to the threats created by Islamic extremism. Ironically, this holds true on both sides of the conflict; the fundamentalist zealots also prefer the simplistic military approach because they are often able to use it effectively. The shock-and-awe strategy of military might simply has not worked. Fundamentalists actually flourish and win the most new recruits amidst overly aggressive military campaigns against them.

Second, *religious extremism is best undermined from the inside rather than smashed from the outside.* The answer to bad religion is not secularism, as all the "new atheists" like to say; rather, it is better religion. And the best antidote to religious fundamentalism of all stripes is—in every case—the genuine faith tradition that is alive and well in most world religions. For example, the best thing that moderate and progressive Christians can do in the struggle with fundamentalism in other faith traditions is to make powerful alliances with the moderate and progressive leaders in those other faith communities. Fundamentalist religion must be countered with prophetic religion, and a new alliance between prophetic religious leaders across our many faith traditions is the best way to defeat the threats of modern fundamentalism.

Third, while the use of force to protect our security and bring perpetrators to justice is justifiable, *defeating the mind-set and motives of terrorists will come with much broader and more creative strategies.* This third principle goes back to Paul's strategy of feeding your enemies to "heap burning coals on their heads" (Rom. 12:20). What the

145

modern Muslim world most needs today is education (especially of its young women), the building of technology and infrastructure, and a principled focus on economic development.

The Middle East in general most needs precisely that kind of assistance from the West, not more weapons and money poured into the coffers of corrupt regimes. The West has not been on the side of democracy or development in the Middle East, and that fundamentally must change. Altering policies in the West will help alter destructive patterns in the Middle East.

But the change most needed in this volatile region must come from within—with the right kind of support from without.

During the summer of 2012, Sojourners worked with local interfaith communities in Joplin, Missouri, to put up billboards that read "Love Your Muslim Neighbors" just blocks from where a mosque had been burned to the ground a few weeks earlier. Sojourners erected another billboard in Oak Creek, Wisconsin, to support the Sikh community after the deadly shootings at its gurudwara in August. And a third sign went up in Murfreesboro, Tennessee, to show our solidarity with our Muslim brothers and sisters there embroiled in an ongoing controversy about a local mosque.

As I was finishing this book, global tensions between Christians and Muslims were high as we witnessed reactions to a very crude and stridently anti-Muslim film rage in many countries. Most of the world heard about this amateurish, hateful video and saw the media coverage of the protests and violence, including a terrorist attack on the eleventh anniversary of 9/11 that took the life of an exceptional US ambassador to Libya, Christopher Stevens, who was mourned in both the United States and Libya.

In the midst of all this, an organization often deemed a hate group decided to run ugly anti-Muslim ads—implying that all Muslims are uncivilized "savages" and jihadists—in New York City subways. Many people of faith from across the nation spoke out against the ads, which NYC transit officials labeled as hate speech and tried to block before a federal judge ruled that the ads are protected by the US Constitution. Sojourners tried to bring a message of love—a light in the darkness—to counter the hate by launching a "Love Your Muslim Neighbor" ad campaign also in the NYC subway system.

These love-your-neighbor ads helped create good and healing conversations in the media and faith communities of those cities where the ugly actions and words were taking place. What we are finding is that such simple and positive peacemaking messages (especially in situations of religious conflict) strike deep and responsive chords in many people, religious and nonreligious alike.

When Jesus said, "Love your neighbor as yourself" (Matt. 22:39), he didn't add stipulations. He didn't offer any extra addendums or qualifiers. Christians around the world need to put those words into action as often as we can, especially where we see hatred like this. And, as we have already described, the Hebrew Scriptures have the same message about loving our neighbors as ourselves, and the Qur'an calls for the same ethic.

Everyone—regardless of race, religion, or creed—deserves to feel welcomed and safe when riding public transit in America or driving through the streets of their hometowns. The reminder of our religious obligations to love our neighbors can bring out the best in people when messages of hate try to bring out the worst. When tensions across the world are especially high, the faith community should do what it can to promote nonviolence in our own backyards and project that message of peace around the world.

Changing the policy. Changing the message. Both are essential if lasting change is to come to the Middle East and the rest of the world.

Since the attacks of 9/11, we have seen a *theology of war* coming from some political leaders in the United States and even from some of our religious communities. It attempts a theological justification for the "war against terror" and even for the particular role of America in prosecuting such an endless war. But, at least for Christians, the words of Jesus at the beginning of this chapter stand directly in the way of that theology of war.

In a world wracked with violence and war, the words of Jesus, "Blessed are the peacemakers, for they will be called children of God" (Matt. 5:9), are not only challenging; they are daunting. The hardest saying of Jesus, and perhaps the most controversial in our post–9/11 world, is indeed, "Love your enemies and pray for those who persecute you" (Matt. 5:44). Let's be honest about the question we raised at the beginning of this chapter: How many churches have heard sermons preached from either of these Jesus texts in the years since America was viciously attacked on the world-changing morning of September 11, 2001? Shouldn't we at least have a debate about what the words of Jesus mean in the new world of terrorist threats and wars of occupation?

The issue here is not partisan politics, and there are no easy answers to the important and complicated questions of national security. No one has a monopoly on the truth. But there is reason to worry about an increasingly religious tone in formulating an aggressive foreign policy that is more nationalist than Christian. Another concern is the use of fear, which is a dangerous basis for foreign policy. Effective campaigns of fear too easily convince anxious people and could lead our nation to decades of virtually endless wars.

The words of Jesus are either authoritative for us or they are not. And they are not set aside by the very real threats of terrorism. They do not easily lend themselves to the missions of nation-states that would usurp the prerogatives of God. Our confession of Christ warns against the demonization of perceived enemies and the assumption that those who fundamentally question American policies must side with the "evildoers." Christian ethics challenge any idea that the world is divided into forces of absolute good and absolute evil.

Empire Stress

As I write in the summer of 2012, approximately seventy thousand US troops remain in Afghanistan, more than ten years after the war began. President Obama has committed to steady withdrawals for the rest of this year and throughout 2013, with all combat troops gone by 2014. But that is not enough. We must make the courageous decision to end the war in Afghanistan much faster than the president has called for. The incremental and gradual drawdown of troops, over more years, is not an adequate response to a failed war.

What began as a response to an attack has become an open-ended war against a Taliban insurgency, which itself is largely motivated to drive out foreign troops and has few designs beyond its own borders. The military operation has so far resulted in the deaths of more than three thousand coalition troops, including over two thousand from the United States. Estimates are that tens of thousands of Afghan civilians have died. And yet Taliban influence continues to spread. Al Qaeda barely exists in Afghanistan, but it has metastasized into Pakistan and has established itself in Yemen, Somalia, and other places around the globe.

Legitimate ethical and moral issues are at stake in Afghanistan: defending US national security from terrorist groups like Al Qaeda, protecting the lives of coalition servicemen and servicewomen, protecting Afghan civilians, defending the rights of Afghan women, supporting democracy, and, of course, saving innocent lives from the inevitable death and destruction that accompany war.

But the past ten years have shown that the United States cannot broker peace in Afghanistan by military force; it is time to transition toward a plan that builds up civil society and provides economic alternatives for Afghans. At a time of economic turmoil, as we are presented with such difficult financial and budgetary decisions at home, we have an opportunity to invest in aid that both supports the people of Afghanistan and saves our country much-needed funds.

In the spring of 2012, a horrible incident in the war in Afghanistan occurred. A thirty-eight-year-old Army staff sergeant, having served three tours of duty in Iraq and now serving another in Afghanistan, left his base near the city of Kandahar in the middle of the night and walked a mile to a nearby village, where he proceeded to go house to house in a murderous shooting spree, killing sixteen civilians as they slept, including nine children, some as young as two and three years old.[15]

Like revelations of torture against Iraqi prisoners that had come to light earlier, and instances of American military personnel deliberately killing civilians in Iraq, this latest incident of horror shocked our nation and created a storm of reaction in the country we are occupying.

15. "Afghanistan Massacre Suspect Named as Sgt Robert Bales," *BBC News*, March 17, 2012, http://www.bbc.co.uk/news/world-us-canada-17411009.

Of course, the vast majority of American servicemen and service-women have not participated in such terrible atrocities, and many have shown courage in humanitarian behavior, even in the midst of conflict. But the *stress* of long wars of occupation has led to great consequences, both for the lives and families of American soldiers and for the people in occupied nations.

We have subjected too many young people to the horrible battle stress of long wars of occupation and multiple tours of duty. Even among those who survive their many tours, hundreds of thousands come home with emotional damage and even brain injuries, and there are now higher numbers of suicides than war deaths. When the suicide of a veteran occurs every eighty minutes, and when soldiers on active duty commit suicide more often (more than one each day) than they suffer casualties, it's time for some much deeper national soul-searching. Can we continue to impose such hardships on our soldiers and their fami-lies—especially when they represent such a small number of Americans, of whom a disproportionate number are lower-income Americans? Is such a strategy either militarily or morally sustainable?

Let's not simply be shocked at the evil we have seen in those hor-rible prison photos or now in the pictures of small children with bul-let holes in their heads; let's instead be sobered and saddened by that same potential in many human beings stressed beyond their break-ing points. When the consequences of psychiatric weakness or social pathology combine with battle fatigue, horrible incidents can result that embarrass the nation and the military and fuel the agendas of the extremists we are there to confront. Brutality is inevitably the consequence of occupation and domination and is an enduring part of the cycle of violence.

In preferring the virtues of human dignity, justice, and even humility, Christianity implicitly teaches that continual war is not the best strategy to fight terrorism. In fact, our wars of occupation often make terror-ism worse by producing tragic behaviors that terrorists use to fuel their murderous agendas. The pictures from Abu Ghraib or of dead children in Kandahar will always be recruiting posters for the next generation of terrorists in the Muslim world.

The Lessons of Humility

My son Jack was born just days before the war in Iraq began. So, for those eight and a half years, it was very easy for me to remember how long that horrible conflict had been going on.

The initial feelings that rushed over me after hearing the White House announcement that the troops would be home for Christmas in 2010 were of deep relief. But then they turned to deep sadness over the terrible cost of a war that was, from the beginning, wrong: intellectually, politically, strategically, theologically, and above all, morally.

The war in Iraq was fundamentally a war of choice, and it was the wrong choice. From the outset, this war was fought on false pretenses and for false purposes. The war literally was sold to the public in the US, UK, and elsewhere with the claim that Iraq had weapons of mass destruction. Many believed it at the time, and an invasion was mounted on what turned out to be false information. A decade of sanctions and United Nations inspections had already undermined the allegations. And in the almost nine years of war, not a single weapon of mass destruction was found in Iraq.

The invasion began with triumphal claims that it would be a "cakewalk" and that US and coalition forces would be welcomed as "liberators." That proved to be initially true with the unexpectedly easy removal of Saddam Hussein from power, which led to the famous picture of a flight-jacket-clad George W. Bush on a US aircraft carrier six weeks after the invasion began, standing under a banner that read, "Mission Accomplished!" The invasion, however, turned into an occupation, and nearly five years of vicious and deadly street warfare, sectarian violence, and constant terrorist bombings were the result.

By the time the heaviest fighting had died down, the Iraqi people were bitterly divided, huge parts of their country had been devastated, and corruption and fraud were rampant. As US and coalition combat troops returned home, they left behind a badly damaged nation that will require years, if not decades, of assistance and humanitarian development. And our responsibility did not end simply because our military presence in Iraq has.

151

Near the end of the war, I met US Representative Walter Jones, a nine-term Republican congressman from eastern North Carolina and a longtime member of the House Armed Services Committee. When he spoke to my students at Georgetown University, he called his decision to give President George W. Bush the authority to go to war in Iraq a "sin."

Even then, he didn't believe or trust the intelligence being used to support a war with Iraq, but confessed he feared the response to a "no" vote among his constituency in a district that includes Camp Lejeune and sixty thousand retired members of the military.

Jones's transformation, which he narrated to the students, came from personal encounters and growing relationships with families who lost their precious loved ones and from the convictions of his own Christian faith. It began when the congressman, attending the funeral of a young man who had been killed, sat next to the deceased's widow and young son, who would now be without their husband and father. It was the first of many funerals and hospital visits.

"We were lied to," Jones told my Georgetown students, and went on to describe his journey to find the truth. For people of faith, "truth matters," he said. Jones learned how the intelligence on Iraq was "manipulated" and "distorted" to justify going to war, and that this was a completely unnecessary war. We were "misled" into war, Jones said, and, so far, nobody has been held accountable for it. There are wars that could be considered "just," he said, but this war was not one of them. Outside Jones's office on Capitol Hill is a wall of "the faces," as he puts it, of those who paid the ultimate price for the manipulation of the truth. And when Jones talks about these young soldiers, you can see how deeply their loss has affected him.

Clearly, religious communities must reach out now more than ever to returning veterans to make sure they have the physical, emotional, and spiritual support they need. One of the most unjust aspects of an unjust war is that such a small minority have borne the brunt of the impact and cost of this war.

Despite this tragically mistaken war, the sacrifices made by many servicemen and servicewomen have been extraordinary. And even in the midst of war's brutalities there have been many acts of real heroism, soldiers risking and giving their own lives for their fellow soldiers and for the lives of Iraqis, who also paid a heavy price. No matter what our view of the war, it is our collective responsibility to be healers for those who are coming home—and for those still left in Afghanistan. The only redemption from the war in Iraq would be to learn from it, from our horrible and costly mistakes.

Representative Jones has become one of the war in Afghanistan's most outspoken critics and has reached across the aisle to coauthor, with Democratic congressman Jim McGovern of Massachusetts, the McGovern-Jones Amendment, introduced in July 2010, which calls for a clear timeline for the withdrawal of troops from Afghanistan. Here are a few excerpts from an interview I did with Jones about the things he has learned—and that we have to learn as well.

> God wanted me to take away from that funeral service [the first he attended of a fallen serviceman, at which he sat with the deceased's widow and child] the pain of a family that lost a loved one for going into a war that never had to have been fought. I realized my mistake and my weaknesses for not voting my conscience.
>
> In 2003, I started writing letters to the families and extended families of people killed in the war. All told, we've written well over ten thousand letters to families and extended families now. This is my penance.
>
> If half the American people could visit Walter Reed [Army Medical Center], we would've been out of Afghanistan five years ago.
>
> I think God wanted to humble me, quite frankly, for not trusting him on that vote. God wanted me to come back to God because I didn't listen. I needed to understand that the world I live in is a world of arrogance and Christ was a man of humility, and in the world of arrogance you will accomplish nothing with arrogance. You have to be humble.[16]

When it comes to how we are going to engage our enemies, humility might be the lesson that we most need to learn.

16. Jim Wallis, "A Convert to Peace," *Sojourners*, September/October 2011, 30–31.

PART 2

Practices for the Common Good

··· 8 ···

Conservatives, Liberals, and a Call to Civility

All that is necessary for the triumph of evil is that good men do nothing.

—attributed to Edmund Burke

It was once said that the moral test of government is how that government treats those who are in the dawn of life, the children; those who are in the twilight of life, the elderly; and those who are in the shadows of life, the sick, the needy and the handicapped.

—Hubert H. Humphrey[1]

There is a war going on today in America's political discourse. And the casualties are many. We've lost our civility, the ability to have public discussion that isn't harsh or dismissive but respectful and genuinely

---

1. Hubert H. Humphrey, remarks at the dedication of the Hubert H. Humphrey Building, Washington, DC, November 1, 1977, in Congressional Record, vol. 123 (November 4, 1977): 37287.

open to dialogue and disagreement. We've also lost our ability to really listen to one another and even to learn from people who don't have all the same views, perspectives, and experiences that we do. We've lost our capacity for political compromise, for actually finding solutions instead of just continually blaming each other for the problems. And we've lost our problem-solving commitment, which sometimes depends on different kinds of contributions and answers from varying points of view. We've certainly lost the kind of news and information outlets that regularly broadcast or publish different and even conflicting political opinions and therefore challenge our previously held thoughts and persuasions.

Perhaps the greatest loss is to the common good—because I believe that both conservative and liberal insights and commitments are necessary for it to exist. In short, I am convinced that the common good requires us to be *both personally responsible and socially just*. These are the two best big ideas of conservatism and liberalism respectively. Let's unpack them.

Your Conservative Uncle or Liberal Aunt

> With it [the tongue] we bless the Lord and Father, and with it we curse those who are made in the likeness of God. From the same mouth come blessing and cursing. My brothers and sisters, this ought not to be so. (James 3:9–10)

Imagine one of your favorite aunts or uncles, or one of your closest cousins, or a very dear friend of your family whom you have known for a long time. Remember all the wonderful times you've had with this person and the memories that will last forever. Now, if you are politically *liberal*, imagine that fond family member or friend is a *conservative*. Or, if you are a political conservative, imagine one that is a liberal. It is a very real experience that many of us actually have; we all know about those family gatherings and holiday dinners that are filled with political humor and even tension.

What do we really think of somebody who is very dear to us, maybe even our mom or dad, or a close brother or sister, who doesn't share our political views and perhaps is on the other side of the political aisle? We certainly all know members of our faith communities, and even our own congregations, who are different from us politically. So we have dear brothers and sisters in faith who do not agree with our political opinions or our voting choices.

Now recall what you have heard conservatives say about liberals, or liberals say about conservatives, on talk radio, cable television, or the screaming covers of best-selling books. "They" are traitors, bigots, disloyal, unpatriotic, stupid, snobs, rednecks, elitists, fascists, socialists, phony Christians, repressive theocrats, anti-Christian, dangerous religious zealots, atheists, fundamentalists, secret Muslims, religious right or left, mean, hypocritical, hateful, liars, without moral values, even demonic, communists, or Nazis—and "they" are clearly threats to our national security, Christian civilization, and democratic society as we know it.

Do you apply those names to your beloved conservative uncle, wonderful liberal aunt, or close family member? Are these the words you first think of when you remember him or her? Likely not. Why is our current political discourse so hostile to people we all personally know and love? Why does it speak so harshly about them, saying terrible things that we know are just not true?

The 24/7 news coverage today, especially on radio, cable, and the internet blogosphere, doesn't really "cover" the news but rather fuels the audience's already-held prejudices about what is happening. Almost all of it is biased, much of it is distorted, some of it is just plain lies, and too much of it is downright hateful. Unfortunately, we are losing genuinely important ideas that the other political side has, which are often critically needed to find more balanced answers to our complex social, political, and economic problems. We've lost our *integrity* in the public arena, substituting ideological warfare for genuine and rigorous political debate, replacing substance with sound bites. Go to the competing networks and top-rated shows to listen to their tone and style; while the politics are very different, the approach and attacks are too often much the same.

In such a polarized, paralyzed, and increasingly poisonous political environment, it is very difficult to find or even discuss the common good. But I believe that both the conservative and liberal philosophies have critical contributions to make in solving our problems and that the best ideas from both are essential for reestablishing a serious public discourse about the common good. What are the best and biggest ideas from each side that we will all need to listen to?

The Best Big Conservative Idea

The best big conservative idea is *personal responsibility*. It focuses on the choices individuals make that determine the direction of their lives, families, communities, nations, and even the world. The famous quote above attributed to Edmund Burke appears more and more often at the bottom of personal emails and on websites from students of mine across the political spectrum. Individuals making good, moral, virtuous, noble, and courageous personal choices are absolutely essential to the well-being of society and the outcome of history. And that is something you cannot legislate or engineer from the top down; it comes from within. My son Jack's travel baseball league is called "Win Within," and the summer baseball camp our boys have gone to for years at the field next door to our house has a slogan: "Talent is what you have, effort is what makes you succeed."

Doing the right thing, the moral thing, the ethical thing in personal decision making is key not only for individual well-being but also, I would argue, for the common good. Honesty, integrity, trust, compassion, and courage are all vital to personal and social relationships. Having your word or promise mean something is fundamental. Being someone whom others can depend on is of critical importance. Recently a friend I was having dinner with said of her father, "He was always a straight shooter. He was and did what he said he believed in." That, she said, had shaped all of his five children, who have now passed that philosophy on to their kids.

Sound moral choices and solid decision making are certainly crucial to the quality of family life, which is absolutely foundational to a nation's health and well-being. Faithfulness and fidelity in marriage are central to that. Infidelity is always based on deception, and the lack of truthfulness in one area of life can affect others. Trust is indeed a bottom line for both our personal and social relationships; if we lose that, other things begin to fall apart.

One critical area of personal decision making is the choice to make our children an absolute priority in our lives, which may be the most important personal and social decision that any of us parents can make. How we raise our young is what will most determine the future, not just for them but for the ripple effect it will have on their own families, communities, and world. Making our child rearing the priority around which other commitments must adjust, instead of the other way around, is the key here. Prioritizing our families is paramount to the common good.

I've asked parents who take clear liberal positions on public policy matters what they think will have the most formative influence on their own children's lives. Will it be what happens in their homes or what the government can do for them? They all know it's their home environment. Most of the things that affect families from the outside, positive or negative, will usually not shape children as much as what the most attentive parenting can do from the inside—or what a lack of parenting will create. I've watched, close at hand, the influence that the pathologies of poverty and violence can have on very poor families, especially if only one parent is available to combat those pressures. But even there, most young people who have escaped poverty give all the credit to a faithful single mom or a special teacher or a life-changing coach. The best ideas of education reform focus on the influence that very attentive teachers, principals, and schools can have. But again, the focus is on personal impact, one student and child at a time. The choices we make about our relationship to children or other people's children shape not only their lives but also the common good in extremely important ways. Of course, many liberal parents emphasize all these same values, but the personal responsibility ethic is core to the conservative philosophy.

Our own Sojourners Neighborhood Center was run for many years in what was then one of the poorest and most violent neighborhoods of Washington, DC. We always stressed the critical importance of *personal choices* with the kids who came in every day. We didn't tell them their lives were trapped in poverty and there was nothing they could do about it until that was changed. We emphasized the importance of their own choices: doing homework (which we helped them with every day at the center), rejecting drugs (through education and disciplined practices), resisting dangerous sexual activity (where self-esteem triumphed over peer pressure), learning how to resolve conflicts (not letting a fight over a jacket become a lethal event), and serving their communities (instead of being a problem or threat). We were always telling and showing them why they had to make clear personal choices, exercise good decision making, and take individual responsibility for their lives.

Similarly, across the country I have observed that those who run youth centers in the most dangerous urban neighborhoods—and who generally support very progressive public policies to combat poverty—are always counseling their young people to make these good personal choices, which could be called *conservative* personal decisions. None of us ever tell low-income kids there is really nothing they can do about poverty; we tell and teach them to take charge of their lives and circumstances by making better personal choices, and then to become activists to change the structures and policies that cause and perpetuate poverty. Most people I know who have escaped poverty usually did so with the help of social assistance, but it always involved clear individual decisions and solid personal choices as well.

Good personal decision making is a central part of the conservative ethic, and conservatives often emphasize it over social programs. But separating good personal decision making and good social programs is more the problem, in my view, than is the focus on individual responsibility, which is a very good and necessary thing. Programs of social uplift, without the ethic of personal responsibility, often don't work and can, indeed, turn into situations and cycles of dependence. Therefore it is right and good, and part of the common good, to emphasize such a conservative ethic in making those good personal choices.

My own parents always emphasized the importance of personal decisions and moral choices in our home. Both of them were very hard-working middle-American Christians and Republicans who voted for Dwight Eisenhower, who they believed represented their own steadiness, competence, and moderation. My dad rose to be one of the youngest executives at Detroit Edison, and my mother ran another company as the CEO's executive secretary, while they both started and led a new evangelical church. They raised five kids who always knew that love and values—both expressed in solidly "conservative" ways—were most important.

Those strong and solid personal values, choices, and decisions are at the heart of the conservative ethic of personal responsibility. Although many liberals have and live many of those same values too, liberalism tends not to use the language of personal responsibility and family values as much as conservatives do. But in a society adrift in narcissistic self-gratification and moral relativism, it is an absolutely critical language, and many long for that old ethic of personal responsibility again.

The Best Big Liberal Idea

The best big liberal idea is *social responsibility*. Being responsible for oneself and even one's family isn't enough. There is also our "neighbor," and even other neighbors we don't think of as such, as our previous discussion of the Good Samaritan gospel parable demonstrated. Compassion is an essential social virtue and should not be confused with political systems. Hubert Humphrey, quoted above, expressed it well: "Compassion is not weakness, and concern for the unfortunate is not socialism."[2] This great liberal icon identified the people for whom social compassion is most often necessary: those in the dawn, twilight, and shadows of life. The question of who will take responsibility for them is a soul-searching one from liberals, especially if those in need are outside of our own families and groups.

From an ethical or religious point of view, and certainly from a democratic point of view, we also have social responsibilities alongside our personal ones. There is a personal *and* a social gospel. Good, strong families are essential, but so is the health and vitality of *the commons* in our society: those places where we come together as neighbors and

2. "Hubert H. Humphrey Quotes," http://thinkexist.com/quotation/compassion_is _not_weakness-and_concern_for_the/209236.html.

citizens to share public space. We shouldn't need to have everything ourselves; we should also value the things that we share as part of the common good. And those interactions and relationships that come from that common sharing are essential to our own good. Our parks and playgrounds are crucially important, not just our own backyards. Everyone's health care is vital, and, ultimately, it will affect the health of my family and children. Education isn't just crucial for my kids, but for all the children of our society; so I shouldn't just support the schools when my own children are of school age, but for the whole of my life.

Forgive another baseball analogy, but we do live right next door to the field! Every night during the spring and summer months, the four adjacent baseball fields are filled with players, parents, siblings, friends, and neighbors who come to watch the games. While we're sitting up on the grassy hill overlooking the kids, coaches, and umpires, a real community event is taking place. Conversations are struck up, connections found, and new friends made. These are lovely evenings when everyone is relaxed and focused on our children, which is good not only for our own souls but also for the soul of the community. The place is even called, funnily enough, Friendship Field. And that is what happens there, especially over many seasons and with many siblings. It's not unusual for the field to become the place where a problem is shared, a heartache acknowledged, a need expressed, and help found. The carpooling, often done to get kids to games and practices, does lead to a kind of "life-pooling," in which more than rides are offered and shared.

My wife, Joy, is an Anglican priest who also happens to be a Little League baseball commissioner and the president of our school parent-teacher association. She isn't working in a church at the moment but is rather a "village priest," quietly serving that role in the broader community of school, sports, kids, parents, and life. The "field" becomes part of her parish, and it isn't unusual for it to be a place where a serious familial problem is shared or a cancer diagnosis revealed to the response of cries, hugs, prayers, and support. Our Friendship Field has become a paradigm for me, a microcosm of what a neighborhood, community, and even society is supposed to be—suffused with an ethic of social responsibility and the common good.

The history of our democracy includes the steady inclusion of those who have been thought to be "the other" by the majority culture. Religious communities, at their best, have often led the way toward that inclusion, but the society eventually comes along. Much of that leadership has come from those who are called "liberals." With some notable exceptions, conservatives mostly missed the civil rights movement, for example, while liberals were at the center of it. Again, liberals, more than conservatives, have been the supporters of equality for women in society and in the religious community. Now the inclusion issues pertain to undocumented immigrants, American Muslims, and gays and lesbians.

Again, my parents, in their own way, also expressed this liberal ethic alongside their conservative values. We had dinner together each night as a family. But often others joined us for a meal around the table, for an evening or a day or for much longer. The family whose house burned down would come and stay with us. A young person who needed a place to stay would be invited to take the room of one of us kids who had left for college. People who had needs would somehow gravitate to our home; or our parents would gravitate toward them, and we would ultimately find them at our house. My father was known in his company for hiring and promoting African Americans and women. And my mother, despite the conservative rules about women's roles in our church, demonstrated every day the powerful leadership that women could have and mentored many younger women in the process.

Such values are passed down. Our house, next to the baseball field, is a kind of "clubhouse" where kids and parents often congregate. One night before dinner, our then-seven-year-old Jack asked if he could pray for the meal. We all bowed our heads, but there was just silence. Finally, I peeked open my eye and saw Jack looking around the table. "What's the matter, Jack?" I asked. He replied, "I don't think there are enough people here." It was just us that night, and apparently Jack didn't think we had a prayer quorum.

The "value" of other people becomes important along with our own traditional personal values. And the value of social responsibility is the necessary complement to the value of personal responsibility we've already discussed. Robert Kennedy said it well:

For the fortunate among us, there is the temptation to follow the easy and familiar paths of personal ambition and financial success so grandly spread before those who enjoy the privilege of education. But that is not the road history has marked out for us. . . . The future does not belong to those who are content with today, apathetic toward common problems and their fellow man alike. . . . Rather it will belong to those who can blend vision, reason and courage in a personal commitment to the ideals and great enterprises of American Society.[3]

When I was a student, the quote from Bobby Kennedy that won my heart was this: "Some people see things as they are and say why? I dream things that never were and say, why not?"[4] The strength of the conservative ethic is to preserve the critically important good of what has gone before. But the liberal ethic is aimed at the future hope of new possibilities. Let's now get specific and tackle two controversial subjects that conservatives and liberals could do better on and perhaps find some common ground by moving to higher ground: strengthening marriage and ending poverty.

Strengthening Marriage

From a book tour for a previous book, I have a vivid memory of an interview I did at the offices of one of the most liberal, progressive magazines in the country. The young woman interviewing me was a Christian, the only one on the staff. After a terrific conversation, she said she had something personal to share with me and then whispered, "I'm getting married!" I remember replying, "Wonderful, but why are you whispering?" She said, continuing in her whispered tones, "If the people around here knew I was getting married, they would think me bourgeois and patriarchal."

3. Robert F. Kennedy, as quoted by Edward Kennedy at his funeral, June 8, 1968, http://abcnews.go.com/blogs/headlines/2009/08/take-a-moment-read-ted-kennedys-euology-of-bobby.
4. Kennedy was quoting George Bernard Shaw. See Robert F. Kennedy, remarks at the University of Kansas, March 18, 1968, http://www.jfklibrary.org/Research/Ready-Reference/RFK-Speeches/Remarks-of-Robert-F-Kennedy-at-the-University-of-Kansas-March-18-1968.aspx.

Marriage was not a positive value at this bastion of liberalism. That is a serious problem. Marriage is actually on the decline now around our country across all classes, but especially among low-income people.[5] Research from across the political spectrum—from the liberal Brookings Institution to the conservative Heritage Foundation—shows that marriage is one of the most critical factors in assessing the well-being of children and the common good—period. Children from married households do far better in life than children from unmarried households in regard to success in education, avoiding substance abuse and crime, and staying out of poverty. Obviously, having jobs that pay enough to support a marriage and family is a critical component of that success. Marriage is clearly an "antipoverty measure," as conservatives are prone to say—and so are jobs that pay a living wage, as liberals often say. How about public policies that are friendly to both? Seldom do we hear that possibility from liberal or conservative leaders locked in ideological warfare around subjects like marriage.

During a press conference on welfare reform a number of years ago, one of the liberal speakers, promoting better funding for child care, said this: "Oh sure, marriage is an antipoverty measure all right—that is, if you marry a millionaire!" It was an embarrassing moment to have a liberal leader so completely distort the facts and caricature an important argument. Here are the facts: the poverty rate in the US for married couples in 2008 was 6.4 percent, while for nonmarried, single-headed households, it was 36.5 percent. According to analysis from the Heritage Foundation, "marriage drops the probability of poverty by 80 percent."[6] Researchers at the Brookings Institution agree; their analysis shows that "if we had the marriage rate we had in 1970, the poverty rate would fall by more than 25 percent."[7] Isn't it time to get beyond the sound bites and examine the barriers to marriage in low-income communities—for

5. Pew Research Center, *Barely Half of U.S. Adults Are Married—A Record Low* (December 14, 2011), http://www.pewsocialtrends.org/files/2011/12/Marriage-Decline.pdf.

6. *Marriage and Poverty in the U.S.: By the Numbers* (Heritage Foundation, 2010), http://thf_media.s3.amazonaws.com/2010/pdf/wm2934_bythenumbers.pdf.

7. *Combating Poverty: Understanding New Challenges for Families* (Washington, DC: Brookings Institution, June 5, 2012), http://www.brookings.edu/research/testimony/2012/06/05-poverty-families-haskins.

example, our broken criminal justice system and the massive incarceration rates for men of color from poor communities? Or the lack of the kind of jobs that can support a family in vast stretches of poor urban and rural America? Or the number of jobs low-income people need to have to pay their bills, and the time that working so many hours takes away from children and family? Yes, let's talk about renewing marriage and family values and overcoming the real obstacles to it.

Why can't liberalism also extol the personal and social benefits of marriage, along with conservatives? I am married to one of the first women ordained in the Church of England. One day our first son was watching his mom celebrate the Eucharist. Luke was about five years old when he turned to me and asked, "Daddy, can men do that too?" In my household and in millions more around the country, the freeing notion of mutuality has replaced old ideas about male headship. That movement must continue until it replaces old patriarchal ideas and structures of marriage.

Liberals could change the conversation if they really affirmed the ideal and goal of marriage to young people who are shying away from such an important commitment. They shouldn't just affirm gay marriage, as liberals are more prone to do, but lift up the personal, spiritual, and social strength of marriage for everyone, and then work to find ways to include same-sex couples in those benefits, as conservatives have argued for in naming marriage as a conservative institution that society critically needs.

Ending Poverty

In working to end poverty, we face a series of false choices—or political preferences between liberals and conservatives. Conservatives stress the *cultural* factors that can cause and further entrench poverty in regard to weak family structures, educational performance, work habits and experience, or substance abuse; and they observe that having children outside of marriage is a huge factor in creating and sustaining poverty. Liberals stress *policy* matters and the need for well-paying jobs, better education, quality child care, stable housing, and affordable health care.

But why are we forced to choose between these two agendas? Why is it *either/or*? Why not *both/and*? Many of us who work on issues of poverty see such political polarization and paralysis around these issues and often consider ourselves politically "homeless." We often talk to each other about the need for a "both/and" politics in this nation.

Columnist Charles Blow summed up the problem this way: "Three out of four of those below the poverty line work: half have full-time jobs, a quarter work part time."[8] That means that most poor people *are working* but are just not making enough to sustain their lives and families. When I hear conservative friends talk about government social programs in the language of "dependency," I often ask if they actually know any low-income people or families in those programs—and they usually don't. When I tell them, for example, that 75 percent of "food stamps" go to families with children, that those families mostly work, and that the programs are usually temporary, to get people through difficult times, and are seldom long-term or permanent, they are quite surprised and say, "You should get that information out!"

Isn't it time to move from our ideological analysis of problems to practical solutions that would promote the values of both personal and social ethics? Mike Huckabee, the conservative talk show host and former US presidential candidate, put it this way in an interview I did with him: "Given the choice between a hungry person and a government program, I'll take the government program."[9] He said a hungry person means that the society's web of family, relationships, economic systems, and social protections has broken down; but when that happens the government needs to make sure the person is being taken care of—and this comes from a conservative. Huckabee says he disagrees with those in his party who are opposed to government programs to combat poverty under any circumstances and who would just let people go hungry for the sake of their ideology. Our whole society needs to work better, according to Mike, and not simply depend on government programs to solve everything. But part of government's responsibility

8. Charles M. Blow, "For Jobs, It's War," *New York Times*, September 16, 2011, http://www.nytimes.com/2011/09/17/opinion/blow-for-jobs-its-war.html?ref=charlesmblow.
9. Author's conversation with Mike Huckabee for a radio show pilot, December 2011.

is to take care of those who are hurting, and sufficient social safety nets should be a commitment of both political parties.

There are indeed those who see government as the only answer to poverty and who miss the crucial role that civil society can play, not only in providing social services but also in encouraging the kind of personal and social values that help lead people out of poverty. The importance of the "mediating" institutions of the civil society is something that both conservatives and liberals ought to be able to agree on. Multi-sector solutions and a balance between the public and private sectors, government and civil society, cultural and policy strategies, and stressing both personal and social responsibility are the way of the future and the path to success.

So why are we at war? Most of the social problems we are trying to solve will need *both* of these ethics strengthened and neither one diminished. The ethics of personal and social responsibility are both clearly important and necessarily complementary. The best personal choices and the most compassionate behavior toward those in need are both essential.

From Winning to Governing, from Blame to Solutions

Winning or losing US elections takes place every two, four, or six years, depending on the office of the public official. And in between, there is this idea called *governing*. But we seem to have lost that. Politics seems to be in constant campaign mode now. Our politicians are always running for office, always battling their opponents, always getting ready for the next election. Their political opponents are thought of more as enemies than as colleagues, and working with them is less important than planning how to defeat them next time. Party leaders now even admit this; their goal at the beginning of an opposing party's presidential term is simply to defeat the new president, not to find ways to work with him or her until the next election. This language is especially prevalent from our most stridently ideological radio and television talk show hosts—who now seem to set the political agenda for their political parties.

Living in Washington, I have often described what I increasingly see taking place. As I wrote earlier, politicians take a problem and do two things with it. First, they try to make people in the public arena *afraid* of the problem. Then they try to *blame* the problem on the other political side. This is now a regular procedure of both political parties and is the theme of most political campaign advertising. And while most people say they are disgusted with negative political ads, the data show that these ads clearly do work. But what they also do is increasingly diminish the public's respect and trust for politics and politicians, which is now at its lowest ebb in many years.

We are going to have to turn *governing by problem solving* into a political ethic expected of those whom we elect. How effectively our political leaders are actually solving problems must be scrutinized in great detail. We must no longer be content merely to listen to politicians lecture us on why we have such problems: "It's the other side's fault."

Even on some of our most divisive issues, we could perhaps find some common ground if we were really looking for it. Those who are deeply committed to the sacredness of human life and those deeply sensitive to a woman's control over her own body could perhaps agree to work together to prevent unwanted pregnancies and commit themselves to a national goal of reducing the number of abortions by supporting low-income women's health care, offering alternative choices, and strengthening adoption. Criminalizing a woman's tragic and often desperate choice might not save as many unborn lives as would offering alternative options, and it can create many new dangers and problems for women in crisis.

Similarly, disagreement on the theological and moral issues around homosexuality should not prevent people on all sides of the debate from supporting equal protection under the law for all people, regardless of their sexual orientation. We could develop new and creative strategies for overcoming poverty by combining both the cultural and policy choices discussed above. And even in areas like economics, believing that big banks and corporations need more public accountability does not prevent us from overhauling the regulations on small businesses that many people on both sides of the aisle believe need fresh scrutiny.

There are many more examples of creative, common-ground problem solving in policy debates—if we were willing to listen to one another and work together.

One criterion for examining the problem-solving ability and commitment of elected officials is to see where and how they work with people on the other side of the political aisle. Today, politicians are sometimes afraid to work across partisan lines for fear of being criticized by the extremists (particularly on talk radio and cable television) for consorting with the enemy. To be honest and fair, the attacks on working with the other side have been most extreme, of late, on the conservative side; but neither can liberals continue to blame all our problems on the conservatives. We must turn that around, demanding to know what they are actually trying to solve and whom they are trying to solve it with. But for that, we are going to need a better political discourse.

From Ideological Warfare to Civil Discourse

It's time to move from endless conflict to mutual respect.

The phone calls began a few years ago. Deeply concerned veteran members of Congress would call me to express a real despair about the alarming level of disrespect, personal attacks, and even hateful rhetoric they observed among their colleagues, reflecting a degeneration of public debate in our national culture. Political debate, even vigorous debate, is a healthy thing for a democracy, they all said; but to question the integrity, patriotism, and even faith of those with whom we disagree is quite destructive to democratic discourse. There were now even threats and implications of the possibility of violence toward those whose politics or worldview differed—an alarming sign of moral danger, and indeed, a sign of democracy's unraveling. Some members expressed real fears about threats of violence they and other elected officials had experienced that were directed against themselves and even their families.

A group of more than 130 former legislators, both Republicans and Democrats, released a letter urging civility and encouraging candidates, once elected, to focus on cooperation in facing our country's greatest challenges: "None of us shrank from partisan debates while in Congress or from the partisan contests getting there. During our time in Congress, partisans on the other side may have been our opponents on some bills and our adversaries on some issues. They were not, however, the enemy."

These former Congressmen and Congresswomen pointed the finger at both parties for this breakdown, observing how legislators hold on to "wedge issues" to run on, as opposed to finding common-ground solutions. The letter also recognized the outside forces at work: "The divisive and mean-spirited way debate often occurs inside Congress is encouraged and repeated outside: on cable news shows, in blogs, and in rallies. Members who far exceed the bounds of normal and respectful discourse are not viewed with shame but are lionized, treated as celebrities, rewarded with cable television appearances, and enlisted as magnets for campaign fund-raisers."[10] These public servants are no longer in office but did us a great public service with their letter. They sounded the alarm about the direction of our public discourse. Sadly and unsurprisingly, the media mostly ignored their appeal.

The Shooting of Gabby Giffords

I was working out in the gym one day when a picture of a friend came on the television screen I was watching. Gabrielle Giffords, a young Congresswoman from Arizona, had been shot at a small outdoor gathering. A young man kept shooting until fourteen people were wounded and six people killed, including a district court judge and a nine-year-old girl who was a member of her student council. At that time Gabby, as everyone calls her, was one of the most beloved political leaders in the Congress and in her home state of Arizona. Almost everyone on both sides of the aisle liked her. One of her colleagues remarked that if there was a list of the most vitriolic politicians in the country, Gabby's name would be near the very bottom. Gabby was known as one of the

10. Former Members of Congress for Common Ground, *Letter to Congressional Candidates*, October 4, 2010, http://i2.cdn.turner.com/cnn/2010/images/10/04/fmoc.letter.pdf.

warmest, brightest, and most open members of Congress, and one of its best listeners. She was listening to her constituents that Saturday at the shopping center when the young man pointed a gun at her head and shot her at point-blank range.

I had been with Gabby just a week before the shooting, as both of our families celebrated the New Year's holiday at a retreat for families in South Carolina. I count her as a friend, and so do many others. We had discussed her very tough and close election, which she won by only a few thousand votes in one of the most divided states in the nation, and where the political rhetoric had become more and more personal and poisonous—much like in the rest of the country.

Gabby is always engaging but never polarizing, and was the least likely person to be targeted by an angry and unhinged man. But she was. Miraculously, she survived the attack, although others around her did not. Now she is slowly recovering in a story that seems like a miracle in itself, but she is no longer a member of Congress. As the county sheriff in charge of the criminal scene in Tucson said that horrible day, this must be an occasion for national "soul-searching."

How do we deeply reflect on the ways we speak to and about one another? How do we create environments that help peace and civility to grow or allow violence and hatred to enter? Many of us would never consider "violence of the fist," but have been guilty of violence in our hearts and with our tongues. We need to be able to relate to others with whom we disagree on important issues without thinking or calling them "evil." The words we say fall on the balanced and unbalanced, stable and unstable, the well-grounded and the unhinged alike.

How Did We Get Here?

How did we get to this place, I asked Michael Sandel, Harvard professor and author of the book *Justice: What's the Right Thing to Do?* Michael said, "The reason for the breakdown of civil discourse is not that we have too much moral argument in politics, but that we have too little. What we really have are ideological food fights—assertions hurled back and forth on cable news. . . . What we don't have is a serious engagement with the competing moral and spiritual convictions that citizens bring to public life."[11] We don't need to give up our values, water them down, or throw out our convictions to have civil discourse. It is exactly these beliefs that allow us to engage in real dialogue. I think there are three lessons of particular importance.

First, there is a religious issue. I am a Christian, and we must always be willing to say that while we Christians are politically diverse, we are united in Christ. Too often the church has reflected the political divisions of our culture rather than the unity we have in the body of Christ. The church in the United States should be able to offer a message of hope and reconciliation to a nation that is deeply divided by political and cultural differences. We can disagree, but how we disagree with one another is a question of our witness for Christ.

Second, we should speak the truth and seek it. Much of our worst political rhetoric these days is based on outright lies that "go viral." I know pastors who now tell their congregations that it is morally irresponsible to forward "rumor emails" without first checking the facts. Too often we focus on media caricatures of political figures instead of treating them with honesty and fairness. Political falsehood and damaging lies are now the substance of politics, and that must be directly and visibly confronted.

Third, we must hold to the early American statement, "Out of many, one." *E pluribus Unum* was not an admission of weakness but a proclamation of strength. The health of our democracy depends on not only the outcomes of elections but also on how those elections happen. We should all be able to say, in the humorous but painfully appropriate words of Jon Stewart, "I disagree with you, but I'm pretty sure you're not Hitler."[12] How do we model civil discourse and call our congregations, media, politicians, and nation to accountability?

11. Jim Wallis, "Doing Justice," *Sojourners*, December 2009, 52, http://sojo.net/magazine/2009/12/doing-justice.

12. Joanna Walters, "Daily Show's Jon Stewart Calls on American Voters to Rally for Sanity," *The Guardian*, September 18, 2010, http://www.guardian.co.uk/media/2010/sep/19/jon-stewart-daily-show-rally.

A Covenant for Civility

Truth and civility are too important to lose. The political polarization of our society has now reached a new and dangerous level. Honest disagreements over policy issues have turned into a growing vitriolic rage against political opponents, and threats of violence against lawmakers have been credibly reported and even carried out.

Several members of Congress who have expressed their concerns and fears to me are also people of faith and are asking the faith community to help them lead in this dangerous moment.

So a group of Christian leaders began talking, praying, and discerning how the churches might lead by example to help create a more civil and moral tone in our national politics. We confessed that too often we Christians have merely reflected the divisions in the body politic instead of trying to heal them in the body of Christ. People of faith from all our religious traditions could help create much-needed safe, civil, and even sacred spaces for better public discourse at this critical moment in our nation's history. What came from that prayerful discernment was "A Covenant for Civility: Come Let Us Reason Together."

One hundred diverse church leaders from across the political and theological spectrum—who have voted Democratic, Republican, and independent in recent elections—joined together around the civility covenant, and the breadth of the signatories is a powerful statement in and of itself. Together we offered what we feel is a strong biblical statement motivated by deep concern about our present situation, and we invited thousands of pastors and laypeople in all of our churches to sign the covenant and seek to implement it in our congregations, communities, and nation.

The "Covenant for Civility" begins:

> As Christian pastors and leaders with diverse theological and political beliefs, we have come together to make this covenant with each other, and to commend it to the church, faith-based organizations, and individuals, so that together we can contribute to a more civil national discourse. The church in the United States can offer a message of hope and reconciliation to a nation that is deeply divided by political and cultural differences.

176

Too often, however, we have reflected the political divisions of our culture rather than the unity we have in the body of Christ. We come together to urge those who claim the name of Christ to "put away from you all bitterness and wrath and anger and wrangling and slander, together with all malice, and be kind to one another, tenderhearted, forgiving one another, as God in Christ has forgiven you" (Ephesians 4:31–32).[13]

We made seven biblically based commitments, seven steps we all could take for truth and civility today. We suggested that Christians should carry these seven commitments with them as a reminder for themselves and a challenge to others. Candidates need to know that voters care not only about who wins but also about *how* they win. And these commitments contain the essentials for creating for our nation—both its religious and its nonreligious citizens—a better and more civil discourse.

The covenant states:

1. We commit that our dialogue with each other will reflect the spirit of the scriptures, where our posture toward each other is to be "quick to listen, slow to speak, and slow to become angry" (James 1:19).

2. We believe that each of us, and our fellow human beings, are created in the image of God. The respect we owe to God should be reflected in the honor and respect we show to each other in our common humanity, particularly in how we speak to each other. "With the tongue we bless the Lord and [God], and with it we curse those who are made in the likeness of God . . . this ought not to be so" (James 3:9–10).

3. We pledge that when we disagree, we will do so respectfully, without falsely impugning the other's motives, attacking the other's character, or questioning the other's faith, and recognizing in humility that in our limited, human opinions, "we see but a poor reflection as in a mirror" (1 Corinthians 13:12). We will therefore "be completely humble and gentle; be patient, bearing with one another in love" (Ephesians 4:2).

4. We will ever be mindful of the language we use in expressing our disagreements, being neither arrogant nor boastful in our beliefs: "Before destruction one's heart is haughty, but humility goes before honor" (Proverbs 18:12).

13. "A Covenant for Civility," March 25, 2010, https://secure3.convio.net/sojo/site/Advocacy?cmd=display&page=UserAction&id=341.

5. We recognize that we cannot function together as citizens of the same community, whether local or national, unless we are mindful of how we treat each other in pursuit of the common good, in the common life we share together. Each of us must therefore "put off falsehood and speak truthfully to his neighbor, for we are all members of one body" (Ephesians 4:25).

6. We commit to pray for our political leaders—those with whom we may agree, as well as those with whom we may disagree. "I urge that supplications, prayers, intercessions, and thanksgivings be made—for kings and all who are in high positions" (1 Timothy 2:1–2).

7. We believe that it is more difficult to hate others, even our adversaries and our enemies, when we are praying for them. We commit to pray for each other, those with whom we agree and those with whom we may disagree, so that together we may strive to be faithful witnesses to our Lord, who prayed "that they may be one" (John 17:22).

We pledge to God and to each other that we will lead by example in a country where civil discourse seems to have broken down. We will work to model a better way in how we treat each other in our many faith communities, even across religious and political lines. We will strive to create in our congregations safe and sacred spaces for common prayer and community discussion as we come together to seek God's will for our nation and our world.[14]

The late Chuck Colson and I, often on different sides in policy debates, wrote a column about the need for this civility covenant in the evangelical magazine *Christianity Today*. We said:

The working of democracy depends upon these virtues of civility. Standing for principle is crucial to moral politics, but demonizing our opponents poisons the public square. Therefore we must strive for both truth and civility. To be able to pursue the common good and to preserve the peaceful transition of political power means a commitment to both moral and civil discourse.[15]

14. Ibid.
15. Jim Wallis and Chuck Colson, "Conviction and Civility," *Christianity Today*, January 24, 2011, http://www.christianitytoday.com/ct/2011/januaryweb-only/convictioncivility .html?paging=off.

I believe these are principles that are useful whether we are religious or not. We need to behave differently, for the sake of both our spiritual integrity and the health of our democracy. We have forgotten some of our key values, and it is time to recover them for the common good.

···9···

Redeeming Democracy

The political temperament which lives by arrangements and compromises, and the prophetic temperament which lives by meditation and spiritual valor, cannot as a rule co-exist in the same person. For great concerted actions it is indispensable that we bring men of both kinds into reciprocal and complementary action: otherwise the prophets in their isolation will turn to vain imprecation, while the tacticians become entangled in their own maneuvers.

—Emmanuel Mounier[1]

"Politics" should be a good word, but in many democracies today it is not. The cynicism around politics has reached a historic high. Democracy is the result of the steady expansion of human rights and opportunities, and yet we seem to have lost our belief in it or our ambition to take it to the next level. And, perhaps most alarmingly, the vocation of politics is not drawing our best leaders to it but rather turning them away.

1. Emmanuel Mounier, *Personalism* (1950; repr., Boughton Press, 2008), Kindle edition, locations 1707–10.

Politics is secular, open to all people and citizens of any religious belief or none—and it is supposed to be that way. Theocracy is a threat to democracy, and religion is not meant to *control* the public square. Yet without moral values, the public square can become naked, as many have warned. And religion, when employed to serve politics rather than dominate it, can be one important source of those values. I believe in the separation of church and state but not the segregation of moral values from public life. So how do we bring the prophetic character and qualities of faith but not its parochial or partisan interests?

There is a theology of democracy, especially for people of faith. For us, the foundations of democracy are rooted not only in political philosophy but also in biblical teaching about the human person, our relationships to one another, and our created task to be just and faithful stewards of the earth and its resources.

A Theology of Democracy

So God created humankind in his image, in the image of God he created them; male and female he created them. God blessed them, and God said to them, "Be fruitful and multiply, and fill the earth and subdue it; and have dominion over the fish of the sea and over the birds of the air and over every living thing that moves upon the earth." (Gen. 1:27–28)

Democracy, both in its pitfalls and its promises, is rooted in the theological assertion that human beings are made in the "image of God," *imago Dei* in Latin. This is how Genesis begins.

If humankind is created in the image of God, certain *political* facts follow.

First is the absolute *worth* of every human person—of every citizen in every nation. People have value that comes directly from their being the children of God, and they must be treated as morally and politically valuable by the governing authorities they live under. Therefore, a fundamental *respect* for every individual is a requirement for any political system or government. And any disrespect or devaluing of persons or citizens undermines their being made in the image of God.

There could be no deeper or more powerful assertion of the respect that political systems owe to their people than to root their treatment in their very nature as human beings created in the image of God. So, most fundamentally, the political rights that each citizen has derive not just from the political promises of the founding documents of the citizen's country but, even more deeply, from their status of being made in God's own image. Politics must always show respect for that most basic worth of every person because of the recognition that "the people" are made in the very image of God and are the children of God; this narrative is rooted in the creation story in Genesis.

Second is *equality* among all who are made in the image of God. One person or group of people is not politically more important than another person or group. We've already seen how all the human tribes are welcome in God's beloved community, and the radical assertion of equal rights for *all* of God's children has been the driving impulse of democracy's steady expansion in the United States and around the world. Human differences in talent, effort, accomplishment, and influence are natural, even positive, and will always exist. But the fundamental equality of the rights of all human beings—rights to political participation and social opportunities—is essential for democracy and is, again, rooted in the creation saga itself, about who people are and in whose image they are made.

These two qualities of worth and equality are *substantive* and should shape both the theory and practice of democracy. They are fundamental principles that must not be violated by governments. To be made in the image of God is to be a mirror image of God's essential nature. Thomas Aquinas spoke of the capacity of human beings to think and reason, setting them apart from other creatures. That is also true of the human capability to reflect God's love, grace, justice, and forgiveness. The ability to make moral decisions is a distinctive human quality. All this allows God to be manifest in human behavior when we act in ways consistent with God's purposes for the world. In the image of God, humans are mental, moral, and relational beings—and they must function as all three to support a democracy.

And it is our *relational* capacity that makes democracy possible. Theologian Karl Barth said it was our human ability to make and maintain complex and intricate relationships that made us like God. That is also what makes democracy a successful relational system. Self-actualization is a part of that, which democracy should enhance; but democracy's existence also owes much to the human need for community. From Adam and Eve onward, we were created for community, and it is through our human relationships that God's purposes and plans can be carried out. The interests we have in each other and in the creation that surrounds us are the building blocks of forming democratic relationships.

The creation narrative even suggests the *functional* purposes of democracy when it tells us to "be fruitful and multiply," to "fill the earth and subdue it," and even to have "dominion" over all the other creatures and the earth itself. That word "dominion" is often interpreted as if it meant "dominance," but the true meaning of the Hebrew word is actually more in keeping with a vision of "stewardship," a faithful caring and nurturing of the whole earth and its many creatures.

There are tasks associated with our being created in the image of God—meaning there is still work to do. When we are most conscious of our role as God's children, we are also more creative about how we can help fulfill God's purposes for the world. There is a strong biblical and theological sense of even being "cocreators" with God in service of those purposes. The Christian conception of God is a "Trinity" of Father, Son, and Holy Spirit, implying not only doctrinal mystery but community. And when God makes humans in God's image, male and female, creating all our diverse tribes, we are being invited into the very community of God. Our social life and even governmental life are not about making sure we are each left alone, but rather that we are in good and life-sustaining relationships together. Modern libertarian views of individual separation and self-sustainability fly right in the face of that biblical theology. The radical individualism of the Tea Party right wing denies the social conscience that is present in the best of both conservatism and liberalism. Clearly, a *biblical theology of democracy leads us not only to the personal good but also to the common good.*

Redeeming democracy for the sake of the common good will require several things: turning consumers into citizens, widening political involvement, confronting the greed and power that subvert democracy, and overcoming the final barrier to democracy: the control of money over politics. Only those major commitments can turn political isolation into participation, take us from polarization to progress, and move us from paralysis to solutions. And we must remember that voting is only the beginning of democracy. We now see citizens engaging in community organizing and mobilizing around public issues that take them beyond narrow electoral goals and into a whole new world of making our life together better.

Barriers to Democracy

If *worth* and *equality* are values derived from the belief that human beings are made in the image of God, then respecting both should be a primary task of democratic political systems. That implies a number of things about how democracy ought to work practically.

First, everything that can be done to make access to voting and political participation more possible for more people *should be done*. Voter registration and identification should be made as easy as possible, not difficult and less accessible. No matter which party benefits from a particular voter or group of voters being most completely brought into the political system, it should be the priority of all parties to do so.

But procedures and processes for voter registration, identification, and even access to the polls on election days have all become highly contested political issues themselves. That is because each party sees voters as holding good or bad potential for its success. Each party, obviously, wants to register and secure the votes that are most likely to be cast in its favor, and each is much less interested in seeing votes cast against it—and even hopes those votes will be reduced.

We are unfortunately seeing the other side of a party's attempts to increase its voters' registration and access, a phenomenon called *voter suppression*. A party that is able to hinder or even block the registration of potential opposition voters by making their participation much

185

more difficult will often do so, and we have seen growing evidence of such tactics. Low voter turnout can secure election victories as much as high turnout can—it all depends on *who* is voting.

Requiring more extensive voter identification is one way voting is being suppressed today. Everyone wants to prevent fraud at the voting booth on election days, and some form of credible voter identification is absolutely necessary. But the threat of fraud has been used and over-used, even when there is little evidence of it, as a justification for more complicated registration procedures and more rigorous and restrictive voter identification. Those tactics have especially been aimed at voters who are more socially vulnerable. Voter suppression works best against lower-income voters, including those from ethnic minorities or poor communities, who often have fewer forms of identification like driver's licenses and less knowledge of and access to the voting process. Elderly voters can be the targets of tactics to discourage or prevent participation. Younger voters are especially vulnerable to efforts at voter suppression because they often have less-stable permanent addresses and fewer forms of identification, with student IDs, for example, sometimes being disallowed.

Voter suppression has historically been used against racial minorities in America, with notoriously excessive demands for voter registration and participation at the ballot box, including poll taxes and even poll tests that few white voters would have been able to pass if administered to them—although they never were. It took a national Voting Rights Act, passed in 1965, to outlaw many of those abusive practices that were aimed at denying black citizens their right to vote. But methods of voter suppression are now coming back, again aimed at the poor, at minorities, and at the elderly and the young. In 2012, such efforts were predicted to potentially deny almost five million former voters the right to vote.

The politicization of voting rights is becoming more and more obvious. According to a recent report by the Brennan Center for Justice, "the states that have already cut back on voting rights will provide 171 electoral votes in 2012—63 percent of the 270 needed to win the presidency." The report goes on to say that "of the 12 likely battleground states [in the 2012 presidential election] . . . five have already cut back on voting rights."[2] In those places where who votes, and for which party, have the biggest ramifications for the election's outcome, it is possible that we will see large numbers of people being disenfranchised.

While there are strong campaigns under way to protect these voting rights and counter the newest attempts at voter suppression, the issues here are not just political, at least for people of faith. They are also *theological*, if we are going to respect both the worth and the equality of all those citizens who are made in the image of God. Voter suppression is an assault not only against citizen rights and the democratic vision but also against the identity of those same people as children of God.

To respect the worth and identity of all God's children in a democratic context means to make voter registration and voting itself work effectively with the highest levels of participation. That means enacting many of the reforms that have worked best to ensure those higher levels of citizen involvement, such as easy voter registration, including same-day registration at the voting place; the wide recognition of any and all credible forms of voter identification; sufficient numbers of polling places for maximum citizen access; effective voting procedures and equipment to prevent long waiting periods at the voting sites; easy and generous practices for absentee and early voting; and perhaps, as has been successfully done in many other democratic countries, making each voting day a holiday—a day off work—so people have sufficient time and space to enable them to vote.

The basic principle is this: maximum voter participation ensures the truest expression of democracy, which is both a political value and a theological value—if we are truly attempting to respect the worth and equality of all our citizens. Voter suppression is not only bad politics, it's also rooted in bad theology. It is an aggressive attempt to deny the worth and equality of all those made in the image of God.

2. Wendy R. Weiser and Lawrence Norden, *Voting Law Changes in 2012* (New York: Brennan Center for Justice, 2011), 1, http://brennan.3cdn.net/92635ddafbc09e8d88_i3m6 bjdeh.pdf. This study pinpoints troubles for the 2012 election, but it seems likely that voter suppression will be an ongoing problem in future elections as well.

The Last Great Barrier to Democracy

Running for political office is more expensive in the United States than anywhere else in the world today—and no other democratic country even comes close. Here are the facts: to run for a seat in the US House of Representatives now costs an average of *more than $1 million per election*.[3] Therefore, to become and remain a member of Congress in the United States of America will cost you tens of millions of dollars, depending on the district and state you are running in. For the Senate, the cost is much higher: *on average over $7.5 million per (victorious) senator in 2008*.[4] It costs hundreds of millions of dollars to become and remain a US senator in the world's most famous democracy.

Senators have told me that they need to raise at least $20,000 *per day*, on average, to have enough money to run for office the next time. They say it with a weariness of voice that suggests how much they would rather be going about the business of governing instead of the endless task of fund-raising, which means continual cultivation of and conversation with donors.

The cost of running for the presidency is now almost *one billion* dollars. To be elected the president of the most important democracy in the world means that you also must become the world's biggest fund-raiser. No other country in the democratic world comes anywhere near to requiring those expenses for public office.[5] What does that mean about American leadership or about the real quality of our democracy?

To have the highest-costing elections in the world today means simply this: to be an elected official in the United States of America you must either be a very wealthy person or be dependent on very wealthy people—or both. When I share just the fund-raising numbers with candidates for the parliaments and legislatures of other nations around the world, they are incredulous and always say something like: "How

3. "The Cost of Winning an Election, 1986–2008" (Washington, DC: Campaign Finance Institute, 2010), http://www.cfinst.org/data/pdf/VitalStats_t1.pdf.
4. Ibid.
5. In comparison, spending in the 2010 UK general election amounted to around $50 million; in the 2008 Canadian federal elections, around $300 million. Most elections in continental Europe are publically funded, at least in part, specifically so the most-financed candidates do not have an unfair advantage over other candidates.

could I possibly serve everybody equally, or even fairly, if I had to raise that much money and be dependent on those who had it?"

But are things getting better with all the talk about campaign finance reform? Is the dependence on wealth in our democracy diminishing? Sadly, the distance between the control of big money and the real prospects of democracy is now growing faster than ever before.

In one of the most defining Supreme Court decisions in American history—the ruling in the *Citizens United* case in 2010—a narrow majority ruled that corporations and unions will no longer have any restrictions on the amount of money they can contribute from their treasuries to elections or to candidates. The *Citizens United* decision virtually overturned the beginnings of campaign finance laws in the United States. In this Supreme Court ruling, American democracy has now been severely set back, and the political situation has been set up for America's richest individuals and corporations to dominate the nation's politics as never before.

It was one of the most disastrous judicial decisions in American history, one in which true democracy was completely undermined and the chances for genuine democratic progress seriously diminished. In *Citizens United v. Federal Election Commission*, the conservative Supreme Court, in a narrow 5–4 decision, ruled that corporations are "people" too, and that the First Amendment "prohibits Congress from fining or jailing citizens, or associations of citizens, for simply engaging in political speech."[6]

But as we have seen, political "speech" in America is hardly "free," and whoever has the most money will dominate the political conversation. Elections are determined by paid speech, not free speech—and you cannot join the conversation without media coverage, which is certainly not free. It is free in many other democratic countries, where candidates can offer their ideas and perspectives to the voting public around election time without cost and as a public service—but not in the United States. The *Citizens United* decision has made American

6. Supreme Court of the United States, Syllabus, Citizens United v. Federal Election Commission (October term, 2009), 33, http://www.supremecourt.gov/opinions/09pdf/08-205 .pdf.

189

electoral politics more expensive and less transparent than ever before in the modern era.

Representing the dissenting opinion of four Supreme Court members, Justice Stevens said the decision "threatens to undermine the integrity of elected institutions across the Nation. . . . A democracy cannot function effectively when its constituent members believe laws are bought and sold."[7]

Laws *are now bought and sold* in American legislatures across the country, and most of the American people know that, leading to a growing political cynicism. Eighty percent of the American public was against the Supreme Court ruling, but democracy lost there too. Stevens, quoting an earlier judicial opinion, wrote that "the appearance of undue influence and 'the cynical assumption that large donors call the tune could jeopardize the willingness of voters to take part in democratic governance.'"[8] Now public cynicism about our elections could seriously diminish American voter turnout at election time, a turnout rate already lower than that of most other countries in the Western world.

But diminishing participation is exactly what the wealthiest and most politically active corporations are indeed hoping for. Serious critics are now suggesting that senators, in the future, should perhaps be named the senator from Exxon Mobile, the senator from Bank of America, or the senator from Goldman Sachs, and so on—just to be completely transparent.

Stevens went on to write that "corporations have no consciences, no beliefs, no feelings, no thoughts, no desires. Corporations help structure and facilitate the activities of human beings, to be sure, and their 'personhood' often serves as a useful legal fiction. But they are not themselves members of 'We the People' by whom and for whom our Constitution was established."[9]

I would carry the point even further. To turn corporations into "people" is not only a profound legal, historical, and political misstep, it is a theological error and a deeply offensive one. Remember, people are

7. Ibid., 63.
8. Ibid., 60.
9. Ibid., 76.

made in the image of God, and corporations are not. Corporations are not human beings. And to give corporations the same rights as people is a grave theological mistake. A better theological understanding of the role of corporations is found in what the epistles of Ephesians and Colossians say about the "principalities and powers":[10] they are institutions with which we have to wrestle in "spiritual warfare"; and many people who work for the biggest corporate enterprises can tell you a great deal about how that works practically. Our largest corporations do not generally act like people or even as if they care about people; but they often need to be continually held accountable to people's needs—even those of the people who work directly for them. If our large corporations are usually not the "people" you would pick for your best friends, how friendly are they likely to be toward democracy when their own interests clash with those of "we the people"? The Supreme Court has given corporations the rights of political free speech that nobody but them will any longer be able to afford.

Justice Stevens concluded:

> At bottom, the Court's opinion is thus a rejection of the common sense of the American people, who have recognized a need to prevent corporations from undermining self-government since the founding, and who have fought against the distinctive corrupting potential of corporate electioneering since the days of Theodore Roosevelt. It is a strange time to repudiate that common sense. While American democracy is imperfect, few outside the majority of this Court would have thought its flaws included a dearth of corporate money in politics.[11]

Another Supreme Court justice from an earlier court predicted this problem and offered the country a choice. Justice Louis D. Brandeis said, "We may have democracy in this country, or we may have great wealth concentrated in the hands of a few, but we can't have both."[12] The current Supreme Court's majority has made its choice.

10. Eph. 6:12; Col. 2:15 (KJV).
11. *Citizens United*, 90.
12. "Louis D. Brandeis Quotes," Brandeis University website, http://www.brandeis.edu /legacyfund/bio.html.

One Person, One Vote?

In America, the final barrier to democracy has now become the control of money over politics. We've seen the steady progress of democracy in history. Governments first advanced from monarchies and oligarchies to republics, and these were first voted in by landed gentry. But over time, the democratic promise was extended to all ordinary men, then to women, then to racial minorities, then to oppressed majorities in South Africa and other developing countries around the world, and now to the Middle East with the Arab Spring.

It's time we stated the obvious truth: the last remaining obstacle to democracy is the dominant power of rich people, their money, and their institutions over the political process, a power that absolutely corrupts democracy. We salute the ideal of "one person, one vote" and herald new democracies in places like South Africa when they achieve it. But in America, we don't have "one person, one vote." Let's be honest. Does anyone truly believe that ordinary citizens have the same influence or real number of votes as the nation's wealthiest citizens and the large corporations that represent their own economic interests? How many thousands—or tens or hundreds of thousands—of votes, or their political equivalent in influence, does each rich donor or large corporation really have? Whom do members of Congress and senators mostly listen to? Who can most easily get appointments with them? Whom do our elected officials spend most of their time with—those who have little or no money to offer to their fund-raising political war chests, or those who keep them full?

The phenomenon of the "Super-PACs" (political action committees), set up to buy hugely expensive campaign ads for and against candidates, has dramatized these distorted realities even further. During the 2012 presidential primaries, it was often just a small handful of donors, or even *one* hugely wealthy superdonor, who determined whether a primary candidate was even viable or how long he or she could compete in the race.

Again, this is not just a political problem but also a theological evil. Any notion of the worth and equality of all citizens as people made in

192

the image of God is destroyed by the unequal control of money over the political process, which enshrines the worth not of the many but only of the millionaires and billionaires. The worth of the wealthy trumps the worth of the nation's citizenry. Until this politically offensive and theologically flawed system of money controlling politics is fundamentally reformed, we will make no more progress toward true democracy in America.

With the power of money becoming even more dominant now, it is difficult to describe America's political system as a genuine democracy. Terms like "plutocracy" and "moneyed oligarchy" are—painful to admit—more truthful and descriptive. And with Washington's dependence on that big money on both sides of the political aisle, it will take a long-term citizens' movement to change the system. It will also take an overturning of the terrible and tumultuous Supreme Court decision if we are going to move the promise of democracy forward once again. But the control of money is the biggest and most influential reality of politics today and has led to a great many of our political demons.

Theodore Roosevelt, in his famous speech at Osawatomie, Kansas, in 1910, focused the issue of democracy with great clarity when he said:

> At many stages in the advance of humanity, this conflict between *the [people] who possess more than they have earned and the [people] who have earned more than they possess* is the central condition of progress. In our day it appears as the struggle of freemen [and women] to gain and hold the right of self-government as against the special interests, who twist the methods of free government into machinery for defeating the popular will.[13]

That struggle now goes on in our day too.

Such dominance of money will need to be *exorcised* from American politics for democracy to be redeemed. And it will take a moral and political movement for that to happen. This will be one of the most important spiritual and political tasks of the next generation. It's finally time, right now, to begin changing money and politics in America.

13. See http://www.theodore-roosevelt.com/images/research/speeches/trnationalism speech.pdf (emphasis added).

From Consumers to Citizens

Citizens are now related to as consumers, something reflected in the mind-set of the professional consultants, pollsters, and advertising agencies who produce all the costly political attack ads, with their innuendos, outright lies, and prophecies of doom if the other candidate gets elected. Candidates are sold as products, and voters are turned into consumers at election time. Members of the public say they hate the barrage of negative ads and phone calls they are bombarded with in the weeks before an election; but these tactics all seem to work. How different and wonderful would it be if, instead of filling the airwaves with loud and distorted attack noise, those who run political campaigns would give us a chance to clear our heads and do some serious thinking before making such important electoral decisions? What if our nation required the media, as other democratic countries do, to offer free time for the positive presentation of all the candidates' views and positions and just let the voters decide?

At their best, political ads can be used to clarify and inform voters of the policies and priorities at stake in an election. At their worst, they are used only to confuse, distort, and manipulate. This has become a business now, a growing one. It turns politics into just another advertising campaign, turns politicians into salable products, and really does turn citizens into mere consumers. The negative ads and robo-calls, which serve only to throw mud on the other candidate, cost an enormous amount of money, which is a terrible waste, especially in hard economic times. The huge amounts being spent on campaigns and, specifically, on the most noxious ads are already disturbing, but when compared to what else that money could be spent on, they are downright offensive.

Why a Broken System Can't Fix Itself

Time and again, I have heard from presidential candidates down to members of Congress that Washington was broken and they were running to fix it. But early in their time in office, they and their teams have then told me how the system was more broken than they had imagined,

194

how special interests were even more powerful, and how the influence of money over everything was almost complete. So they decided to work within that broken system and try to get a few things done. And that is their mistake.

Change is easier, they tell me, if you're just talking about tinkering around the edges. Change is harder if you actually dig in and try to deal with the structural problems that have long impeded progress. What they find is that as long as the system is broken, *any* change is very difficult, even when you just tinker around the edges. We've seen their tinkering around the edges when it comes to the poor, our financial and banking system, our tax code, immigration reform, and the wars of occupation in Iraq and Afghanistan. Clearly, these systems don't just need tinkering; they need substantial change.

Every White House and Congress needs prophetic truth-telling and courageous witness—rather than just quiet advice—from people who believe in change, and especially from faith leaders. Our candles for reform must burn brighter with the hope that comes not from Washington or from politics but from our theological convictions about what democracy is supposed to be.

It takes the power of movements to change politics. Change never starts in Washington or in our legislatures or houses of government; it almost always begins outside of politics. If public momentum can be built among millions of people, change eventually arrives in the nation's capital.

At the deepest level, what are lacking are vibrant and visible social movements that empower and enable genuine democratic reforms. Both the Occupy and Tea Party movements are a step in that direction (albeit from different directions), seeking to challenge the control of Wall Street and Washington. The question, of course, is whether these are or will remain genuine populist movements or be taken over by the political elites on both sides.

The accomplishments of the FDR era in protecting workers, seniors, and the most vulnerable, and the accomplishments of the Kennedy/ Johnson years in promoting racial justice and effective poverty reduction, were due in no small measure to robust workers' movements and the civil rights movement. The activism of those independent social movements *created the space* for major reforms and made those presidencies memorable.

The lack of "street heat" is often at the center of our problems today in changing political systems. Social change requires more than having a genuine "progressive" in the White House; it requires a movement outside of the White House and Congress to make fundamental reforms possible. We have to relearn the choreography of the outside/inside "dance" that real change requires.

History demonstrates that presidents need prophets and movements. But it is also true that prophets need politicians to remind them of what is possible in the real world, the here and now. I am often concerned about the deep disappointment I sense among those who believed that swift and sweeping political change was coming after a fresh election.

I am not just speaking of the ideological disappointment of the political left or right. Rather, I refer to the racial minorities who overcome their cynicism to believe that another United States might be possible; the low-income voters who make the effort to vote, believing somebody might be listening to them for a change; or, most of all, the younger voters of every stripe who defy the conventional wisdom about youthful political passivity and act like citizens with a real stake in the future.

What they must all learn is that we really need political *movements* and not just another transfer of power. Hope for that kind of movement can be real, but when disappointed it can disappear rapidly. Those who had that hope for change may retreat into an even deeper cynicism than before. Extraordinary challenges confront genuine reformers, especially in a time of political crisis; but it is precisely a real crisis that makes a bolder style of leadership more necessary and even more possible.

Historically, political leaders committed to change need to have the *wind of a movement* at their backs to accomplish anything of real significance. But they will also need a movement at their front, to clear the path and pull them along when necessary.

This requires a change in perspective on the part of political leaders—to see independent movements on the outside as necessary and worth supporting (even calling for), rather than, at worst, as a threat or as a constituency that must be appeased.

Inside/Outside

Just as Lincoln needed Frederick Douglass, Kennedy and Johnson needed King, and Roosevelt needed a robust labor movement, so also political leaders today who are serious about reform need the kind of social movements that are always necessary to make real change in Washington and other world capitals. No one can do this alone, as every election winner quickly realizes upon taking office.

The critical relationship between the inside and the outside is eloquently summed up in a book titled *Personalism* by Emmanuel Mounier, a French Christian existentialist, who correctly describes the complementary vocation of prophets and politicians. His contrast of the "political temperament" and the "prophetic temperament," quoted at the beginning of this chapter, makes the critical point that both are indispensable. They have the kind of reciprocal relationship and perform the kinds of complementary actions that are required for social change and political reform.

Leaders from various constituencies must always be ready to mobilize social movements. They should always be willing and ready to do that, even if political leaders decide on a more cautious direction. We are in a time that needs more independent and critical social movements. Many of us in the faith community have charted a prophetic course on behalf of the issues that are central to us. And we will continue to reach out directly to the people in our pews, our parishes, and our communities, empowering ordinary people to resist political cynicism and become citizens, in the true sense, again.

Today, social movements are growing again, hitting the streets and the web with compelling calls to make democracy real and concrete. At the local level we see a new emphasis on community organizing that is based on the face-to-face relationships people have with one another in their own neighborhoods and communities. And the institutions most frequently chosen now as the base for that contemporary community organizing are faith congregations; tens of thousands of them are now involved across the nation.

At both the national and international levels, direct action is spreading across the internet in the mobilization of both vast resources and very large numbers of people who, together and quickly, can focus on a country, a cause, or a campaign for human rights or democratic progress. All around the world, we see the power of social media as a new tool for reaching and mobilizing more people than ever before. Some of the results have been breathtaking. Visiting the websites of groups like 350.org or Avaaz will give you an indication of just how significant and influential these online movements are becoming. Sojo.net is a growing mobilizing network in the faith community.

At the heart of all these movements for greater democracy is the vision of the common good. Special interests are being transcended by the public interest. This takes us back to where we began this chapter, with the creation narratives setting out our purposes as human beings made in the image of God. We are truly the children of God, not mere demographics on somebody's list to be exploited for political power. How we view our human identity as God's children and cocreators for a better world has profound implications for democracy.

··· 10 ···

Economic Trust

The truth is that the economic and social order isn't a self-contained affair, separate from actual human decisions about what is good and desirable. Certain kinds of political and economic decisions have the effect of threatening the possibilities for full humanity.

—Archbishop of Canterbury Rowan Williams[1]

"To be *generically against* markets," says Indian economist Amartya Sen, "would be almost as odd as being generically against conversations between people."[2] The market produces continual conversations, interactions, and transactions about economics. As a mere mechanism, the market is amoral. But the events of the last few years and the consequences of the Great Recession the world has experienced are now demanding a *new moral conversation* about the market and *how* it

1. Rowan Williams, "Human Well-Being and Economic Decision-Making" (a keynote address at TUC [Trades Union Congress] Economics Conference, Congress House, London, November 16, 2009), http://www.archbishopofcanterbury.org/articles.php/767/human-well-being-and-economic-decision-making.
2. Amartya Sen, *Development as Freedom* (Oxford: Oxford University Press, 1999), 6.

should operate—which individual human beings make moral decisions about every day. Or as I asked of a plenary session at the 2009 World Economic Forum in Davos, Switzerland, right after the 2008 global financial meltdown, "What happens when the invisible hand lets go of the common good?"

Adam Smith, who wrote famously in his *Wealth of Nations* about "the invisible hand" of the market, wrote earlier in his book *The Theory of Moral Sentiments* concerning what happens when economics forgets ethics. Smith said capitalism can't function properly without a moral framework. Another proponent of capitalism, Austrian economist Joseph Schumpeter, agreed and said that without ethics, the market ends up devouring everything else and, finally, even itself. That's what happened on Wall Street to begin the current economic crisis. While the market may be amoral in itself, it takes place within a moral structure, either good or bad.

A Moral Economy

> But those who want to be rich fall into temptation and are trapped by many senseless and harmful desires that plunge people into ruin and destruction. For the love of money is a root of all kinds of evil. (1 Tim. 6:9–10)

The World Economic Forum now calls for a "moral economy"[3] and has begun new studies and "global action councils" on values and the role of business. We have lost the ability to speak in moral terms about economics, and many are feeling the need to recover an ethical and values-based language about the economy. After having little to say about market behavior for many years, the religious community has reengaged in the moral conversation about the financial crisis, and it claims that the recent failures of some of our leading banks and corporations are breaches of moral and even religious principles.

The road for that moral conversation is becoming clearer. We will see it by focusing on what we have learned, or need to, from our recent

3. World Economic Forum, *Faith and the Global Agenda: Values for the Post-Crisis Economy* (Geneva: World Economic Forum, 2010), v.

financial catastrophe and the massive economic suffering that resulted. It is about remembering and reestablishing neglected but critical virtues that could help us get from where we are to a new and better place. How to get there isn't entirely clear yet, but where we need to go is becoming more so.

Here is the road for a new moral economy: from massive inequality to decent equity; from the narrow definition of shareholders to a broader vision of stakeholders; from short-term to long-term thinking and acting; from the ethics of endless growth to the ethics of sustainability; from doing well to also doing good; and from broken social contracts to a new social covenant between citizens, business, and government. And that is the new road we now need to travel. Let's look at what it would mean to start moving toward a more moral economy that could enhance rather than undermine the common good.

Repent, for the End May Be Near Again

We are all familiar with the famous pop-culture image of a street evangelist holding up a sign reading, "Repent, for the end is near!" But repentance is actually a fundamental religious theme, and one that's often misunderstood. With the recent recession, we could imagine a group of pastors, priests, rabbis, and imams holding up a sign on Wall Street for the titans of the financial industry to see, reading, "Repent, or the end could be near again."

As we discussed in chapter 3, the biblical meaning of repentance is to turn around and take a new path. In a religious framework, it means realizing you have made a moral mistake and deciding to change your behavior. It's not enough to feel guilty or sorry for something; genuine repentance requires a change in decisions and actions, moving in a different direction. Merely admitting you were wrong is not enough. You have to change.

In these past few years, I've had serious conversations with financial leaders about ethics, morality, and even faith. Some come like Nicodemus—a religious leader who came to talk to Jesus in private—at night. Many have felt remorseful about what happened on Wall Street and how it has hurt so many people. They describe the behavior in their profession with words such as "greedy," "risky," and "reckless."

In one conversation with a senior trader at a leading financial investment company, I asked if the trader's firm had practices and products that led to this crisis. The answer was yes. Then I asked what my conversation partner had done to raise these issues at the highest levels of the company, to which the reply was, "We can't do that." Many of the business and banking leaders do feel sorry, but *repentance* means that remorse must be coupled with a change in the behaviors that led to the problems. And that has yet to happen on Wall Street.

Alan Blinder, professor of economics at Princeton University and a former vice chairman of the Federal Reserve Board, said in an op-ed for *The Wall Street Journal*:

> When economists first heard [Gordon] Gekko's now famous dictum "Greed is good," they thought it a crude expression of Adam Smith's "Invisible Hand"—which is one of history's great ideas. But in Smith's vision, greed is socially beneficial only when properly harnessed and channeled. The necessary conditions include, among other things, appropriate incentives (for risk-taking, etc.), effective competition, safeguards against exploitation of what economists call "asymmetric information" (as when a deceitful seller unloads junk on an unsuspecting buyer), regulators to enforce rules and keep participants honest, and—when relevant—protection of taxpayers against pilferage or malfeasance by others. When these conditions fail to hold, greed is not good.
>
> Plainly, they all failed in the financial crisis. Compensation and other types of incentives for risk were badly skewed. Corporate boards were asleep at the switch. Opacity reduced effective competition. Financial regulation was shamefully lax. Predators roamed the financial landscape, looting both legally and illegally. And when Treasury and the Federal Reserve rushed in to contain the damage, taxpayers were forced to pay dearly for the mistakes and avarice of others. If you want to know why the public is enraged, that, in a nutshell, is why.[4]

4. Alan S. Blinder, "When Greed Is Not Good," *Wall Street Journal*, January 11, 2010, http://online.wsj.com/article/SB10001424052748703652104574652242436408008.html?mod=rss_opinion_main.

Those who led us down the path to financial ruin or helped to accommodate it—causing millions of people to lose their homes, jobs, and savings—now have some serious repenting to do. Yet the statements and behavior of many Wall Street executives, and the revelations in the media about what is going on inside some of our leading financial institutions, make it painfully clear that repentance and public accountability are still far from many economic minds.

I keep coming back to the concepts of forgiveness and grace. When the government tried to save the economy from meltdown, real grace was extended to the big banks—but now the banks seem unwilling to extend that forgiveness and grace to anyone else, including homeowners struggling to make mortgage payments. They have decided instead to reward themselves. As a founder of Citigroup, John S. Reed, told *The New York Times*, "There is nothing I've seen that gives me the slightest feeling that these people have learned anything from the crisis. They just don't get it. They are off in a different world."[5]

When you preach, one of the most important parts of preparing is selecting a text relevant to the issue of the day. A clear and obvious biblical text for this crisis is 1 Timothy 6:9–10, quoted above: "the love of money is a root of all kinds of evil." Or, as Jesus succinctly put it, "You cannot serve God and wealth" (Matt. 6:24).

The critics of Wall Street call it putting self-interest above the public interest. But the Bible would just call it sin. We could call it the sin of putting personal profit and gain above the common good, above the good of your customers and consumers, and even above the good of your clients and investors. My friend Robert Lane was the CEO of John Deere and is also a person of faith. He speaks of the market as a tool that, like any tool, can be used for good or harm. He once told me "the market was meant to be a means and not the end." But when the market is an end unto itself, it runs the danger of what religion might call "market fundamentalism." And when that happens, there are times when outside pressure is needed to change destructive behaviors—times like now.

5. Louise Story and Eric Dash, "Banks Prepare for Big Bonuses, and Public Wrath," *New York Times*, January 9, 2010, http://www.nytimes.com/2010/01/10/business/10pay.html.

America and other democracies have always had a love-hate relationship with both business and government. The climate shifts like a pendulum between eras of an "anything goes" mentality and periods of more careful public oversight and government regulation. The excesses of the 1920s, leading to the Great Depression, were followed by the reforms of Franklin Roosevelt's New Deal, including the creation of the Securities and Exchange Commission, the Federal Deposit Insurance Corporation, and new rules of the road for banks and investment companies intended to protect citizens from excessive risk and abuse.

But over the last forty years, many of these regulations were relaxed (by both Republicans and Democrats dependent on the political contributions of Wall Street), while new financial realities, products, and practices have developed for which there were no regulations. Because of the Great Recession, a new financial regulation debate is now raging.

The Bible does not prescribe any economic system, nor does it lay out an ideal means of economic governance. And while religious leaders will not often get into the details or partisan wrangling, there are some principles that—from a moral and even religious viewpoint—should guide those economic deliberations.

The Church of England's General Synod 2009 report on the financial crisis was summarized this way: "The dominant assumptions in our economic system may be innately un-Christian—assuming that human beings are strangers who relate to one another only with the aim of maximizing profits and pleasure. Economics is not simply a science for experts. It contains assumptions about the nature of human beings, which is a moral and theological question."[6] Former Archbishop of Canterbury Rowan Williams, quoted at the beginning of this chapter, went further by saying that "certain kinds of political and economic decisions have the effect of threatening the possibilities for full humanity."[7]

In October 2011, a new and quite direct pontifical statement came from the Vatican expressing the perspective of the Roman Catholic

6. Arabella Milbank, Adam Atkinson, and Angus Ritchie, "Christian Responses to the Financial Crisis: A Briefing Pack for Clergy and Parishes," http://www.londonpen.org/wp-content/uploads/2011/11/responding-to-the-financial-crisis.pdf.
7. Williams, "Human Well-Being and Economic Decision-Making."

Church on the reforms needed after this financial crisis. It was a note of real warning about massive inequality and against the assumption that self-interest alone can ensure the common good. It specifically provided a theological rationale for new public regulation and accountability. It reads:

> Recognizing the primacy of being over having and of ethics over the economy, the world's peoples ought to adopt an ethic of solidarity as the animating core of their action. This implies abandoning all forms of petty selfishness and embracing the logic of the global common good which transcends merely contingent, particular interests.
>
> In economic and financial matters, the most significant difficulties come from the lack of an effective set of structures that can guarantee, in addition to a system of governance, a system of government for the economy and international finance.
>
> In this process [reform of international financial institutions], the primacy of the spiritual and of ethics needs to be restored and, with them, the primacy of politics—which is responsible for the common good—over the economy and finance.[8]

What principles should guide us?

First, provide transparency and accountability. Given the human condition and the many temptations of money, we need transparency and accountability in financial markets and instruments, including high-risk and questionable instruments such as the now infamous "derivatives." We need regulators who are genuinely independent of the industries they regulate rather than those who come from and go back to the very companies they are supposed to hold accountable. To protect the common good, we need to enact better oversight of all elements of the banking industry. Earlier regulations—now discarded—had enforced a clear separation between day-to-day banking and speculative banking, and this separation desperately needs to be reintroduced.

8. Pontifical Council for Justice and Peace, "Towards Reforming the International Financial and Monetary Systems in the Context of Global Public Authority" (Vatican City: Pontifical Council for Justice and Peace, 2011), http://www.news.va/en/news/full-text -note-on-financial-reform-from-the-pontif.

Second, protect consumers. Any pastor can tell you stories of how parishioners are mistreated, cheated, and damaged by current banking practices. My good friend Joel Hunter, pastor of a large church in Orlando, Florida, says the major credit card debts of his parishioners have put people "in bondage."[9] A survey in his church showed that the average debt of his parishioners (excluding home and car debts) was $31,000! Many clergy strongly favor protecting consumers from predatory financial lending practices, either by payday lenders or by credit card companies. We need something like a strong independent consumer finance protection agency, with jurisdiction and enforcement power over companies in the financial sector and over those who run the credit card businesses, in order to protect people from fraudulent, misleading, and abusive behavior. Those long and confusing credit card contracts are now full of abusive procedures and practices devised to cheat people and turn them into debtors, a familiar biblical category of injustice. It's time to level the playing field by introducing clarity and transparency and taking on the exploitative behavior of the small number of huge banks who now control most of the credit card industry—the ones most opposed to public openness and accountability.

Third, change the banks that were "too big to fail" and were therefore bailed out at public expense. This may mean limiting the size of financial institutions or the risks they can take. Give a stronger voice to shareholders and investors, and perhaps other stakeholders, in institutional practices and policies—including determining executive compensation and the now-infamous bank executive bonuses. If banks have become too big to fail, they perhaps have become too big not to be held publically accountable, just as public utilities in the energy industry are. Right now, these banks are just too big to care about the common good.

Fourth, address the volatility of increased financial exchanges, which create great riches for some but great instability for economic systems. In the mysterious and secret global transactions between investment bankers and hedge fund traders, the profits continue to grow. From

9. Joel C. Hunter, "Freedom Begins with Christ! 2011 Sermon Series Preview by Pastor Joel Hunter," NorthlandChurch.net, December 30, 2010, http://www.northlandchurch.net /blogs/set_free_a_sneak_preview_of_where_were_headed_in_2011/.

1973 to 1985, the financial sector peaked at 16 percent of US domestic corporate profits. In the 1990s it reached postwar-period highs by climbing to between 21 and 30 percent. But this decade the financial sector's share of corporate profits hit 41 percent.[10] These profits weren't from products, and they weren't always from finding the best use for capital; they were from money making more money for a new class of super-rich financial traders. Even traders from some of those banks, some of whom are people of faith, privately tell me that when the percentage of corporate profits from the financial sector grows from 15 to 40 percent, something has gone terribly wrong with the economic system. The financial industry, they say, was meant to facilitate a productive capitalism, not become the primary engine of a casino-like economy for financial gamblers. A number of groups, including several religious institutions, have suggested reforms such as the banning of tax havens and the institution of a new taxation on those financial transactions (the Tobin, or "Robin Hood," tax) with the revenues going toward needed global development.

Fifth, begin church-inspired campaigns against exploitative lending practices on the basis of both biblical and early-church teaching against usury. Such campaigns aim at setting limits on what lenders can charge. Theologian Luke Bretherton describes how issues of money and lending are fundamental to the Scriptures:

> At the heart of the story of salvation we find the power of money and liberation from debt is a central concern. The admonition that we cannot serve both God and Mammon (Matt. 6:19–24) is not a trivial matter: the central drama of salvation history is an act of liberation from debt slavery. To put the pursuit of money before the welfare of people, and use money to re-enslave and exploit people, especially the poor and vulnerable, is to turn your back on God's salvation and deny in practice the revelation given in Scripture of who God is.[11]

10. Simon Johnson, "The Quiet Coup," *Atlantic*, May 2009, http://www.theatlantic.com /magazine/archive/2009/05/the-quiet-coup/7364/#.

11. Luke Bretherton, *"Neither a Borrower nor a Lender Be"? Scripture, Usury and the Call for Responsible Lending* (London: Contextual Theology Centre, April 2011), http://www.londonpen.org/wp-content/uploads/2011/11/bretherton-on-usury.pdf.

These principles—clarity, transparency, accountability, and protecting the common good against private greed—are not just economic policy matters. On a more transcendent level, they provide the metrics of real repentance for those who have behaved badly and must now change. Perhaps we need some sermons on repentance for Wall Street, some pastoral care for the financial giants who sit in our pews, and maybe even some prayer vigils outside the nation's biggest banks. If the banks fail to repent, another financial meltdown could be near.

But I am also reminded of what writer G. K. Chesterton once said when asked what was most wrong with the world. He reportedly replied, "I am." We are all going to need some deeper moral reflection on the meaning of this Great Recession. We do need real reform of our financial institutions and systems. But it will also require the "reform" of ourselves—our own economic choices, desires and demands, and lifestyle requirements. Our consumption-soaked culture was on an insatiable binge when the recession hit. *New York Times* columnist Tom Friedman wondered about the deeper meaning of the Great Recession when he asked, "What if it's telling us that the whole growth model we created over the last 50 years is simply unsustainable economically and ecologically and that 2008 was when we hit the wall—when Mother Nature and the market both said, 'No more'?"[12]

The Un-Economy

At the deepest level, our global economy is not fulfilling the role that economics is meant to fulfill. It has instead become the "un-economy." In an international meeting with economists, business executives, nonprofit organizational leaders, and theologians, my colleague Stewart Wallis of the New Economics Foundation succinctly summed up the problems of the current global economy: it's *unfair, unsustainable, unstable,* and is making many people *unhappy.*[13] These issues of the "un-economy"

12. Thomas L. Friedman, "The Inflection Is Near?," *New York Times*, March 7, 2009, http://www.nytimes.com/2009/03/08/opinion/08friedman.html.

13. Stewart Wallis, "A Great Transition," New Economics Foundation blog, September 27, 2011, http://www.neweconomics.org/blog/2011/09/27/a-great-transition.

were at the heart of our discussions at the World Economic Forum *and* the Occupy Wall Street encampment I had visited in New York City just days before. Let's use Stewart's framework and expand on it.

Unfair

Since the Occupy Wall Street movement began, the issue of massive *inequality* has been brought to public attention. In our discussions about the economy, this has been the elephant in the room that few wanted to discuss out loud. The "occupiers" have given voice to the unspoken feelings of countless others that something has gone terribly wrong in our societies. And this message has resonated widely. In the last hundred years, there have been two peak periods of great inequality in American society: just before the Great Depression in the late 1920s, and in 2008, right before our current Great Recession.

The Occupy movement has created the space for a new conversation, a moral discussion, about inequality. The 1 percent and the 99 percent are now a metric and a template that is widely discussed and is changing the cultural and political framework. What is fair, what is just, and what is right are all on the table now. And both economics and politics will have to answer those questions.

Of course, the many differences between talent, opportunity, contexts, work efforts, and sheer luck will always create human inequality. Opportunity and creativity make inequality inevitable and even necessary. But the *level* of that inequality is the moral question, along with whether those levels are making fairness and opportunity even less possible. The Bible treats extreme inequality in a very negative way, and the extent of our inequality today has now reached biblical proportions.

At the end of the nineteenth century, the ratio of the richest 20 percent in the world versus the poorest 20 percent was about 7 to 1; at the end of the twentieth century, it was 75 to 1.[14] Eighty percent of the real increase in wealth in the United States between 1980 and 2005 went to only 1 percent of the population.[15] In the United States now, the richest

14. Ibid.
15. Ibid.

400 people have as much wealth as the poorest 155 million people. The top 1 percent controls more wealth than the next 95 percent.[16] A *Wall Street Journal* poll found that more than three-quarters of Americans say the country's economic structure is out of balance and "favors a very small proportion of the rich over the rest of the country."[17]

In most advanced countries the ratios of chief executive officer salaries to the pay of the average worker in their companies has risen astronomically over the last thirty years. In the United States, that ratio has grown over the last three decades from about 30 to 1 to about 500 to 1! Inequality has grown rapidly in most of these countries, often fueled by corruption and extreme greed.

In contrast, from 1949 to 1979 all income groups in the United States saw gains from prosperity, but the largest gains went to the bottom 20 percent.[18] Since 1979, the top 5 percent have seen their real family incomes increase by 72.7 percent, while the real family income for the bottom 20 percent has dropped 7.4 percent.[19] From a religious point of view, there is a great moral difference between those two very different eras of prosperity. When prosperity is inclusive of everyone, especially those near the bottom of society, religion and the Bible seem to approve; but when prosperity is skewed mostly toward those on top, it is attacked by our Scriptures and by the religious affirmation of the common good.

As Richard Wilkinson and Kate Pickett demonstrate in their book *The Spirit Level*, excessive inequality, even more than poverty, harms everybody in society. Countries with dramatic inequality have far more social problems, including crime, corruption, and lower trust levels; and everybody's well-being is depressed in such countries when compared to ones with more equality. In a similar vein, Nobel laureate Amartya

16. Michael Moore, speech to protesters in Madison, Wisconsin, March 5, 2011, http://www.youtube.com/watch?v=wgNuSEZ8CDw&feature=player_embedded. This fact was substantiated by *PolitiFact Wisconsin*, http://www.politifact.com/wisconsin/statements/2011/mar/10/michael-moore/michael-moore-says-400-americans-have-more-wealth-/.

17. Jonathan Weisman, "WSJ/NBC Poll: Most Americans Say U.S. Economy Favors 'Small Portion of the Rich,'" *Wall Street Journal*, November 7, 2011, http://blogs.wsj.com/washwire/2011/11/07/wsjnbc-poll-most-americans-say-u-s-economy-favors-small-portion-of-the-rich.

18. "Comparing the Growth of US Family Incomes," United for a Fair Economy, April 28, 2011, http://faireconomy.org/node/1713.

19. Ibid.

Sen has argued that those who suffer from great inequality (even in wealthy societies) face a diminution in their basic economic and political freedoms, such as their ability to achieve political efficacy.

Underneath it all, a deeper issue of *mistrust* is being raised—that leaders have betrayed the public trust, that systems aren't fair, that the rules of the game don't apply to the people at the top, and that most people are really on their own in this modern economy. The levels of economic and political inequality that we now experience, along with the social immobility also being revealed, undermine the public sense of ownership and belonging in society. People have little trust in their governments and economic institutions, believe they are penalized for the mistakes of others who continue to reap handsome rewards, and do not believe they themselves are rewarded fairly for their efforts. People are fearful for their future, their old age, and the prospects for their children. More and more people now have little stake in society. Opportunity is a lost hope for many, as social mobility in America is now lower than in Western Europe.

When the risk taking, greed, and selfishness of the wealthiest created a crisis for many others, we bailed them out and left everyone else to suffer in the economic wilderness of unemployment, home foreclosures, pension losses, deep middle-class insecurity, and shamefully rising poverty rates. If you search the Scriptures, you'll find that God cares not only about poverty but also and especially about real unfairness and shameful inequality. That's what the young people "occupying" Wall Street and so many others are angry about.

Inequality is an inevitable part of the human condition. But when it becomes too extreme, it is a moral and even a religious issue. Something has gone terribly wrong in the United States when the middle classes have experienced stagnant wages for decades, the poverty rate is the highest in fifty years, and the richest just continue to get richer and exercise more and more political power—which they are using toward their own selfish advantage, as we discussed in the last chapter. When human inequality and its resulting injustice become so great, God becomes angry too, as the biblical prophets testify.

Unsustainable

Economies are also ecosystems. If everyone had a Ferrari, the planet could not survive. The earth groans as the ethics, or nonethics, of endless growth are measured only by corporate shareholders in quarterly profit-and-loss statements. "Short-termism" is a phrase heard over and over again now in the broad conversations about values at the World Economic Forum. A global economy based on dirty energy creates unjust regimes, angry populations, endless terrorism and war, and dangerous warming of the planet, which is all clearly unsustainable. Add to that an advertising industry that systematically, psychologically, and even spiritually turns "wants" into "needs," and you have a formula for human and ecological disaster.

It's time to move from a narrowly defined shareholder economy to a stakeholder economy that includes workers, consumers, the environment, and future generations in our economic calculations and decision making.

Theologically speaking, we have been witnessing a massive despoiling of God's creation. We were meant to be stewards of places like the Gulf of Mexico, where many faith leaders, including me, traveled to see the consequences of the BP oil spill. We saw what happened to the wetlands that protect and spawn life, to the islands and beaches, and to all of God's creatures who inhabit the marine world. At the root, we saw the results of an ethic of endless economic growth, centered on carbon-based fossil fuels, that is ultimately both unsustainable and unstable.

It's not just that BP had lied, even though they did—over and over—to cover up their behavior and avoid their obligations. It is that BP *is* a lie; what it stands for is a lie. It is a lie that we can continue to live this way, a lie that our style of life is stable and sustainable, and a lie that these huge oil companies are really committed to a safe and renewable energy future.

Many people now apparently agree with the new direction of a "clean energy economy." And we know this will require a rewiring of the energy grid. But it will also require a rewiring of *ourselves*—our demands, requirements, and insatiable desires. Our *oil addiction* has led us to environmental destruction, endless wars, and the sacrifice of young lives, and it has put our very souls in jeopardy.

We need a new beginning and a new direction for our energy future; we must turn away from oil and fossil fuels toward cleaner and renewable energy sources. And we must start by mitigating the effects of climate change and beginning the critical process of adapting to a new energy future. For that adaptation, much more help will be needed for the world's poorest people—who will be first and most impacted by climate change—and the world's more affluent countries must lead the way.

There is not just one answer to these calamities, but many: corporate responsibility, serious government regulation, public accountability, and real civic mobilization to protect our endangered atmosphere, waters, coasts, and species, as well as people's livelihoods. But at a deeper level, we need a conversion of our habits of the heart, our energy sources, and our lifestyle choices. And somebody will need to lead the way. Who will dare to say that an economy of endless growth must be confronted and converted to an economy of sustainability, to what the Bible calls stewardship? There is hardly an issue more central to the common good than that.

Unstable

One of the most critical conversations taking place around the world is about dangerous and growing conflicts over food, water, land, and energy resources. Conflicts, both present and future, will not be over ideology alone but over survival in the face of resource scarcity and highly unequal resource distribution. Contrast our global maldistribution to the fundamental principle of God's economy: there is enough, if we share it.

Both the instability and sustainability issues are huge factors here. Where poverty is the greatest, people live in far more vulnerable environments and have much less influence on political decision making. While much is made about the politics of the conflicts in places like Darfur and the Middle East, the matter of resource scarcity is often at the core of many conflicts today. In both western Sudan and the Palestinian territories the battles over *water* are absolutely central, as will soon be the case in many other parts of the world as well. The location of oil reserves is also very entwined with the politics of why "ethnic cleansing" continues in southern Sudan and why countries like China and Russia take the wrong side in such conflicts because of their own energy needs and investments. And there is little doubt that oil is the fuel that keeps the fires of conflict raging in the Middle East. Awful pictures of hand-to-hand fighting over the limited food and water from relief trucks in many situations of conflict are simply a metaphor for the future global battles over what is necessary for human survival.

The most hopeful talk about economic stability is occurring around the myriad of new economic approaches based on local, cooperative, and sustainable models of market activity. My goddaughter, Korla Masters, is engaged in the mushrooming urban gardening movement in my hometown of Detroit, and she tells me that if only half the vacant land in the city were cultivated, it could provide up to three-quarters of the needed vegetables and fruits in the Motor City! A local economy like this could have profound effects on the food industry, dramatically reducing the amount of energy used to transport food across the globe. Vibrant local economics are likely the most productive path to a more stable economic future—both locally and globally.

Unhappy

Being rich doesn't make you happy. Of course, happiness and well-being are connected to a modicum of economic security that we all need. But "enough is enough" is proving to be a better guide to a happy life than the maxim "greed is good." The logic of a manic consumer economy is that you are never *supposed* to be satisfied with what you have but should always demand *more*. That endless striving and never-ending desire is *not* making people happy but rather has led us into a lifestyle of constant stress.

An advertisement from Hargrave Custom Yachts captures the spirit of what a consumer culture believes makes people happy. It reads: "We used to sell yachts as luxury items—in today's world they're really a necessity." It goes on, "Successful people have now become the target."[20] But in Detroit, we are seeing the burgeoning urban gardens producing several things: jobs, healthy food, and a sense of community—all of which are ingredients for a happy life.

At its core, this is also a spiritual crisis. More and more people are coming to understand that underlying the economic crisis is a values crisis, and that any economic recovery must be accompanied by a moral recovery. This should be a moment to reexamine the ways we measure success, do business, and live our lives—a time to renew spiritual values and practices such as simplicity, patience, modesty, family, friendship, rest, and Sabbath.

We need nothing less than a pastoral strategy for the financial crisis. We must use our religious teachings to develop Christian, Jewish, and Muslim responses to it. What should people of faith be thinking, saying, and doing now? What is the responsibility of churches, synagogues, and mosques to their communities, to the nation, and to the world? I keep hearing about churches that are starting adult Sunday school classes on economic values, personal finances, and community social responsibility.

Pastors, lay leaders, and innovative faith-based practitioners are suggesting creative answers: mutual aid, congregational and community credit unions, and new cooperative strategies for solving such problems as hunger, homelessness, and joblessness. If these initiatives succeed, the economic crisis may offer congregations an opportunity to clarify their missions and reconnect with their communities.

Going Local

One step that many people are now taking is to go local with their own household economies. When I wrote that my wife, Joy, and I had decided to close our account at Bank of America and move our money to a local bank that has behaved more responsibly, I was amazed at the response. Religious leaders and pastors from around the country called to say that they too were ready to take their money out of the big banks that have shown such shameful immorality and instead invest according to their

20. *Yachts International* (September/October 2011): 89, http://viewer.zmags.com/publi cation/d0a6cd6a#/d0a6cd6a/91.

215

values by putting money into more local and values-based community institutions. Websites have created searchable databases of community banks and credit unions. The idea is beginning to spread.

Local congregations and national church denominations alike should reflect on where they keep their money and how their investments reflect their faith. Some congregations are creating checklists to evaluate whom they do business with, and national church bodies are even taking a deep look at where they invest their pension funds, which are very substantial. Christians, Jews, and Muslims are all asking these questions. Already we are hearing reports of whole congregations, groups of churches, and faith-based organizations from California to New York deciding to transfer their funds to local banks and credit unions.

While the actual effect on banks will take some time, statements of moral integrity are being made. The "unrepentant" banks, whose greed helped destroy our economy, who relied on us to regain their health, and who are now simply back to business as usual, are being sent the clear message that we find their behavior unacceptable. Removing our money can help send that message. And we see seemingly small personal stories and campaigns going viral when they resonate with people in the same situation—such as the story of a young woman whose protest against Bank of America's fee hike drew hundreds of thousands of other people to the cause and forced the bank to back down.[21]

Economic reform will take both external regulation and self-regulation for the nation's leading institutions, both external accountabilities and the internal moral compass that comes from embedding values in a business. Klaus Schwab, the founder and executive chairman of the World Economic Forum, years ago wrote about the need for business to take into account not only the interests of *shareholders* but also those of the many other *stakeholders*—including employees, consumers, the poor, the environment, and future generations.

21. For the original petition against the fee, see http://www.change.org/petitions/tell -bank-of-america-no-5-debit-card-fees, and for Bank of America's statement announcing their change of policy, see http://mediaroom.bankofamerica.com/phoenix.zhtml?c=234503& p=irol-newsArticle&ID=1624356&highlight=.

That the World Economic Forum would take these issues very seriously, and would turn to faith community leaders for help, is good news indeed. But a *New York Times* article on an opening day of the 2011 Forum indicated that we still have a long way to go: "Intentionally or not, Davos [Switzerland, the meeting place of the WEF] will focus attention on one of the most striking consequences of the most recent technological revolution and the spread of globalization that has transformed the world economy in the past 30 years or so: the emergence of an international economic elite whose globe-trotting members have largely pulled away from their compatriots."[22] Many of those superrich are at Davos; and the only people whose lives seem to have gotten back to "normal" since the financial crisis began are those whose behaviors helped to cause it in the first place. They are back to record profits, while we see dramatic and devastating unemployment around the globe, especially for young people.

Moral Facts and a Religious Response

The fundamental facts and *morality* of the current economy are now very clear. The very top end of the economic order is receiving most of the benefits from current growth and profits. The middle parts and people of the economy have experienced decades of stagnating income, declining wealth, and a growing insecurity. Other periods of prosperity, like the thirty years following World War II, saw great gains and a hopeful social mobility for many people in all sectors of the economic class structure—including people who had been at the bottom. But prosperity over the last thirty years has been extremely skewed to the increasing advantage of those at the highest end. The reasons why have to do with political decisions directly shaped by the wealthiest people and institutions in our society and by the politicians of both parties whom the rich have been able to influence. Meanwhile, most people are more insecure than ever before, and those at the bottom face a literal

22. Chrystia Freeland, "Working Wealthy Predominate the New Global Elite," *New York Times*, January 25, 2011, http://dealbook.nytimes.com/2011/01/25/working-wealthy -predominate-the-new-global-elite.

struggle for survival. And that is simply and morally wrong. It's been a long time since "the rising tide" has "lifted all boats." Another euphemism, "the rising tide lifts all yachts," is not simply a clever variation but an accurate description of the stark reality we now face.

Then add the global reality in which 1.3 billion people live in the extreme poverty of less than a dollar a day, and half of God's children—three billion people—live on less than two dollars a day. The unbelievable truth is that more than *twenty-five thousand children die each day* due to utterly preventable hunger and disease. And the rest of us live with that fact every day because we simply do not care enough to change it. That lack of will offends a just and loving God and should shame and motivate us.

Such a situation of economic clarity requires a religious clarity in response. Such massive inequality and economic injustice is an affront to biblical principles and direct disobedience to God, who demands that prosperity be shared and the poor be protected. These are no longer just financial matters but, rather, matters of faith. It's time for the religious world to tell the financial world that God requires a different kind of economy—both domestically and globally. To make that happen is a moral imperative and a test of faith.

Building a New Social Covenant

Old social contracts have unraveled. Former assumptions and shared notions about fairness, agreements, reciprocity, mutual benefits, social values, and expected futures have all but disappeared. The collapse of the financial systems and the resulting economic crisis have not only caused instability, insecurity, and human pain; they have also generated a growing disbelief and fundamental distrust in the way things operate and how decisions are made. Over the last twenty to thirty years, we have witnessed a massive breakdown in trust between citizens, their economies, and their governments. This is true whether we look at Occupy or at the Tea Party.

We urgently need a new social covenant between citizens, businesses, and government. Contracts are what have been broken, but a *covenant*

adds a moral dimension to the solution that is now essential. By definition, this will require the engagement and collaboration of all the
"stakeholders"—governments, businesses, civil society groups, faith
groups, and especially young people. Social covenants should be discussed
in many contexts, and their results will vary from place to place. But they
should all include shared principles and features, such as a value basis
for new agreements, an emphasis on jobs that offer fair rewards for hard
work and real contributions to society, security for financial assets and
savings, a serious commitment to reduce inequality between the top and
the bottom of society, protection or stewardship of the environment, an
awareness of future generations' needs, a stable and accountable financial
sector, and the strengthening of both opportunity and social mobility.
Such a covenant would aim at the promotion of human flourishing,
happiness, and well-being as social goals and affirm the movement from
a shareholder model to a stakeholder model of corporate governance.

Such new social covenants are already being drafted and discussed
in a variety of settings and countries. The discussion itself will help
produce the conversation leading to the results that we need.

A moral conversation about a social covenant could ask what a "moral
economy" should look like and whom it should be for. How could we
do things differently, more responsibly, more equitably, and yes, more
democratically? In forums where business and political leaders meet,
the conversation should focus on the meaning of a moral economy as a
way to safely interrogate our present failed practices. Such a discussion
could lead to new practices driving both ethical and practical decisions
about the economics of our local and global households.

Lack of trust is bad for politics, bad for business, and bad for overall
public morale. It undermines people's sense of participation in society
as well as their feelings of social responsibility, and makes them feel
isolated and alone—more worried about survival than interested in
solidarity. Because the "contract" was broken, a sense of "covenant" is
now needed, fused with a sense of moral values and commitments. And
the process of formulating new social covenants could be an important
part of finding solutions. What better conversation could we have for
the common good?

··· 11 ···

A Servant Government

Man's capacity for justice makes democracy possible; but man's inclination to injustice makes democracy necessary.

—Reinhold Niebuhr[1]

I am a democrat [proponent of democracy] because I believe in the Fall of Man. I think most people are democrats for the opposite reason. A great deal of democratic enthusiasm descends from the ideas of people like Rousseau, who believed in democracy because they thought mankind so wise and good that everyone deserved a share in the government. . . . The real reason for democracy is just the reverse. Mankind is so fallen that no man can be trusted with unchecked power over his fellows. . . . I reject slavery because I see no men fit to be masters.

—C. S. Lewis[2]

1. Reinhold Niebuhr, *The Children of Light and the Children of Darkness: A Vindication of Democracy and a Critique of Its Traditional Defense* (1944; repr., Chicago: University of Chicago Press, 2011), xxxii.
2. C. S. Lewis, "Equality," in *Present Concerns* (San Diego: Mariner Books, 2002), 17.

There is hardly a more controversial political battle in America today than that around the role of government. The ideological sides have lined up, and the arguments rage about the size of government: how big or how small should it be? Some famously have said government should be shrunk so small that it "could be drowned in a bathtub."

But I want to suggest that what *size* the government should be is the wrong question. A more useful discussion would be about the *purposes* of government and whether ours is fulfilling them or not. Rather than big or small, we need a *servant government*. What are the proper *functions* of government, and how can we hold our political leaders to them? Ensuring smart and effective government, which serves its proper purposes and functions, would be a far better use of our energy than determining an arbitrary size. Here is where some of our biblical texts can help us.

Let Every Person Be Subject

> Let every person be subject to the governing authorities. . . . For rulers are not a terror to good conduct, but to bad. . . . Do what is good, and you will receive [authority's] approval; for it is God's servant for your good. . . . Therefore one must be subject, not only because of wrath but also because of conscience. For the same reason you also pay taxes, for the authorities are God's servants, busy with this very thing. Pay to all what is due them—taxes to whom taxes are due, revenue to whom revenue is due, respect to whom respect is due, honor to whom honor is due. (Rom. 13:1, 3–7)

> I saw a beast rising out of the sea. . . . It opened its mouth to utter blasphemies against God. . . . It was allowed to make war on the saints. . . . It was given authority over every tribe and people and language and nation. (Rev. 13:1, 6–7)

The words of Paul in the thirteenth chapter of Romans are perhaps the most extensive teaching in the New Testament about the role and purposes of government. Paul says those purposes are twofold: to restrain evil by punishing evildoers and to serve peace and orderly conduct by rewarding good behavior. It's pretty straightforward. Government should not be "a terror to good conduct, but to bad. . . . Do what is good, and you will receive [authority's] approval" (Rom. 13:3). And civil authority is designed to be "God's servant for your good" (13:4). Government is supposed to be our servant for good. Today we might say "the common good" is to be the focus and goal of government. In the First Epistle to Timothy, Paul says we should pray for people in high political authority "so that we may lead a quiet and peaceful life" (1 Tim. 2:2).

N. T. Wright puts the Romans 13 paragraph in the context of the end of Romans 12 (which we have discussed in chapter 7), where Christians are told not to repay evil for evil but to overcome evil with good and try our very best to live peaceably with all, clearly leaving vengeance to God.

> When we put these verses back into their context, right here in the letter, we start to see what Paul is getting at. He has just said, strongly and repeatedly, that private vengeance is absolutely forbidden for Christians. But this doesn't mean, on the one hand, that God doesn't care about evil, or, on the other, that God wants society to collapse into a chaos where the bullies and the power-brokers do what they like and get away with it. . . . We don't want to live by the law of the jungle. We want to live as human beings in an ordered, properly functioning society. That is almost all that Paul is saying, making the point as he does so that the Christians, who were regarded as the scum of the earth in Rome at the time, must not get an additional reputation as trouble-makers. . . . They are indeed a revolutionary community, but if they go for the normal type of violent revolution they will just be playing the empire back at its own game. They will almost certainly lose, and, much worse, the gospel itself will lose with them.[3]

The Romans text is clearly not meant merely to describe the government authorities and how they always act but rather to describe what is the ideal for them, what God wills for them to do. Paul and the early church certainly understood that government doesn't always

3. N. T. Wright, *Paul for Everyone: Romans Part 2* (Louisville: Westminster John Knox, 2004), Kindle edition, locations 1366–78.

live up to these ideal purposes. And the Romans text is certainly not an endorsement of everything governments do, nor does it command blind obedience to their demands. Repressive and unjust governments have sometimes even used Romans 13 to attempt to create both silence and submission to their unjust dictates, such as the Afrikaner regime of apartheid in South Africa and their white Reformed Church, which sought to give them theological justification. But that is a distortion of the text. Rather, these are the purposes that God intends for governments—punish the evil and reward the good—and Christians are allowed and encouraged to actually hold governments *accountable* to those rightful purposes. And they have often done so over the years, as the black churches in South Africa prophetically did, to cite just one example.

Paul himself on at least two occasions decided to vigorously stand up for his "rights" as a Roman citizen when he was mistreated by the governmental authorities. Clearly, government doesn't always live up to the ideals that God desires. Wright comments:

> The Christians are called to believe, though, that the civic authorities, great and small, are there because the one true God wants his world to be ordered, not chaotic. This does not validate particular actions of particular governments. It is merely to say that some government is always necessary, in a world where evil flourishes when unchecked. Of course Paul knew that quite often one might do the right thing and find the rulers doing the wrong thing. You only have to read the stories of his escapades in Acts to see that. But notice, in those stories (his visit to Philippi in Acts 16, for instance, or his trial before the Jewish authorities in Acts 23), that precisely when the authorities are getting it all wrong and acting illegally or unjustly Paul has no hesitation in telling them their proper business and insisting that they should follow it.[4]

The National Association of Evangelicals puts it this way: "God has ordered human society with various institutions and set in place forms of government to maintain public order, to restrain human

4. Ibid., 1382–88.

evil, and to promote the common good. . . . Government must fulfill its responsibilities to provide for the general welfare and promote the common good."[5]

The Beast from the Abyss

About forty years after the writing of Romans 13, the apostle John was imprisoned on the island of Patmos, a place then used for political detainees, where he wrote the book of Revelation. It is revealing how different Revelation 13 is from Romans 13. Most biblical scholars and commentators believe that John's references to "the beast from the abyss,"[6] the "whore of Babylon,"[7] and all the "dragons" and the "beasts"[8] who rise up to command the obedience of all the peoples and nations, and even "make war against the saints,"[9] are code words for the Roman Empire. The Roman government had become even more oppressive and brutal under Nero and Domitian, claiming divine status for emperors and waging campaigns of violent persecution against Christians and other dissidents who would not submit to the Roman "gods." The apostle John's Revelation 13 depicts the state as a totalitarian beast—a metaphor for Rome, the persecutor of the early Christians.

John's critique of Rome and promise of God's ultimate triumph over the beasts and dragons in Revelation has become a much broader metaphor for resistance to all totalitarian governments ever since. We have, obviously, seen many examples of that kind of totalitarian state and the resistance to it, often by Christians. I think of Dietrich Bonhoeffer and the Confessing Church in Germany, which stood up to the Nazi regime of Adolf Hitler. Political power can indeed turn demonic, replacing its proper civic role with the aspiration to absolute power and even trying to take the place of God.

5. National Association of Evangelicals, *For the Health of the Nation: An Evangelical Call to Civic Responsibility*, 5, 10, http://www.nae.net/images/content/For_The_Health _Of_The_Nation.pdf.
 6. Rev. 11:7.
 7. Rev. 17:5.
 8. Rev. 13:1.
 9. Rev. 13:7 (NIV).

N. T. Wright again makes very clear what New Testament texts like Romans are saying: "What Paul says is clearly anathema to the totalitarian: the point about totalitarianism is that the ruling power has taken the place of God; that is why it is always *de facto*, and frequently *de jure*, atheist. For Paul, the 'state' is not God. God is God, and the state is thus relativized, as are the powers precisely in Colossians 1:15–20, where they are created and reconciled but not divine."[10]

The Revelation passages serve as a clear warning about the abuse of governmental power. A power-hungry government is clearly an aberration from what it is intended to be and a violation of the proper role of government in protecting its citizens and upholding the demands of fairness and justice. To disparage government per se—to see government as the central problem in society—is simply not a biblical position. But to not see the potential danger of dictatorial government power is also to ignore the biblical warnings.

So there is a biblical tension when it comes to the role of government. Government can be either a minister of God or an instrument of Satan. The Bible sees government not only as important and necessary because of the real evil in the world but also as provisional, temporary, and ultimately subject to the authority of God. The role of government is therefore a paradox that includes the terms of both Romans 13 and Revelation 13. And holding governments accountable to the former is the best defense against the latter. Jesus says in Mark's Gospel, "Render unto Caesar the things that are Caesar's, and unto God the things that are God's" (Mark 12:17 ASV). And God decides what is rendered to Caesar, not the other way around. Remember, Jesus also called Herod "that fox"[11]—not a very positive term for his most immediate political ruler in occupied Palestine.

The word "conscience" is also invoked in the Romans text, and sometimes the only way to honor the *office* of government, or its intended purposes, is to disobey it in conscientious acts of civil disobedience, as we have seen in the nonviolent actions of Martin Luther King Jr., Mahatma Gandhi, or Desmond Tutu. But those who "honor" government by

10. N. T. Wright, "The New Testament and the State," *Themelios* 16 (1990): 15.
11. Luke 13:32.

disobeying it when it is wrong must also be willing to pay the penalty for their civil disobedience, which has often led to changes in the law itself. When I have been a part of civil disobedience, I've had the experience of judges saying that they respected what we had done around the cause we believed in, but that we still had to go to jail, which we were willing to do. I remember one magistrate who was so conflicted that she asked us to write essays about law and conscience for her while we were in jail!

The Bible is discerning about government, calling for us to "be subject" to it, to "honor" it, and to pay our taxes, but it never implies that submission means complete or unquestioned obedience or that honor is the same thing as fear. Rather, to be subject, to honor, and to pay taxes means to recognize the standing of government and its legitimate and necessary role in society. We have what Wright calls "ties of obligation" to our fellow humans and must understand that God "has called his human creatures to live in harmony with each other."[12] These obligations are to be enshrined in the laws that governments make.

To Protect and Promote

So the purpose of government, according to Paul, is to protect its people from the chaos of evil and to promote the good of the society: to *protect* and *promote*. Preserving the social order, punishing evil and rewarding good, and protecting the common good are all prescribed, and we are even instructed to pay taxes for those purposes. Practically, what does that mean? What is a government supposed to do, from a biblical perspective? First, government is supposed to *protect* its people. That certainly means protecting its citizens' safety and security. Crime and violence will always be real in this world, and that's why we have the police, who are meant to keep our streets, neighborhoods, and homes safe. When law and order break down, as they sometimes do in the aftermath of natural disasters, for example, we see how quickly chaos, looting, and random violence can break out, pointing again to the need for the maintenance of civil order and protection.

12. Wright, "New Testament and the State," 15.

227

Governments also need to protect their people judicially and make sure our legal and court systems are procedurally just and fair. The biblical prophets regularly rail against corrupt court decisions and systems, in which the wealthy and powerful manipulate the legal processes for their own benefit and put the poor into greater debt or distress. Arbitrary injustice is a regular target of the prophets, who hold the courts accountable to justice. The prophet Amos speaks directly to the courts (and government) when he says, "Hate evil, love good; maintain justice in the courts" (Amos 5:15 NIV).

Along with protecting, governments should *promote* the good of society. The prophets hold kings, rulers, judges, and even employers accountable to the demands of justice and fairness, therefore promoting those values.

The Scriptures say that governmental authority is to protect the poor in particular and promote their well-being. The biblical prophets are consistent and adamant in their condemnation of injustice to the poor and frequently follow their statements by requiring the king (the government) to act justly. That prophetic expectation did not apply only to the kings of Israel but was also extended to the kings of neighboring lands and peoples. The justice requirement is not simply for "the people of God" but for all kings or governments, wherever they happen to be.

Jeremiah, speaking of King Josiah, said, "He defended the cause of the poor and needy, and so all went well." And the subsequent line is very revealing: "'Is that not what it means to know me?' declares the Lord" (Jer. 22:16 NIV). Of Solomon, the Scriptures say, through the words of the queen of Sheba, "Because the LORD loved Israel forever, he has made you king to execute justice and righteousness" (1 Kings 10:9). Psalm 72 begins with a prayer for kings or political leaders: "Give the king your justice, O God, and your righteousness to a king's son. May he judge your people with righteousness, and your poor with justice. May the mountains yield prosperity for the people, and the hills, in righteousness. May he defend the cause of the poor of the people, give deliverance to the needy, and crush the oppressor" (Ps. 72:1–4). There is a powerful vision for promoting the common good here, a vision of prosperity for all the people, with special attention to the poor and to "deliverance" for the most vulnerable and needy, and even a concern for the land.

Ron Sider, in his book *Fixing the Moral Deficit*, summarizes the biblical meaning of the justice required of kings and governments by focusing on the Hebrew words for "justice."

> The biblical understanding of justice clearly includes both procedural and distributive aspects. That the procedures must be fair is clear in the several texts that demand unbiased courts (Exodus 23:2–8; Leviticus 19:15; Deuteronomy 1:17; 10:17–19). That distributive justice (i.e., fair outcomes) is also a central part of justice is evident not just from the hundreds of texts about God's concern for the poor . . . but also in the meaning of the key Hebrew words for justice (*mishpat* and *tsedaqah*).
>
> Time and again the prophets use *mishpat* and *tsedaqah* to refer to fair economic outcomes. Immediately after denouncing Israel and Judah for the absence of justice, the prophet Isaiah condemns the way rich and powerful landowners have acquired all the land by pushing out small farmers (Isaiah 5:7–9). It is important to note that even though in this text the prophet does not say the powerful acted illegally, he nevertheless denounces the unfair outcome. In another text Isaiah denounces the powerful who used "unjust laws" to "deprive the poor of their rights" (Isaiah 10:2). . . . The prophets clearly teach that justice includes fair economic outcomes, not just fair procedures.[13]

Notice that Sider says "fair outcomes" and not "equal outcomes." The political right continues to accuse all who would hold governments accountable for justice of asking for equal outcomes from public policy. But that simply is not true. Rather, we are asking for *fair outcomes*. Indeed, the historical attempts by many Marxist governments to create equal outcomes have dramatically shown the great dangers and fallacies of that approach. Individual freedom has been crushed, and the concentration of power in a few government hands has led to totalitarian results.

The radical economic sharing of the early Christians, recorded in the book of Acts, left "not a needy person among them" (Acts 4:34).

13. Ronald J. Sider, *Fixing the Moral Deficit: A Balanced Way to Balance the Budget* (Downers Grove, IL: InterVarsity, 2012), 54.

But that was voluntary economic redistribution on the basis of faith, not the forced distribution of communist regimes, which have proven, as evidenced by the lifestyles of their dictatorial rulers, to be oppressive and hypocritical. The theological reason for that outcome is indeed the presence and power of sin and the inability of such fallible human creatures to create social utopias on earth.

Yet the biblical prophets do hold their rulers, courts and judges, and landowners and employers accountable to the values of fairness, justice, and even mercy. The theological reasons for that are, in fact, the same: the reality of evil and sin in the concentration of power—both political and economic—and the need to hold that power accountable to justice, especially in the protection of the poor. So fair outcomes, not equal ones, are the goal of governments.

Checks and Balances

Here is where the comments of Reinhold Niebuhr and C. S. Lewis above are very important. Lewis says, in effect, that his pessimistic view of the human condition is his reason for supporting democracy. Democracy is important not because of how good we are but, in fact, because we are often not very good. Lewis continues: "The danger of defending democracy on those [optimistic] grounds is that they're not true. . . . I find that they're not true without looking further than myself. I don't deserve a share in governing a hen-roost, much less a nation."[14] Human fallibilities, illusions, and the will to control are the reason a theologian like Niebuhr, who knew many of the politicians of his day, called democracy a necessity in combating our human "inclination to injustice."

What the theologians are calling for here, and what the biblical texts clearly suggest, is a political system of checks and balances. In the United States, we have such a system already built right into the government, at least theoretically, with the constitutional separation of powers between the three branches—executive, legislative, and judicial. And we have seen government acting in our history to provide a check on powerful

14. Lewis, "Equality," 17.

people, institutions, and interests in society that, if left unchecked, might run over their fellow citizens, the economy, and certainly the poor.

Does anyone really think it isn't necessary for the government to have the power to try to make sure our food is kept clean, our waterways unpolluted, and our air fit to breathe? What kind of bad theology suggests that we could trust all our big companies to voluntarily protect the safety of their consumers or be good stewards of the earth? Is there any evidence that we don't need government to check the behavior of private corporations to keep us all safe and secure?

What do those saying they want to make government so small it could be "drowned in a bathtub" really mean in light of these biblical passages and theological warnings about the fallen behavior and selfishness of humanity and its institutions? Without civil authority having the strength or capacity to *protect* the people, who would protect us from the biggest, wealthiest, and most powerful persons, interests, and corporations, for example, which are now larger than many governments around the world?

The antigovernment voices clearly don't believe in a "sinless government," and neither do I. There are myriad examples of government bureaucracy not doing a good job, standing in the way of good social outcomes, or stifling necessary innovation and creativity. This is why the need for reform of our governments is constant, and why we have regular elections in democracies. But do those government critics really believe in a "sinless market"? Should market forces be set free to create an economic wilderness free of any values or constraints? Should big economic enterprises be allowed to become all-powerful and virtually unaccountable to us as citizens? If government is rendered unable to "punish the evil" or "reward the good" when it comes to the behavior of huge corporations and banks, for example, exactly who else is going to do that? The radically antigovernment stance of the current right-wing Tea Party ideology is simply contrary to a more biblical view of government, the need for checks and balances, the sinfulness of too much concentrated power in either the government or the market, the responsibilities we have to our neighbor, and the God-ordained purposes of government in serving the common good.

Jubilee

In the Scriptures, the most important resource for people is land. Many texts tell how people should be treated in relationship to the land. Landowners are instructed to leave the edges of their fields unharvested for the poor. Illegal and even legal behavior by large landholders that took away the land of smaller owners was vigorously condemned.

In the biblical tradition of Jubilee, three things were commanded to be done periodically: setting slaves free, forgiving the debts of debtors, and returning land to its original owners. Three things are worth recognizing about the Jubilee laws. First, these are not minor references in the Scriptures, but a teaching and tradition that begins in the book of Deuteronomy and runs right through the Scriptures to the first words of Jesus at Nazareth about his mission "to proclaim the acceptable year of the Lord" (Luke 4:19 ASV). Second, these are not suggestions that individuals do certain things voluntarily; they are structural requirements. Third, these laws dealt with the critical elements of society that could easily lead to great injustice and inequality, and they are meant as periodic and corrective measures.

Today, with only about 1 percent of Americans owning farm land,[15] those critical elements that contribute to injustice and justice will be very different. But the principle of corrective measures that are structural is still very important.

Unfortunately, the issue of slavery is still with us, with 2.5 million women and children being sexually and economically trafficked, silently and invisibly, at any given time, not only in the developing world but even in major American cities.[16] A primary goal and purpose of government protection should be to combat the sexual trafficking and economic exploitation that are today's slavery. Powerful faith-based movements are growing around the world to abolish the modern slavery of trafficking, but often without the active and focused help needed from many governments.

15. US Department of Commerce Economics and Statistics Administration, *Who Owns America's Farmland?* (Washington, DC: United States Census Bureau, 1993), http://www.census.gov/apsd/www/statbrief/sb93_10.pdf.

16. United Nations Office on Drugs and Crime, "Human Trafficking: An Overview" (New York: United Nations, 2008), 6, http://www.ungift.org/docs/ungift/pdf/knowledge/ebook.pdf.

Financial capital now holds the place that land once did. Today there are so many violations of ethics around financial capital that governments need to address them just as they do other ethics violations. Predatory lending practices (such as payday lending) that principally target low-income people are a great injustice that perpetuates poverty and even leads to violence. Contracts for credit cards and home mortgages have grown into many impossible-to-understand pages, with the purpose of cheating people and enslaving them to debt. Young people and low-income people are especially susceptible to abuse by credit card companies. Slavery to debt is another form of modern slavery that government should address—both the procedures and outcomes. Simply making procedures and contracts clear, aboveboard, understandable, and accountable to fairness would make a great difference for many people.

It is now clear that both unethical and criminal behavior on the part of half a dozen banks and financial institutions led to the financial meltdown of 2008 and the resulting Great Recession, which has caused much suffering for many people. Some criminal penalties have been imposed (though hardly at levels befitting the crimes), and embarrassing revelations about the practices and products of some of the nation's leading financial institutions have been splashed across the op-ed pages of our newspapers by former employees disgusted with their firms' greedy and immoral behavior.[17]

There *had been* rules and regulations that might have prevented those behaviors, but they were repealed in the Congress by the senators and representatives who came to represent those banking interests and whose campaigns had been financed by them. Most of those historic rules were based on old usury laws that had their origin in the religious community, but they began to be suspended in the 1980s. Elizabeth Warren, the first acting director of the new Consumer Financial Protection Agency, put it like this to my class at Georgetown: "We were protected by usury laws, all the way from the Code of Hammurabi until 1980."

17. See, for example, Greg Smith, "Why I Am Leaving Goldman Sachs," *New York Times*, March 14, 2012, http://www.nytimes.com/2012/03/14/opinion/why-i-am-leaving-goldman -sachs.html?pagewanted=all.

It is very necessary for civil government to employ those kinds of laws, rules, and regulations consistently in order to protect the people and the economy. To push them aside because of the political power of wealthy interests is simply a violation of that legitimate public role and trust.

Perhaps the most important resource today, like land was in ancient biblical times, is education. Here is where some of the greatest injustices in our society are occurring. Many schools in our most deprived urban neighborhoods, where poor children of color are forced to go, should not be called schools at all but prisons, because they do not educate, but simply imprison the next generation in poverty and maintain an endless cycle of impoverishment from one generation to the next. A good education is today's clearest and best way out of poverty.

The goal of the reform and renewal of our educational system should be one of the most important purposes of government. That doesn't mean that government must do all the educating but rather that it makes sure it is being done and done well, especially for those who have been trapped in educational poverty. Like land in ancient biblical times, the asset of accessible education for all should be a basic concern of government. Fortunately, there is a growing educational reform movement now that is bipartisan and focuses on the most important ingredient: the teachers and principals we desperately need. Real reform requires the political and financial commitments of our public policy makers. Supporting that movement focused on teachers and prioritizing resources for educational transformation will be one of the best ways to pursue the positive role of government in our day. It is a very contemporary example of stopping the evil and rewarding the good.

Finding the Balance

Today we are facing political philosophies that hold individual rights as their supreme value and consider government the major obstacle. The "just leave me alone and don't spend my money" opinion has shaped the political debates around debt crises and deficits. But the enshrinement of individual choice is not the only or preeminent Christian virtue when it comes to a biblical view of government. Emphasizing individual rights at the expense of others' needs and rights violates the whole idea of the common good. The Christian answer to the question of whether we are our brother's keeper is decidedly yes. Jesus tells us that the greatest commandments are to love God with our whole being and to love our neighbor as ourselves. In so doing, he gave a proper regard to looking after oneself but put it in the context of having the same concern for our neighbors.

Loving your neighbor is a better Christian response than telling your neighbor to just leave you alone. We have seen how both compassion and social justice are fundamental Christian commitments. And while the Christian community is responsible for living out both commitments in the world, we can see how government is also held accountable to the requirements of justice and protection of the poor.

A thoroughly antigovernment ideology simply isn't biblical. In Romans 13, Paul describes the role and vocation of government in addition to that of the church, and the apostle teaches that government also plays a role in God's plan and purposes. Of course, debating the size and role of government is always a fair and good discussion, and most of us would simply prefer smart and effective to "big" or "small" government.

But a supreme confidence in the market is also not consistent with a biblical view of human nature and sin. The exclusive focus on government as the central problem ignores the problems of other social sectors, and in particular, the market, which I addressed in chapter 10. When government regulation is the enemy, the market is set free to pursue its own self-interest without regard for public safety, the common good, or the protection of the environment, which Christians regard as God's creation. Those who believe in what I call the myth of the sinless market seem to think that the self-interest of business owners or corporations will always serve the interests of society, and that if they don't, it's not government's role to correct it. That's more than bad politics; it is also bad theology.

Such antigovernment theorizing also ignores the practical issues that the public sector has to solve. Should big oil companies like BP simply be allowed to spew oil into the ocean? And is regulating them really "un-American"? Do we truly want no one inspecting our water, making sure our kids' toys are safe, or guarding our health care procedures and products? Do we really want owners of restaurants and hotels to be able to decide whom they will or won't serve, and should liquor store owners also be able to sell alcohol to our kids?

Given the reality of sin in all human institutions, doesn't a political process that provides both accountability and checks and balances make both theological and practical sense? Again, we need democracy not because people are essentially good but because they often are not. Public accountability to democracy is essential to preventing the market itself from becoming a beast of corporate totalitarianism.

Of course, excessive government spending is a legitimate concern, and those with more positive views of government are more vulnerable to ignoring that problem. But to mainly attack social programs for the poor, rather than the billions and trillions of dollars in other more protected areas of spending such as "corporate welfare" or Pentagon waste, is morally inconsistent. Coming to a better moral balance in achieving fiscal responsibility while protecting the poor should be a bipartisan effort, as we discussed in chapter 4.

Looking to government first to solve all our social problems is a common mistake of pro-government forces. We need to forge new partnerships between the public sector, private sector, and nonprofit civil society, which also includes communities of faith. Innovation, new solutions, creativity, and multipurpose projects often come from the NGO (nongovernmental organization) world. Social entrepreneurs from both the private and public sectors are rolling up their sleeves to actually find solutions to many social problems today. But questions of scale are important. Major philanthropists such as Bill and Melinda Gates come to Washington regularly to remind our politicians that their foundation's billions are not enough to ensure basic health for the world's poorest—that public investment in global health on the part of governments is absolutely crucial. Charity is insufficient, and that's why justice is the preferred biblical solution to injustice, as the Scriptures clearly demonstrate.

Common Ground for Higher Ground

As we have already discussed, the solutions to problems like poverty concern both policy *and* cultural matters. For example, marriage and healthy families *are* a critical antipoverty solution, as are living wages, stable housing, earned income and child tax credits, and affordable child care. Public policies that promote and are friendly to all those crucial factors are much needed. And the vocational and unique role of nonprofit organizations and faith communities in changing cultural habits and behaviors is also essential.

Ultimately, these should not be such partisan matters, despite all the current battles around the role of government. We have seen support across the political aisle for effective initiatives aimed at overcoming poverty, shoring up international aid and development for the most vulnerable, and supporting critical agendas, such as encouraging the international adoptions of marginalized children and fixing the broken domestic foster care system. Indeed, some of our efforts to combat poverty and disease, especially efforts against HIV/AIDS, malaria, and massive hunger in the poorest parts of Africa, have even brought liberals and conservatives together.

Some of that support comes from the agenda of "compassionate conservatism," in which political leaders who are fiscally conservative, favor small government, and believe in the free market also believe that government should and must partner with the private sector—especially nonprofit and faith-based organizations—to help lift people out of poverty, both abroad and here at home. Such a conviction requires two things: a genuine empathy and commitment to the poor on the one hand, and a more balanced and positive view of government on the other. It expresses both conservative principles and social conscience, with particular concern for the poorest and most vulnerable. The compassionate conservative space is vital to the health of the nation and the future of the poor, and therefore preserving it is essential. Such space is open to the kind of bipartisan cooperation we have had before and now desperately need again.

Mike Gerson, former speechwriter for and policy adviser to President George W. Bush, and now a columnist for the *Washington Post*, is one of the most eloquent spokespersons for this compassionate conservatism, and I count him as a friend and ally. Mike and I helped to create something called the Poverty Forum,[18] which brought together policy experts from both Republican and Democratic administrations and Congresses to propose commonsense steps to reduce poverty. The project produced a surprising level of consensus, as participants focused on practical solutions that are proven to work rather than on ideology.

I saw that energy again at a reception that Bono and his ONE Campaign hosted for World AIDS Day on December 1, 2011. Earlier in the day, three US presidents—Barack Obama, George W. Bush, and Bill Clinton—had spoken at a televised gathering, celebrating the real successes achieved over the last thirty years in the battle to end the scourge of AIDS and committing to finishing the job.

When making a difference in the lives of poor and vulnerable people is seen as a nonpartisan issue and a bipartisan cause (as the battle against AIDS has been), then we make the most progress. In a *New York Times* op-ed that same day, Bono celebrated the success against AIDS and gave shout-outs to people as diverse as evangelicals and the gay community, Democratic senator Pat Leahy and former Republican senator Rick Santorum, and ideological foes such as Nancy Pelosi and Jesse Helms![19]

The victories that have been won in the global battle against AIDS are the result of the efforts of many—Republicans, Democrats, conservatives, liberals, Christians, Jews, Muslims, and people of no particular religious predilection—and most big gains for the poor will require support from both sides of the political aisle of government to serve the common good.

Government can do good things and bad things. Some of the good things are big, and some are little. And we can all point to horrendous things done in the name of government, with its complete political authority. My friend Richard Land is a political conservative, but we agree that the GI Bill and FHA (the Federal Housing Authority) made a big and positive difference in the lives of our families and so many

18. http://www.thepovertyforum.org/.
19. Bono, "A Decade of Progress on AIDS," *New York Times*, November 30, 2011, http://www.nytimes.com/2011/12/01/opinion/a-decade-of-progress-on-aids.html.

others by educating fathers and making first family homes possible after our dads came home from World War II. Most people who have Medicare are very happy with it, and Social Security rescued an older generation from poverty. But some government programs don't work, and we need to be completely honest about that.

For people of faith, government is never ultimate but needs to play the important and modest role of servant. The criteria for evaluation and judgment of civil authority are whether it is serving the people, whether it is guarding their security, whether it is maintaining a positive and peaceful social order, whether it is helping to make the lives of its citizens better, and, in particular, whether it is protecting the poor. Because of the human will to power, political leaders must always be held accountable, and the best governments are characterized by checks and balances. To be opposed to government *per se*, especially when that opposition serves the ultimate power of other wealthy and powerful interests, is simply not a biblical position. Transparency, accountability, and service are the ethics of good government. "Of the people, by the people, and for the people" is still a good measure and goal of civil authority. But people of faith will ascribe ultimate authority only to God, to whom civil authority will always be accountable.

···12···

Making Things Right

It is from numberless diverse acts of courage and belief that human history is shaped. Each time a man stands up for an ideal, or acts to improve the lot of others, or strikes out against injustice, he sends forth a tiny ripple of hope, and crossing each other from a million different centers of energy and daring those ripples build a current which can sweep down the mightiest walls of oppression and resistance.

—Robert F. Kennedy[1]

The term "social justice" comes under attack these days, especially from media pundits on the political right. Why are they so afraid of social justice? And why are they especially afraid of the biblical imperatives for *justice*? Is it because these imperatives make their calls for mere *charity* inadequate? Justice must indeed be "social," as the Bible makes very clear. But this issue is not political or about the size of government, as

1. Robert F. Kennedy, "Day of Affirmation Speech" (University of Cape Town, Cape Town, South Africa, June 6, 1966), http://www.jfklibrary.org/Research/Ready-Reference /RFK-Speeches/Day-of-Affirmation-Address-news-release-text-version.aspx.

the right-wing talk show hosts want to suggest. The real biblical concern is what it takes to *make things right*.

Afraid of Social Justice

> But let justice roll on like a river,
> righteousness like a never-failing stream! (Amos 5:24 NIV)

My wife, Joy, was taking my nine-year-old, Jack, to school. A song called "Waiting on the World to Change" was on the radio.[2] The song describes many of the things that are wrong with the world, then goes to the refrain "We're waiting on the world to change." Jack was listening and quickly responded, "Mom, that's wrong! We can't just wait for the world to change. We have to change it ourselves!"

That's the response of a new generation.

It's very controversial to talk about social justice in America. The question has become politicized. Those who speak about justice are accused of being "socialist." Advocating for justice means you believe in "BIG GOVERNMENT!" according to some. You might even be called a "communist" by certain TV talk show hosts who put up your name on their "blackboard."

I've learned that you can also be attacked so vehemently around your speaking invitations in some very conservative parts of the country (often led by the most zealous disciples of the media pundits) that your teenage son asks you, "Dad, do those people who hate you so much have guns?" And many of them do.

What is clear is that some people in this society—some of our media talking heads, some of our political leaders, and even some of our church leaders—are *afraid* of social justice.

They want us to focus on *charity*—just charity. They like charity. Everyone likes charity. Just help the poor as best you can. But *justice*, that word scares some people.

2. John Mayer, "Waiting on the World to Change," on *Continuum*, Aware Records LCC, 2006.

Compassion is indeed a wonderful and powerful thing. It's how we start to engage, and it is usually the doorway we walk through to gain a deeper understanding of what's wrong in the world. Compassion is often the doorway to justice. Acting out of compassion toward those who are the victims of things that are wrong often helps us to understand why things are wrong and how we might be able to make them right.

So how do we understand justice in a biblical way? It's not about socialism, at least not with me, because I think socialism is a system that gives too much ownership and power to government; nor is it about communism, because we've seen what has happened to millions of people under that system. It's not even about "big government." I've never done the math, but if you cut from government many of the things I don't support—like a military budget that dwarfs the rest of the world's defense spending, or spending trillions on wrong wars, or the billions in corporate subsidies we dole out, or the unnecessary overpayments in skyrocketing health care costs—and just focused on the things government is supposed to do to protect its people, my ideal government might even be *smaller* and more focused than its current form. Justice is not really about any of those "isms" or political philosophy or a particular size of government.

Biblical Justice and Righteousness

The God of the Bible is not just a God of charity; the God of the Bible is a God of justice. But what does that mean?

Our understanding of biblical justice has been diminished by how the Greek and Hebrew words that were originally used have been translated. In Hebrew, there were at least three words to articulate the concept of justice, as we understand it today—each with its own nuances and subtleties. According to *Baker's Evangelical Dictionary of Biblical Theology*, the Hebrew words *tsedeq* and *mishpat* and the Greek *dikaiosyne* are all used to describe "justice" in the Bible.[3] We began discussing the meaning of those terms in the last chapter.

---

3. "Justice," in *Baker's Evangelical Dictionary of Biblical Theology Online*, http://www.biblestudytools.com/dictionaries/bakers-evangelical-dictionary/justice.html.

The biblical words for "justice" are interchangeable with and inter-related with the words for "righteousness." What is "just" and what is "right" are essentially the same. The original Hebrew and Greek words for "justice" are the same as those rendered "righteousness." And in about half the cases in which we have "just" or "justice" in the King James Version and the American Standard Revised Version, the words have been changed to "right" or "righteous" or "righteousness" in later versions.[4]

We must remind ourselves that the two ideas are essentially the same; "justice" and "righteousness" are deeply connected in the Bible. They are richly applied to many things, from fair weights and measures, to just legal proceedings, to good personal conduct, to honesty and truthfulness, to an individual's right or just claim, to employers' eco-nomically just behaviors, to judges' fair decisions, to the governmental responsibilities of kings and rulers.

The clear meaning of "justice" is "what is right," "rightness," or "what is just" or "what is normal," the way things are supposed to be. Fair and equal treatment under the law and the fairness of laws are common biblical concerns. Throughout the Scriptures, God is the defender and protector of the poor, the alien, the debtor, the widow, and the orphan. Justice can also mean "deliverance" or "victory" or "vindication" or "prosperity"—but for all, and not just a few. Justice is part of God's purpose in redemption.

One of the clearest and most holistic words for justice is the Hebrew *shalom*, which means both "justice" and "peace." Shalom includes "wholeness," or everything that makes for people's well-being and security and, in particular, the restoration of relationships that have been *broken*. *Shalom*, the Bible's best word for justice and peace, is about restoring relationships. Justice, therefore, is about *repairing* the relationships that have been broken: our relationships both with other people and to structures and systems, systems of courts and punish-ments, money and economics, land and resources, and kings and rulers.

Shalom is a wonderfully creative and expansive idea that can be ap-plied to all of our personal and social relationships and even to imagining

4. "Justice," in *Bible Justice Online*, http://www.bible-history.com/isbe/J/JUSTICE.

how our societies can be changed. It's all about repairing relationships and making our social lives healthy again. The deeply biblical idea of shalom is the reason why justice always has to be "social." We can begin to imagine how the reform of our criminal justice system could be based on "restorative justice" rather than mere retribution. Employer-employee relationships could be brought into the idea of shalom as well—fixing what has been unfair, unjust, or exploitative. Economic systems, structures, and interactions can be judged by how they serve or destroy good and healthy relationships. Even government can be evaluated by how it ignores problems, creates dependencies, or actually facilitates better relationships between citizens in a civil society.

Justice is about fixing and healing relationships that have been broken—things that have gone wrong—and making them right again. Finally, it's about restoring our broken relationship with God and to what God intends for us, which includes our role in God's purposes for all of God's creatures and for the world that God has made. Injustice is about broken relationships—broken relationships between people and systems and the creation and finally the Creator.

Justice as an Act of Worship

The biblical words for justice all relate to the justice and fairness of God, the judgment of God, the love and faithfulness of God, and the blessing and healing of God. And it is clear that justice is also part of our *worship* of God. Listen to the prophet Amos:

> I hate, I despise your religious festivals;
> your assemblies are a stench to me.
> Even though you bring me burnt offerings and grain offerings,
> I will not accept them.
> Though you bring choice fellowship offerings,
> I will have no regard for them.
> Away with the noise of your songs!
> I will not listen to the music of your harps.
> But let justice roll on like a river,
> righteousness like a never-failing stream! (Amos 5:21–24 NIV)

This is some of the strongest language in the Bible about worship and justice, and it clearly makes a connection between the two. God "takes no delight" (as some other translations say) in the "noisy" worship of his people if their worship is disconnected from justice—from making things right for those who are poor and oppressed. Exuberant worship can even distance us from the realities of an unjust world, and that distance creates a distance from the God of justice, who is passionate about the world he has made and about all of his children. Even worse, we have even seen how worship can serve as a cover-up for injustice, how we can act in our religious gatherings as if everything is all right—as in the Sunday services in apartheid South Africa or America's segregated South—or North. And that is likely what the prophet means when he says that such false worship is a "stench" to God.

The only way worship can be made pleasing to God again is to "let justice roll on like a river, righteousness like a never-failing stream." There is the interrelationship between justice and righteousness in God's eyes. Clearly a worshiping community is not acceptable to God if its members are not acting every day to make justice more possible in the world. Acting on behalf of justice and righteousness in the world is really an act of worship too.

So justice, most simply, means making things right—putting things right again. Justice means fixing, repairing, and restoring broken relationships. And doing justice restores our relationship with God and makes our worship of God authentic.

That should be our justice lens for viewing any society—*looking at what's wrong and figuring out how to make things right*. Justice is as basic as that. And acting for justice shows that we love and worship the God of the Bible, who is a God of justice.

The Fight for Justice

The fight for justice begins when somebody sees that something is wrong. As quoted at the top of this chapter, Robert Kennedy once eloquently said, "Each time a man stands up for an ideal, or acts to improve the lot of others, or strikes out against injustice, he sends forth a tiny ripple of hope . . . and . . . those ripples build a current which can sweep down the mightiest walls of oppression and resistance."[5]

That is how every movement for justice starts. There are things on our minds, things that bother us, things that have gotten our attention that we think are *wrong*. Movements for justice often start when a new generation comes to believe that something is wrong. Something captures the attention of young people.

We always need that from young people, and, indeed, I believe it's always part of the vocation and obligation of the next generation. When young people believe something is wrong, that is often the starting point for new social movements. On the other hand, when young people don't see anything wrong, when nothing gets their attention, when their only concern is themselves—how they look, how they feel, what they want to eat or drink, who they like, or who likes them—*the society is in big trouble*. And if they are Christian young people, and they're caught up in themselves, then *the church and the gospel are in big trouble*.

Part of the job of each new generation, part of the vocation of young people, and part of the faith obligation of Christians is to learn to see what is wrong, unfair, cruel, and unjust in the world around them: what broken relationships are hurting God's children and God's world, or what is breaking the heart of God.

Paying attention to what is wrong, and then figuring out how to make it right—that's exactly what people of faith are supposed to do.

As I have already described, I was a young Christian in Detroit and sensed something was very wrong in the area of race, with the relationships and systems between whites and blacks. I could see a problem in my city and my country, and I wanted to make it right. But I had to leave the church and join the civil rights and student movements of my time because my church would not embrace my desire for racial justice. I came back to faith only when I found that concern for justice in the Bible and learned how Christians had acted to make things right in times past and led many of the most important social justice movements in history. I learned that whatever it takes to make things right

5. Kennedy, "Day of Affirmation Speech."

is the work of justice—see what is wrong and figure out how to make things different and better. I learned to trust my questions as a young person and to encourage other young people to trust their questions as well—and to act on them.

Rescue the Victims or Make Things Right

Let's take some contemporary examples of issues that are touching the minds and hearts of a new generation and awakening a passion for justice. All these deeply serious issues compel the compassion of the young and lead them to consider how to make things right again.

Millions of young Christians today have discovered the issue of human sexual trafficking. They obviously believe it is wrong and have become deeply involved in campaigns to rescue women and children caught up in the trafficking, and those efforts are critically important. But the numbers being trafficked are growing, and the rescues are increasing. So how do we end it, change it, and stop the trafficking? Only by asking the justice questions: Who's making the money and running the systems, and which politicians are covering it up or might even be involved? What could stop this: what financial measures, what public revelations, what legal battles, what new laws would confront the brothel systems, expose the perpetrators and participants, and protect the victims? What would make things right?

It's critically important to rescue the women and children, but clearly not enough. How do we make things right? In answer to that question, a new abolitionist movement has begun not only to rescue the victims but also to try to stop the trafficking. It shouldn't matter what political philosophy one has—what does matter is what it will take to make things right so that so many women and children will no longer suffer such vicious brutality.

We can ask the same question with a host of other issues and concerns. Take homelessness. Many congregations, faith-based organizations, and social service groups are feeding, sheltering, and caring for the medical and social needs of homeless individuals and families. But what that movement has found is summed up in the phrase "Housing First," which is a commitment to first provide safe and stable housing and then start solving all the other problems that cause or relate to homelessness. This is the strategy that has proven to work best and makes things right and normal again for those who have become homeless.

Millions of people are involved with tutoring young school kids who need some extra help, a community service that my own teenage son has become involved in. But what will bring genuine reform to badly performing schools for our poorest students, and who will make that happen? A new and broadly nonpartisan education reform movement is now afoot, and the focus is on finding and producing the right kind of teachers and school principals. This movement comes from the experience of learning that tutoring isn't enough—a fundamental transformation of our educational system, especially in our poorest neighborhoods and communities, will be required to set things right.

Faith communities and other civic organizations are involved in feeding the hungry through food pantries, food banks, and soup kitchens, serving regular meals and providing bags of groceries for families who come up short each week. But here is where public budgets are important. The well-respected Bread for the World Institute's analysis on hunger in America "consistently shows that the amount of food provided by government programs dwarfs charitable contributions by more than 9 to 1."[6] When the funding is cut for food stamps and other critical programs, the faith community and nonprofits are overwhelmed with the long lines and new emergency needs. That's why faith-based organizations and churches have formed a circle of protection around the most critical programs for low-income people, telling politicians that they should go somewhere else to find the money needed for deficit reduction. Going to where the real money is instead of balancing budgets with the most painful costs for the poor is clearly a justice question about how we set things right. We discussed this hopeful development in chapter 4 (see "The Circle of Protection").[7]

6. "Government Food Assistance: Why It's Needed," Bread for the World Institute website, http://notes.bread.org/2011/11/government-food-assistance-why-its-needed.html.
7. "Circle of Protection for a Moral Budget," *Sojourners*, http://sojo.net/get-involved/action-alerts/circle-protection-moral-budget.

With as many as twelve million undocumented immigrants now in America, more and more churches and synagogues are getting involved with those in jeopardy. In doing so, they are especially motivated by the increasingly harsh immigration laws being passed in states around the country. As we also described in chapter 4, the heart of the problem is the two invisible signs up at the border between Mexico and the United States. One sign reads "No Trespass" and the other says "Help Wanted." And now millions of vulnerable families are caught in the conflict between those two signs.

We clearly have a broken system. And what we need is the solution of comprehensive immigration reform. But that continues to be postponed because of politics, while everything keeps getting worse for undocumented people. State laws have been enacted that attempt to make life much more difficult and painful for the undocumented and that pressure them to leave voluntarily ("self-deportation") because their lives have become so unlivable, which I would call *deportation by cruelty*. Even acts of Christian ministry toward those who clearly fit the biblical category of "the stranger" could now be deemed illegal as harboring or transporting those named as "illegal aliens." But those ministries to undocumented people are continuing to grow, and clergy are even deciding to break those laws until we find a way to make things right—by passing new comprehensive immigration reform laws that secure the borders and respect the rule of law, provide safe and legal guest worker status, stop the breakup of families, and create an earned path to citizenship for those who have lived and raised their families in this country for many years, even decades. And again, a movement led by evangelical Christians, who vote both Republican and Democrat, is helping to lead the way to make things right, as we also discussed.

The shooting of Trayvon Martin in February 2012 in Sanford, Florida, sparked a nationwide outcry. Young Trayvon and his father were visiting friends inside a gated community, and Trayvon had gone out to get some snacks; he was coming back with some candy and a soft drink when he was spotted by a neighborhood watch volunteer, who chased the unarmed African American teenager and finally shot him to death, claiming self-defense.

The heartbreaking death of a young son and the deep grief of his mother and father cannot be resolved simply by the arrest and trial of the shooter. Resolution should also address the new "stand your ground" laws, which can be used to justify such killings, and the gun laws that make it so easy for any person to acquire even the most dangerous automatic weapons without any checks.

On a deeper level, the only redemption for the death of Trayvon Martin will come from a nation's soul-searching. What has come to the attention of the nation out of this tragedy is how every black father and mother in America—regardless of their status, class, and neighborhood—must have "the conversation" with his or her young son about how to behave in the presence of the police or other armed security personnel. White parents simply don't have those conversations with their sons. And white parents should be asking their black friends—at their kids' schools or on their sports teams—about their experience. Many are shocked to learn that "the conversation" occurs in almost every black family in America. The racial profiling of young and even older African American men is a persistently and profoundly unjust fact of American life and must be changed—must be made right. Only a change in those behaviors, in our culture, and in our criminal justice system will be enough to respond to the killing of Trayvon Martin. And that will take a multiracial movement in America to make things right.

What the Prophets Say

To change and correct injustice, we must confront the systems and logic of our world. British abolitionist William Wilberforce, for example, didn't just call for English Christians not to possess slaves; he wanted to *end* the slave trade, and that required a long political campaign. Martin Luther King Jr. wasn't content to just ask American Christians not to personally practice discrimination against black people; he understood that the nation needed a civil rights law and a voting rights act to stop racial discrimination and fulfill real democracy for African Americans. That required leadership from the White House and votes in Congress. But mostly it took a civil rights movement.

This is what the Bible teaches us. The Scriptures reveal a God of justice, not merely a God of charity. Words such as "oppression" and "justice" fill the Bible. The most common *objects* of the prophets' judgments are kings, rulers, judges, employers—the rich and the powerful in charge of the world's governments, courts, economies, systems, and structures, those who run the world's logic. When those who are in charge mistreat the poor and vulnerable, say the Scriptures, it is not just unkind but also wrong and unjust, and it makes God angry. The *subjects* of the Scriptures' concern are always the widow and the orphan, the poor and the oppressed, the victims of courts or unscrupulous employers, debtors whose debts need to be forgiven, and strangers in the land who need to be welcomed. And the *topics* of the prophets' messages to the powerful are things like land, labor, capital, judicial decisions, employer practices, rulers' dictates, and the decisions of the powerful—all the stuff of justice and politics.

Movements for change begin when something touches people's hearts and strikes a chord. And for some it compels faith. People engage the issue and join with others who care about it, and together they figure out how to make a wrong right—that's justice. Don't let anybody tell you that it's dangerous. It's dangerous only to injustice and to those who have investments in the systems and structures of the world as they are.

Do you want to make fundamental changes in the way the world works? It is really not about commitments to political systems or philosophies, or large or small governments. Instead, it's about going to the root causes of things that are wrong, getting to the core of the problem, and then going far enough to make things right again. That can mean changes in attitudes, cultures, institutions, systems and structures, policies and laws. It may indeed be about changing politics to make something right, but it need not be a partisan cause. And the most successful movements need to attract bipartisan support. Those movements actually change the things that are wrong and make them right—which justice always requires. This is a new generation's time to decide what is wrong and commit to whatever it takes to make it right.

··· 13 ···

Healthy Households

Bidden or Not Bidden God Is Present
Don't Postpone Joy
We Interrupt This Family for Baseball Season

—Three signs up in our household

From the outset of this book we have talked about the common good as that which encourages *human flourishing*. For all the importance and attention we have given to national, institutional, cultural, economic, and political forces, no force, no place, is more formational to human flourishing than the *households* we live in. That's because our households are the places where we have our most primary relationships and because, most important, they are the environments where our young are primarily raised. Our households are usually the most formative places in our lives, for better or for worse. They are the places that most of us leave in the morning and come back to at night. Households are the home base of our existence and the foundation of a society. Households hold our families together, and they are the first place where we learn the lessons of human relationships and community—that is, the lessons of the common good. It is in our households that we must learn to *choose values over appetites.*

Values over Appetites

Point your kids in the right direction—when they're old they won't be lost. (Prov. 22:6 Message)

Our households are the main target of the modern consumer society's relentless stimulation of our appetites, but they are also the place where the primary values of human flourishing can be taught so that we can govern our appetites, which, if unbridled, threaten our very humanity. And a fundamental question regarding the common good is whether our households will form our values or simply feed our appetites.

One night in my household, we had a friend of one of my sons over for dinner, as we often do. Sitting around the table, and just before we started to eat, we all joined hands to say a brief prayer of thanks. Our thirteen-year-old guest's face lit up in a big smile, and he said, "Wow, this is just like in the movies!"

That discipline, and it is a spiritual discipline, of sharing dinner together as much as possible is becoming increasingly countercultural. Family dinners provide a regular respite, or even retreat, from the enormous cultural pressures that now bombard the lives of parents and children every day. The table and what occurs around it offer sustenance, both physically and spiritually.

First, a home-cooked meal is usually better and healthier than the fast-food options that families on the go often settle for. Second, dinners together provide a quiet place and time just to talk and to answer the question, "So, how was your day?" That encourages the habit of regular communication and even actual *reflection* on the things that happened to us during our very different days. What happened and what does it mean? What do we all think about what happened?

Schoolwork, office work, and housework can all be discussed, along with the schedule for tomorrow and the rest of the week. What do we want to happen becomes a question; we don't just react to the events of the day. And yes, it gives us a chance to bow our heads for a moment and give thanks for each other, for all those we love around the table and distant from us, and for a table with enough food to eat if we are fortunate enough to have that. This is obviously an opportunity for relationship around our eating and drinking, reminiscent of the important role that table fellowship played in the life of Jesus and his disciples. With school, work, sports, homework, evening meetings, and always more work to do, spending time together is not always easy, and it takes the commitment of a spiritual discipline to make eating together happen as often as possible.

To be honest, it wasn't until I became involved in starting a family (a little later in life than most people) that I began to more fully understand the meaning and importance of households. I was raised in a strong family household, and the relationships between the five brothers and sisters remain strong today, even since our mom and dad passed. But until you have your own household and find a base and foundation for your life that you never had before, it's hard to understand just how formative households are.

Becoming a father has absolutely changed my life and even my sense of vocation. Things like being a Little League baseball coach have become as important to me as writing books and columns, being a justice advocate, speaking out in the public square, or leading faith-based organizations and coalitions. I build my travel and speaking schedule around baseball practices and games, weekends, Sunday worship, and our family schedule, and my greatest excitement occurs on the baseball field right next to our house just as much as, or more than, in my arenas of activism around the world. So this chapter will be more personal than many of the others in this book.

What happens in our households is absolutely imperative. Are they places where we merely take in the culture from all our "screens" and become the couch potatoes of consumerism? Or are they places of spiritual and cultural formation, teaching household members how to actually live by the values we choose, often counter to the distorted values of popular culture and the consumer lifestyle?

Do our households nurture our values or just encourage our appetites? That is the critical question today. Our popular culture has become a big advertising machine systematically offering us the products, priorities, and personalities of the rich and famous—with all of it aimed directly at our households. But our households also hold the promise of creating an alternative culture that resists and replaces that dominant consumer formation with a much more human one. Therefore, our households are critical places for the practice of human flourishing and for teaching the next generation the meaning of the common good. Our households can become the places where life and joy are abundant, despite all the societal pressures that make our lives tense and anxious.

One day a friend sent me a little sign that read, "Don't Postpone Joy." Because Joy is my wife's name, the sign of course has a double meaning. I placed it on a bookshelf at eye level, right across from my home study desk, where I sit almost every day I am home. I find it a good vision for a household: don't postpone joy.

Coaching Baseball

My iPhone died and I didn't even care. A cooler full of water and ice had just been dumped over my head, soaking not only me but also my phone. The Nationals, the Little League team of my older son, Luke, had just won the Majors championship in Northwest Little League, and the boys were very excited and eager to douse their coach, just like they always see on TV. I was so happy for them that I really didn't care about the soaked iPhone!

I have coached both of my sons' baseball teams. Luke's team was undefeated in the AA League and had won the AAA championship two years before (in the younger kids' division, where I still coach his nine-year-old brother Jack). And now we'd won the Majors, which is the division for the oldest kids in Little League. When asked by other coaches what my secret was in sweeping all three Little League divisions, I pondered the questions thoughtfully and then gave them an honest answer: my secret is having a son who hits in most of your runs and then pitches no-run innings against the other team!

I played baseball as a kid too, until I was about sixteen, but Luke has already gone way beyond what I ever did, and he is just thirteen. He now has "real" coaches (not just his dad) on both his travel team and his middle school baseball squad. He hears the other voices he needs, voices providing great instruction, from serious young men who actually played serious baseball—some through college. Having been coached by me since he was five years old, Luke is now on track to play high school and maybe even college baseball. That's what he has always wanted, even as a little boy, so I have done my job. Luke sometimes still fantasizes about Major League Baseball, like many kids his age who play, but he is realistic enough to know that it is unlikely for even the best kids at his level. He is also now thinking about the other things he would like to do that "have a better chance of changing the world than being a professional baseball player does," as he puts it to his little brother.

But even more than just watching my talented sons play baseball, I have loved coaching them for all these years. It has been a father-son bond that will always be with us. For days after the championship game, Luke would come up to me with a big grin on his face, give me a fist bump or a high five, and quietly say, "We did it, Dad."

I still remember the day we won the AAA title game two years earlier. After the team party at our house, Luke wanted to go back to the field and do a little more pitching. I smiled and said okay. But soon it was dark, and one of us was going to get hit in the head with a ball—likely me. So I suggested we just take a slow walk around the four diamonds that compose our Friendship Field, touching home plate at each one. We discussed the game and all its parts, how well his teammates did, and what a great season we just had. It was very dark when we touched the last home plate, and we could see the lights on at our house, as if welcoming us home. As we left the field to head back to the house, my ten-year-old son looked up into my eyes and quietly said, "Thanks, I love you Dad." It was one of those moments you remember for the rest of your life as a father. And for us, baseball has provided that kind of bond.

Coaching also enabled me to get to know all my sons' teammates and the kids on other teams who are their best friends in the world.

257

When I come home and walk into our family room to a bunch of guys watching a game and say, "Hi, guys," one says back, "Hi, Dad," and the rest reply, "Hi, Coach." That has been a good experience. Our house has always been the team clubhouse, and I'm sure other parents can understand how great that is for us.

Though we have had winning teams, we have never stressed winning as the primary goal or made competition our driving energy. I've always had just three simple rules on our teams: first, have fun—which, after all, should be the whole point of Little League; second, always be good teammates (absolutely no negative talk is allowed from players, parents, or coaches when somebody makes a mistake); and third, learn to love the game of baseball and become better ballplayers. These principles seem to have produced winning teams for us. We all make mistakes, including the coach, but when we do, there is always "next time." And we all learn to love this game. The families become a little community for the season and beyond, and the friendships that are created continue far past baseball.

I know baseball well enough to teach and coach the kids, but expertise concerning skills has never been my strength as a coach. Rather, I bring the qualities from the rest of my life as a preacher and pastor to my Little League team. I try to inspire, encourage, support, and guide the kids in ways that will work not only for baseball but also for the rest of their lives. Their parents often smile and comment on my continual narrative from the sidelines. "Prepare like the ball is coming to you." "Down and ready for each pitch." "Know what you're going to do with the ball." "Stay awake!" "Know you're a hitter." "Protect the plate." "Help your teammates." And always: "You can do this." When I call out words of encouragement or instruction or gather the players around me in a team circle, their parents say that I am teaching them "the lessons of life"! At the beginning of our championship game I gave the kids a little talk (of course!) and predicted who would win the game. "Who will win?" they demanded to know. "Whoever is the most focused today; whoever doesn't let bad calls bother them but just keeps going; whoever is most supportive of their teammates even when they make mistakes; whoever digs deep inside and offers their very best today and leaves everything on the field," I replied. They won a close one, 4–2.

Of course, I feel a sense of joy and even pride when Luke hits another towering home run, or gets the biggest hit in the All Star game, or pitches lights-out and shuts down the other team's batting, or makes a great pick at first base, or throws out a runner stealing second while catching at home. And I try not to act too excited as the dad/coach. But honestly, the deeper delight often comes from the kid whose nervous face is replaced with a big smile when he finally learns to connect with the ball; or from the one who, after making lots of errors all season, ends up making the game-winning play in the field and gets the game ball; or from the parents who tell you long after the season is over that whenever their child is facing tough challenges in school and life, he is encouraged when they remind him to "believe in yourself, just like Coach Jim believed in you." Most coaches will tell you that helping the kids who struggle with the game is often the most satisfying accomplishment.

Now that Luke has aged out of Little League, I'm done coaching his teams. From now on, as I watch his baseball career unfold, I will just be a dad and fan. In his last summer Luke was on the Northwest Little League twelve-year-old World Series team that won the DC championship and went on to represent the nation's capital in the regional World Series Tournament in Bristol, Connecticut. The whole family went for the week, which was the experience of a lifetime for the kids and the families. After all those years of playing together, it was such a treat to enjoy the deep sense of community that had been created among all the parents and siblings of our all-star players. And Luke finally got to play in the Little League World Series Tournament, which we have watched on television as a family every August. It was a great conclusion to a Little League career, and the kids had the greatest time, even if they didn't get to the championship in Williamsport. They all remembered the rules: have fun, be good teammates, love and learn the game of baseball. As far as teaching kids the lessons of the common good, I don't think I've ever had a better chance to do that than in coaching baseball.

My younger son, Jack, has made the nine-year-old traveling team, and my coaching now focuses just on him. We are both very excited.

He's leaner and faster than Luke and will likely be a sure-gloved middle-fielder who is also becoming a good hitter. Now the boys go to the batting cages together, where Luke helps Jack work on his swing. We "drafted" a team full of all his friends from his elementary school and former baseball teams. Jack's big lesson this spring was to deal with the disappointment of breaking his wrist the day before our semifinal play-off game. Ouch! But he was there at the game, with a cast signed by all his teammates, cheering on his pals from the dugout. "You can do it! We can do it!" That's what the kids learn by playing baseball. Recently, when our whole family was speaking together at a Christian conference on youth and family, Jack was given the microphone and began his remarks with "On the eighth day, God created baseball."

Summer is filled with the tournaments now, for both boys' teams. Joy and I drive back and forth between fields, making good on the sign she puts out in front of our home when the spring begins: "We Interrupt This Family for Baseball Season." Coaching has been an anchor for me, a deep connection to my sons, and a critical balance to the rest of my life. Baseball is likely the most practical thing we do as a family to build a sense of real community in our neighborhood and city. And we've also helped to spread baseball around the city to neighborhoods it hadn't been in before.

And guess what? The iPhone dried out and is working just fine!

Father's Day

For our family, Father's Day and Mother's Day are two of the biggest days of the year. We've learned that sometimes the most important things are not at the top of the news cycle and will not necessarily make the most headlines in the world. But we're sure that raising our two boys and working hard to be a good mom and dad will end up near the top of our importance list.

Washington infighting; tea parties, occupiers, and poll numbers; oil gushing and congressional gushing; pompous generals and failing wars:

all will capture the week's headlines, but that doesn't make them the most important things.

After a great Father's Day Sunday, Luke and I got up early one Monday morning in 2010 to attend President Obama's fatherhood speech at a Boys and Girls Club in southeast Washington, DC. It was an honor to be invited and a great opportunity to hear the president—who also loves being a dad—talk about how important he thinks fatherhood is for the country. We expected merely to be part of the audience and were surprised to be asked to sit in the front row of the stage, right behind the president, as he delivered his remarks. (You could tell that we didn't expect our placement; the television coverage showed both of us right behind President Obama, with Luke wearing his shorts and T-shirt!) But sitting where we were, we really had to pay attention!

Listening carefully, I found myself quite moved by the president's words about being a father. I have steered away from naming current politicians in this book, and I hope the points made will outlast our contemporary officeholders. But this event and its theme could and should be a bipartisan one, with key principles and commitments expressed that are essential to the common good. Even those who strongly oppose other parts of Obama's agenda generally applaud his clear commitment to fatherhood, as well they should.

"Fatherhood" was also the name of one of the key task forces of the president's first Advisory Council on Faith-Based and Neighborhood Partnerships, which I was privileged to be a part of. President Obama started his speech by posing a simple question: "How can we as a nation—not just the government, but businesses and community groups and concerned citizens—how can we all come together to help fathers meet their responsibilities to our families and communities?"[1]

He then spoke honestly about all the problems in children's lives caused by the absence of fathers, and spoke personally about his own absent father and how he still felt "the weight of that absence." While affirming the love of a wonderful mother and loving grandparents who

1. "Promoting Responsible Fatherhood" (remarks by President Obama at a Father's Day event, Washington, DC, June 21, 2010), http://www.whitehouse.gov/photos-and-video/video/promoting-responsible-fatherhood#transcript.

raised him, the president said not having a father who is present is "something that leaves a hole in a child's life that no government can fill." Barack Obama's own life experience is a big part of why fatherhood is so important to him and why his two daughters are so central in his life.

In a way that both conservatives and liberals could find inspiring, Obama spoke about the limits of government in such a personal and foundational area of life: "We can talk all we want here in Washington about issues . . . but government can't keep our kids from looking for trouble on those streets. Government can't force a kid to pick up a book or make sure that the homework gets done. Government can't be there day in, day out, to provide discipline and guidance and the love that it takes to raise a child. That's our job as fathers, as mothers, as guardians for our children."[2]

Government, whether you are for or against it in other critical areas of public life, is clearly limited in what it can accomplish in households. Public policy should be as family- and household-friendly as it possibly can, avoiding things that undermine family life and promoting things that nurture the strength of households. And, as President Obama has done, political leaders should use their public rhetoric, their "bully pulpits," to uphold and encourage the absolute importance of parenting—being good fathers and mothers to our children. Because what happens inside our households may have as much, or more, influence on the common good as whatever happens on the outside. I didn't understand that until I was a parent, a father, with a household to nurture. But I think most parents, regardless of their political views about what happens outside of their family life, realize how important life inside their households is, not only to the future of their children but also to the future of the country—in other words, to the common good.

As he often does, Obama spoke about the difference between having a kid and being a father: "The fact is, it's easy to become a father; technically, any guy can do that. It's hard to live up to the lifelong responsibilities that come with fatherhood. And it's a challenge even in good

2. Ibid.

times, when our families are doing well. It's especially difficult when times are tough; families are straining just to keep everything together." From our vantage point on the stage, Luke and I could see the faces of the dads and moms and kids who filled the auditorium. Their nodding heads, knowing smiles, and hearty applause indicated that they knew exactly what the president was talking about. Then Obama zeroed in on the heart of his message for Father's Day:

> Here's the key message I think all of us want to send today to fathers all across the country: Our children don't need us to be superheroes. They don't need us to be perfect. They do need us to be present. They need us to show up and give it our best shot, no matter what else is going on in our lives. They need us to show them—not just with words, but with deeds—that they, those kids, are always our first priority. Those family meals, afternoons in the park, bedtime stories; the encouragement we give, the questions we answer, the limits we set, the example we set of persistence in the face of difficulty and hardship—those things add up over time, and they shape a child's character, build their core, teach them to trust in life and to enter into it with confidence and with hope and with determination.[3]

That our children should be "always our first priority" is a very powerful thing to say, and a very difficult thing to fulfill. Think about what that means for the president of the most powerful nation in the world, or for you, with whatever your responsibilities are outside your household—and they also are very important. It literally means putting our children first in our lives. For me it means my two boys are always my most important "audience," among all the other audiences I may have. I need to reach them, at their deepest levels, with the values that are most important to Joy and me, and that matters more to me than the number of other people I can reach. It means their needs and their schedules have to come first in my schedule, and all of us who have such busy schedules know how much of a challenge that really is.

In our politically polarized environment, it was a refreshing word from a president that should cut across all of our political boundaries. As

3. Ibid.

Obama put it, "Too often when we talk about fatherhood and personal responsibility, we talk about it in political terms, in terms of left and right, conservative/liberal, instead of what's right and what's wrong. And when we do that, we've gotten off track. So I think it's time for a new conversation around fatherhood in this country."

Then the president said something that I know he truly believes and that made me feel very grateful that he does: "The work of raising our children is the most important job in this country, and it's all of our responsibilities—mothers and fathers." The crowd gathered in that recreation center in a tough Washington neighborhood burst into applause, and it was all I could do to not jump to my feet behind him. He went on:

> Now, I can't legislate fatherhood—I can't force anybody to love a child. But what we can do is send a clear message to our fathers that there is no excuse for failing to meet their obligations. What we can do is make it easier for fathers who make responsible choices and harder for those who avoid those choices. What we can do is come together and support fathers who are willing to step up and be good partners and parents and providers. . . . But ultimately, we know that the decision to be a good father—that's up to us, each of us, as individuals. It's one that men across this country are making every single day—attending those school assemblies; parent-teacher conferences; coaching soccer, Little League; scrimping and saving, and working that extra shift so that their children can go to college.[4]

It is both rare and significant when a political leader gets personal in an authentic way. To admit mistakes and failures—of our country and of ourselves—is not something politicians normally do. But when the president spoke of his own struggles and joys as a parent, every dad who heard him could easily identify. "Even when we give it our best efforts, there will still be plenty of days of struggle and heartache when we don't quite measure up—talking to the men here now. Even with all the good fortune and support Michelle and I have had in our lives, I've made plenty of mistakes as a parent. I've lost count of all

4. Ibid.

the times when the demands of work have taken me from the duties of fatherhood. And I know I've missed out on moments in my daughters' lives that I'll never get back, and that's a loss that's hard to accept. But I also know the feeling that one author described when she wrote that 'to have a child . . . is to decide forever to have your heart go walking around outside your body.'"[5]

I felt myself tear up at that one, and I don't think I have ever heard a better description of what is feels like to be a parent: to have a child is to have your heart walking around outside your body.

Obama's 2008 Philadelphia speech about race will be remembered as one of the most important on that subject in many years. Many remember his soaring rhetoric of change in speeches during the campaign, and the promise of hope in the address he gave the night he was elected. But as I sat there, just a few feet from the presidential rostrum, the words that came next seemed to me to be among the most important he will ever speak: "Over the course of my life, I have been an attorney, I've been a professor, I've been a state senator, I've been a U.S. senator, and I currently am serving as president of the United States. But I can say without hesitation that the most challenging, most fulfilling, most important job I will have during my time on this Earth is to be Sasha and Malia's dad."[6]

I believe he means that. And I believe it in part because that is exactly the way I feel about being Luke and Jack's dad. Of all the things I have ever done, or will ever do, this is the job that now feels like the most important one to me. It's also the greatest privilege and blessing I've ever had.

When he finished, President Obama turned and came to greet the people in the front row on the stage. When he got to us, he shook my son's hand and said, "Hey Luke, it's great to see you. What grade are you in now?"

"I'm in the sixth grade," Luke replied as he looked into the eyes of the president of the United States. "That was awesome, Dad," he whispered as the president walked away. "I'm never going to wash this

5. Ibid.
6. Ibid.

265

hand." I reminded him, "Remember, that's your pitching hand, Luke." It was a good day, a great speech, and a presidential commitment that could make more difference in this country than most of the other things the nation talked about for the rest of that day and for the rest of that week.

Marriage, Commitment, and Fidelity

Marriage is in deep trouble in our society, and that is a fundamental threat to the common good. By all the data, marriage is one of the most important factors in combating poverty, juvenile delinquency, crime, drugs, low educational performance, and even bad health. And marriage is in decline among the poorest people in our society, making them even more vulnerable. A 2003 briefing from the Center for Law and Social Policy reported that "children living with single mothers are five times as likely to be poor as those in two-parent families."[7] With more than one-quarter of American children living in one-parent families, these trends are affecting more and more families.[8] We introduced this topic in chapter 8.

Across the economic classes, divorce rates have soared, women and children are being abused in alarming numbers, single-parent families have increased, and "blended" families are now becoming normative in many places.

Stable marriages are at the core of healthy households, and they are critically important for good parenting. Though I have known many single parents who do heroic things for their kids, most of them will be the first to say how hard it is to do all the parenting alone. All of us parents who at times have had the experience of doing all the parenting jobs on our own while our partner was away will also testify to that. "How do single parents do it?" is the question often asked when

7. Mary Parke, *Are Married Parents Really Better for Children? What Research Says about the Effects of Family Structure on Child Well-Being*, Couples and Marriage Research and Policy 3 (Washington, DC: Center for Law and Social Policy, 2003).

8. United States Census Bureau, *Custodial Mothers and Fathers and Their Child Support: 2007* (Washington, DC: United States Census Bureau, November 2009), http://www.census .gov/prod/2009pubs/p60-237.pdf.

a partner comes home. Here is a principle for the common good: without a critical mass of healthy and functional marriages, a society steers into real trouble.

Therefore, an unequivocal social commitment to restore the strength—and people of faith might say the sanctity—of marriage is one of the most important that we can make, if we really do care about the common good. The restoration of a social ethic that drives us toward healthy marriages is essential for good parenting, which is a key for societal well-being. In addition to the value of good parenting, the marriage ethic also nurtures something else that is important for both personal and social well-being: the ethics of commitment and fidelity.

Being faithful in sexual relationships is a value almost continually undermined by a culture of narcissism and consumerism that makes even sexuality a commodity for our consuming pleasure. The commodification of sexuality, and of women in particular, is now a central theme of our entire advertising culture. Many parents feel that the daily assaults of that consumer culture, which teach utter materialism and irresponsible sexual adventurism, are *directed right at our children*. Teaching children the virtues of commitment, integrity, responsibility, and fidelity in their economic and sexual lives has to be a central part of parenting in the consumer culture. And, as we all know, how we *act* as adults and parents will ultimately have more impact on our children than all of the things we *say*.

The belief that sexuality is meant to be *covenantal* instead of *recreational* may be one of the most countercultural convictions in our modern society. But that is both what our Scriptures teach us and what the common sense of a society has always discovered. For many of us that means within the context of marriage. But there is little doubt now that the recreational sexual ethic and the promiscuous sexuality it promotes have become a normative ethic in modern society. Even in the faith community, the ethics of marriage are in great need of repair, with divorce rates that nearly match those of the surrounding society and with sexual irresponsibility embarrassingly common, even among some of our religious leaders.

267

This should not be just a religious or sectarian issue in a secular society. New social research is demonstrating the problems caused by having many sexual partners, having to do with reasons of public health but also with emotional and psychological well-being. Too much intimacy with too many people turns out to be a fragmenting experience for human beings, contributing to our growing sense of insecurity, disintegration, and even isolation.

Covenantal relationships, on the other hand, can help create deeper feelings of wholeness and security and integrate the physical, emotional, and spiritual dimensions of our lives. Many young people, religious or not, are beginning to experience that and are starting to resist the constant social pressure of their consumer society to be sexually active all the time. Many now speak of their need for sexual *healing*, as many of us feel sexually broken by the consuming sexual ethic of our society; and people are finding a new sense of wholeness in covenantal sexual relationships.

How would a new sense of covenantal marriage relate to same-sex couples? Many of us, including a new generation of young Christians, believe that equal protection under the law is an important civil right and must include all people, regardless of their sexual orientation. Most straight young people today have close friends who are gay, most churches have gay members (whether acknowledged or not), and those friends and brothers and sisters in Christ have convinced most of us that being gay is less a choice than an orientation, no matter how or why it happens. Whether equality under the law requires new laws to protect gay people or gay civil unions or gay civil marriage will be worked out democratically in this country, state by state, and around the world, and a new generation's more tolerant attitudes and commitments on gay civil rights will likely determine the future.

In the meantime, our government must seriously commit itself to a religious liberty that fully protects the right of each faith community to work these issues out in light of their own scriptural interpretations and traditions. Faith congregations and communities will continue to wrestle with the theological and biblical questions about sacramental marriage, including the question of how that concept relates to same-sex marriage: Is marriage only between a man and a woman? Or can it include the committed same-sex relationships that most of the biblical passages mentioning homosexuality are not really about and that their authors couldn't have imagined? That is, can the concept of civil or even sacramental marriage be applied to a set of covenantal relationships that includes gay couples? That question is likely to occupy us for a long time, and the biblical and pastoral work needed to answer it is likely to go on for some time. It is critical, in my view, for people on all sides of this debate to respect one another, even in their differences. It is unfortunate that this issue has become so divisive and has taken up so much time in national church meetings and conventions. I do not believe that different views on gay issues and even gay marriage are the most important social question of our time or should be a breaking point for Christian unity in the churches; rather, we should be able to live with and tolerate those differences, as a new generation helps find a way forward with theological, biblical, and relational integrity.

Of course, the issue of gay marriage has become very controversial in any discussion about marriage. While important on their own grounds, the controversies surrounding gay marriage may be preempting—on both the right and the left—the broader issues concerning the weakening of marriage in our society. Marriage is more than a human rights issue; it is, most deeply, a covenantal commitment. And reconnecting sex to covenant is the most important contribution that people of faith need to make for the sake of marriage and the common good. That is what must be restored. The integrity of covenantal marriage should be a commitment prior to the human rights debates over gay marriage. That should be our first priority and central to the way we understand marriage for all couples.

Another important issue in regard to marriage is the commitment that marriage be a good, life-giving, and liberating commitment for *women* as well as men. We still have a very long way to go in making the mutual commitments between men and women that healthy and fulfilling marriages require. If marriage is not good for women, it will not be good for the common good either. And that means we have to be much more demanding of good behavior on the part of men.

Men Behaving Badly

It's a constant story line involving powerful men in politics, sports, business, and even religion: they behave with utter disregard for the dignity and humanity of women, using and abusing them at will, and somehow believe that they are entitled to do so. These men seem to think that the ordinary rules of decent behavior do not apply to them. We have a never-ending cavalcade of disgusting stories about men cheating on their spouses and the mothers of their children, abandoning old wives for new ones, practicing serial philandering as a way of life, sexually harassing and assaulting women, and even committing rape. But when all is said and done, the perpetrators are still playing basketball, football, and golf, still running for political office, and still steering the institutions of the economy, and even the church.

I don't have to mention names, because we all know who we are talking about and, sadly, space prevents us from even listing them all. But as the secret stories are revealed, there is great interest and perverse excitement in the media. The pain and suffering of the women involved, and the invisible hurt of the children, are brushed aside. The women are even subtly and sometimes directly blamed. And sometimes, in all-male circles, there is a wink and a nod, and, most disgustingly, even a little envy of the powerful men who get to break all the rules when it comes to women. The primary outcry is usually and mostly from other women who, in the name of equality and dignity, lament this continual pattern of abuse.

What has been missing from this too-often repeated narrative is the condemnation of these behaviors and attitudes from other *men*, especially men who are in positions of power, authority, and influence. While the primary blame lies with the perpetrators, we should look next at the good men who say nothing. It's time for good men to hold accountable the bad men who abuse women. Those who abuse, cheat, assault, and rape are not real men. They distort and destroy any sense of healthy manhood. It's time to tell our sons that they must never act like these abusers and perpetrators and to make sure to raise our own sons to love, respect, and be faithful to women.

The best use I know of for men who treat women this way is to use them as anti–role models for my two sons. They exemplify what I hope my boys will never become. So here is my little contribution to condemning men who need to be condemned for not behaving. When TV shows with these most abusive and unrepentant men come on, we will change the channel. When movies come out with them on the big screen, we will stay home. When sports games are played with them as stars, we won't be cheering for them. When another media story erupts because of more bad behavior, my boys will be told that men who abuse women are not good men. They might still have money and power, but their abuse of women diminishes their humanity.

Women are already speaking out, and it's time for other men to also say that this bad behavior is not acceptable. Other men must condemn these men, not only as immoral and sometimes criminal but also as the worst examples of what and who we are supposed to be. These men have given their humanity over to their most selfish impulses. And I hope all of these recent revelations are lessons to politicians everywhere: your sin will find you out. We need to establish a firm principle: the abuse of women by men will no longer be tolerated by other men. The voices of more men need to join the chorus to make that perfectly clear. Again, these are not prudish or sectarian religious commitments but rather necessary ethics for the common good.

Food

Why are household values so essential to the common good? Precisely because the formation of values that support and nurture our social well-being can directly and successfully counter the promotion of appetites that are harmful to it. That is certainly true in the parental teaching of commitments and values, the strengthening of marriage, the modeling of faithfulness and fidelity, respect for women by men, and the countering of destructive materialism. But it could also lead to other kinds of social change that are indispensable for a better future.

One area crucial to the common good is good health. I have learned in many ways how important food is to health. And I myself have changed in this area, as I took a time of sabbatical to write this book. I began to study and learn about food, the culture of food, lifestyles of food, the stress and addictions of food, the politics of food, and the spirituality of food—in short, how our eating is instrumental to our health and to the quality of our lives.

America now has what could be called an epidemic of obesity. Yes, an epidemic. Between 1960 and 1980, the obesity rate in America comprised 15 percent of the population. Today, 36 percent of Americans, more than twice as many as just a few decades ago, are obese. If present eating patterns continue, almost *half* of all Americans will be obese by the year 2030. We've now learned that obesity—being too overweight—is responsible for some of our most serious health problems, including many that lead directly to death: strokes and heart problems, diabetes, cancer, high blood pressure, sleep disorders, and even mental health problems and diseases like dementia and Alzheimer's. Obesity shortens the length of life and is becoming one of our leading causes of death. It is growing most among lower-income people, who often have less access to healthy foods, safe exercise, and knowledge of healthy alternatives.

But for many of us on the go, the time needed for healthy shopping, cooking, and eating is more easily spent on a faster lifestyle with faster foods that are far less healthy. And stress, I have now learned, can also cause us to overeat as both a compensation and comfort. In the context of a more relaxed and restful sabbatical, I began to examine my own pace of life, the stresses I live with, and the patterns of eating I had fallen into. Busyness is falsely regarded in our society as a sign of importance, when instead it can be a cause of ill health.

I learned that politics are also involved in eating, as they are in most things. The American epidemic of obesity can be traced directly to the decision of major American food companies to put much more processed food on our grocery shelves, which will last longer and make them more money. Almost all those processed foods are unhealthy. And since our largest food companies turn out to be owned now by the largest cigarette companies, these manufacturers have great experience in making money from products that create addictions and poison people. Government standards for a balanced diet fell in line with the priorities of the food companies, as often happens when government regulators and large corporations collaborate.

So I have completely changed the way that I eat: from processed foods—all the "whites" of sugar, flour, and rice; all the fried and greasy stuff that our brains have been taught tastes good—to a healthy diet of whole foods and grains, vegetables, fruits, fish, and very lean meat, if any. So far, thirty-five pounds have dropped off, and I feel better than I have in years. It isn't a diet but rather a change in eating habits that goes back to how human beings are supposed to eat, and a way of eating that reorients our enzymes and brain back to the ways they worked before we all became so "processed" and addicted to bad food. Along with daily exercise, good eating becomes a way of life and not a new, fancy, exotic, or expensive routine. Most important, preparing and eating good food is a household habit, good for people of any age. It means shopping around the edges of supermarkets, where all the fresh food is, and avoiding the middle of the store with all the processed stuff.

Honestly, when I used to think about addiction I most often thought of other people and alcohol and drugs. But I've learned that food addictions are more and more common today for many of us. Our lifestyles, our schedules, our pressures and stress, and our overwork create an unhealthy situation to start with, and the food companies and fast-food industry have taken advantage with addictive products that are very profitable to them and very damaging to us. Since losing weight and changing my eating habits and routines, I now feel much freer from food than I did before—from thinking about it, worrying about it, or being attracted to it. Now I can really enjoy a good meal, in good time, with good family or friends, around the table fellowship we spoke of at the beginning of this chapter. Exercise—walking, running, other cardio workouts, weight lifting, playing baseball and other sports, and wrestling with my boys—is all much easier now and so much fun. Changing my eating way of life is a personal good for me. And changing *our* eating way of life could become a great common good for all of us. The personal and social transformation of our politics of food is going to become a very big issue for our future.

I have fasted on only water and juice for long periods of time, during Lent in particular, to bring attention to issues such as the way the poor were being treated in our deficit debates or our unnecessary wars. But frankly, the disciplines of good eating are more transformational over the long term than even fasting has been for me, and far better for my health! And good disciplines and habits are at the core of healthy household living.

I am more and more convinced that a fresh understanding of what good household values are can actually begin to heal our materialism, social addictions, stress, ill health, and even our empty overwork. What's good for our families is good for our communities, and what's good for our communities is good for our society. Let's look out for one another as we look out for ourselves. And let us all rewire the way we live in our households, which will enable our human flourishing and help restore the common good.

···14···

The World Is Our Parish

I look upon all the world as my parish.

—John Wesley[1]

One of the sayings in our country is *Ubuntu*—the essence of being human. *Ubuntu* speaks particularly about the fact that you can't exist as a human being in isolation. It speaks about our interconnectedness. You can't be human all by yourself, and when you have this quality—*Ubuntu*—you are known for your generosity. We think of ourselves far too frequently as just individuals, separated from one another, whereas you are connected and what you do affects the whole world. When you do well, it spreads out; it is for the whole of humanity.

—Desmond Tutu[2]

1. John Wesley, *The Journal of John Wesley* (Grand Rapids: Christian Classics Ethereal Library, 1951), 42, http://www.jesus.org.uk/vault/library/wesley_journal.pdf.

2. "Desmond Tutu Explains Ubuntu," in Ik Ben Omdat Wij Zijn, http://www.ikbenom datwijzijn.info/index.php?option=com_content&view=article&id=114:desmond-tutu-ex plains-ubuntu&catid=44:english&Itemid=92.

To speak, live, and act for the common good is ultimately a very personal decision. We *can* just live for ourselves, and most of the daily pressures of our culture and of the market relentlessly push us to do that. But, as we have seen in the wisdom of teachers from Jesus to the most inspiring people in today's world, to live just for ourselves is simply not the best way to be *human*. Our very humanity depends on our relationships with one another, with our neighbors. That is the foundation of the common good, and many of the people who have contributed the most to the common good throughout history have come to understand that. Albert Einstein said, "Only a life lived for others is a life worthwhile."[3] Ultimately, that's what we want to teach our children too, or, as my thirteen-year-old son Luke said recently, "The real measure of success is what we do for other people, right?" Right.

Let's make this last chapter personal too. After reading this book, ask yourself not just how you might think differently, but how you might *act* and *live* differently.

Occupy the Gospel

> Seek the welfare of the city where I have sent you into exile . . . for in its welfare you will find your welfare. (Jer. 29:7)

John Wesley, an Anglican priest and English revival preacher who founded Methodism about three hundred years ago, regarded the whole world as his parish and every place in it as a place to proclaim the "glad tidings" of the gospel. What he meant by salvation was "not barely, according to the vulgar notion, deliverance from hell, or going to heaven; but a *present deliverance* from sin, a restoration of the soul . . . the renewal of our souls after the image of God, in righteousness and true holiness, in justice, mercy, and truth."[4] Wesley taught his legions of converts three centuries ago what this meant:

3. "Life," *Albert Einstein Quotes*, http://www.einstein-quotes.com/Life.html.
4. John Wesley, "A Farther Appeal to Men of Reason and Religion," in *The Works of John Wesley*, vol. 8, *Addresses, Essays, Letters*, version 1.0, Books for the Ages (Albany, OR: AGES Software, 1997), 50, http://media.sabda.org/alkitab-11/V6F-Z/WES_WW08 .PDF (emphasis added).

Do all the good you can,
By all the means you can,
In all the ways you can,
In all the places you can,
At all the times you can,
To all the people you can,
As long as ever you can.[5]

Wesley had a very strong notion of what we are calling *the common good*. And his gospel preaching helped to inspire it. It even inspired a young parliamentarian named William Wilberforce to lead the abolitionist movement that eventually ended the slave trade and slavery in England. The revival Wesley and others led helped to change the conversation in England about what was right and what responsibilities people had to one another.

Three centuries later, it is still the right conversation. That's what many of today's young people have in mind: to find the common good again and to spark a big enough movement to end some obvious injustices.

I was witnessing a drama worthy of a London theater stage. Near the steps of the historic St. Paul's Cathedral, under its magnificent dome framed by twin spires, a ragtag group of tents was pitched. A village of young people had emerged and was engaging its community and the whole world through "Occupy London," one of thousands of sites springing up from a movement that began in New York City as "Occupy Wall Street." Although this movement was criticized for its unclear messaging, its central cry was heard by anyone with the ears to hear: "The world has gone wrong." The structures of the economy are unfair, unjust, unsustainable, and making many people unhappy, just as we discussed in chapter 10. Many people around the world feel those very same things, but a global youth insurgency was now expressing it, making the issues visible and creating a global conversation.

A new generation was saying that the very few (1 percent) had forgotten the great many (99 percent) and had rigged the system to mostly

---

5. "John Wesley quotes," ThinkExist, http://thinkexist.com/quotation/do_all_the _good_you_can-by_all_the_means_you_can/148152.html.

benefit themselves. In this global production, the young were playing what is always their best role—giving voice to the script about society that others may indeed have been privately reading but had not yet been able to move from monologue into dialogue. The young people struck a nerve and sparked a worldwide discussion. The rest of us have jobs and kids and responsibilities. Most can't easily sleep in tents on concrete for long. But the young occupiers did, and in doing so they were creating new space for the honest talk we all need to have.

I was listening to the conversation about worldwide economic inequality just a few meters from one of the world's most historic cathedrals, which was also the site of one of the most famous weddings ever, between Princess Diana and Prince Charles in 1981. As I stood there on the steps of St. Paul's, observing the scene and entering into discussion with the young occupiers, I could hardly believe this compelling picture of protest. What was at that moment the most prominent public forum in the world had now come to the steps of St. Paul's. The world had come to church, in a country where fewer and fewer people do.

You would think that the church might be erupting in thanksgiving for this opportunity, to work and witness in this *parish of the world* that was now at its doorstep. You might have thought to hear their liturgical praise of "Thanks be to God" for this amazing blessing—the chance for mission, hospitality, pastoral care, even evangelism, and certainly prophetic witness. Instead, the powers that be, of both church and state, were working together to try and evict the young protesters who were hoping for a better world. Some younger cathedral canons resigned when St. Paul's began planning the eviction. Now they and some other priests were walking among the occupiers on-site, as they imagined Jesus was already doing.

It was the very beginning of Advent, when Christians await the coming of Christ in the weeks before Christmas. This is the season when the Christian world celebrates the coming of God to earth, in the absolutely ironic scene of a vulnerable baby born in an animal stall. This is what Christians mean by the theological term "incarnation." I describe it this way: in Jesus Christ, God hits the streets. But even though the streets of the world had come to the church in the form of the young Occupy movement, the authorities at the cathedral missed this incarnational moment at Advent—as our churches often do.

I don't know where the Occupy movement will lead, or where it will be when this book comes out. But that London scene was clearly an example of what's happening in our parish of the world today, especially among a new generation. How we relate to the issues raised by a movement like Occupy will show whether our faith is meant to be for this world, in the here and now, or just for the hereafter.

When Occupy Wall Street broke out in New York City, I traveled up to see what was going on in Zuccotti Park. The first young leader I spoke to (they would, of course, call themselves "nonleaders") was involved in the first meetings that planned the initial protests. He told me they expected this to last only, at best, for about three days, and they were as surprised as everyone else when a movement exploded and then rose up around the world.

When I asked him *why* he was doing this, I didn't hear diatribes about the financial markets, policy pronouncements to fix the system, or anarchic or socialist dreams about the future. Instead, my new young friend said, "I have decided that I want to have children; I hope to be a dad. I thought the world was in a pretty bad place right now, so we wanted to change some things—and perhaps make our world a better place to have our children." Ours was a conversation about the common good and one that stressed how family values have been lost in an economy that created so much uncertainty and instability.

I spoke to a young woman who was an economics major but who decided to take her fall semester off to live and study with Occupy Wall Street "to do some real work on alternative investment, business, and commerce," as she told me. When I started to describe the idea of Jubilee in the Scriptures, she exclaimed, "Wow, you mean there is such a thing as biblical economics?"

A young African American man seemed especially interested in the role of the faith community in all these issues—though he was not himself religious. So I asked him how he thought the churches and congregations in New York City and elsewhere should respond to Occupy. "I would suggest three things," he said. First, he thought they could be "counselors, because there are a lot of broken lives around here." Second, he said the movement needed the religious community's "moral authority." Third, he said they just needed our "presence." All his ideas seemed like a pretty good *parish strategy* to me.

I've Been There

Let's go back to John Wesley's expansive vision of the parish. The word "parish" simply means "district." With the Anglican and Catholic churches, in particular, a local church is responsible for a very specific geographical area. St. Catherine's, for example, would be responsible for the fifty square blocks around the church building—and for all the people who lived there, whether they were Christians or not. The parish is one of the simplest yet most powerful ideas for the church's mission in the world. It forces the church to both get outside of itself and also come back down to earth.

I've seen black churches in Boston, after a young man was shot on their church steps late on a Saturday night, or after having a gang cross-fire on their block, be driven to prayerfully decide if they were *responsible* for their neighborhood and their city twenty-four hours a day—whether they were at church or not. Their "yes" decisions helped reduce youth homicide in the city by 70 percent. I saw pastors from churches across the theological spectrum at our weeklong "justice revival" in Columbus, Ohio, come up to the stage with tears in their eyes, join hands together, and declare that the capital city of Ohio *was now their parish*. I've been to a church outside Kansas City, Missouri, that completely rehabilitates public school buildings each summer, then turns the keys of a transformed facility back over to the city in September (and doesn't then ask to run the sex education program!). I've seen a Catholic order supply the seeds for the urban gardening movement that is transforming my hometown of Detroit.

I was on retreat with a small group of US Christians when we were called by Nicaraguan church leaders who asked us to try and stop the threatened US invasion of their country in the 1980s. And I saw how our pledge of resistance, which vowed civil disobedience in the event of such an invasion, spread to eighty thousand people and helped change the minds of Washington decision makers. I've watched a Polish archbishop rally his people to stand up to the Soviet regime in their country and help spark a movement that made communism fall. I was there when South African archbishop Desmond Tutu stood in his pulpit at St. George's Cathedral in Cape Town and simply smiled at the South African Security Police who were literally surrounding his congregation. He told them they were going to lose, and he invited them "to come and join the winning side!" Ten years later, at Nelson Mandela's inauguration, I told Desmond that he had taught me my theology of hope. *I've been there*, as they say, and have seen when churches have decided to treat their neighborhoods, their cities, their countries, and their world as their parish—and how it has changed the lives of people and the history of nations.

Speaking Loudly about God

When Christians do what Jesus has told us to do, when we act on behalf of others, when we really do love our neighbor as ourselves, when we treat the world around us as the parish that we are responsible for, it speaks loudly about God. In the words of the National Association of Evangelicals:

> Jesus calls us as his followers to love our neighbors as ourselves. Our goal in civic engagement is to bless our neighbors by making good laws. Because we have been called to do justice to our neighbors, we foster a free press, participate in open debate, vote, and hold public office. *When Christians do justice, it speaks loudly about God. And it can show those who are not believers how the Christian vision can contribute to the common good and help alleviate the ills of society.*[6]

Of all the religious teachings about the common good, the best and most insightful come from the Catholic Church. Although I am an evangelical Christian, the truth is that I have become a convert to

---

6. National Association of Evangelicals, *For the Health of the Nation: An Evangelical Call to Civic Responsibility*, 3, http://www.nae.net/images/content/For_The_Health_Of _The_Nation.pdf (emphasis added).

Catholic social teaching. Here is what it says about the common good: "Common good is the whole network of social conditions which enable human individuals and groups to flourish and live a fully, genuinely human life, otherwise described as 'integral human development.' All are responsible for all, collectively, at the level of society or nation, not only as individuals."[7]

The Catholic Church could hardly be described as an institution of the "religious left," and its teachings on a variety of subjects cross the traditional boundaries of the political left and right. But Catholic teaching makes absolutely clear what the responsibilities of public officials are, no matter where they stand on the political spectrum:

> Public authorities have the common good as their prime responsibility. The common good stands in opposition to the good of rulers or of a ruling (or any other) class. It implies that every individual, no matter how high or low, has a duty to share in promoting the welfare of the community as well as a right to benefit from that welfare. "Common" implies "all-inclusive": the common good cannot exclude or exempt any section of the population. If any section of the population is in fact excluded from participation in the life of the community, even at a minimal level, then that is a contradiction to the concept of the common good and calls for rectification.[8]

When it comes to all the controversies regarding the role of government, Catholic social teaching helps us to sort out the ways in which solutions are meant to be found. Push things to the most local levels possible but make sure that public policies have the scale to actually solve problems. That creates a dynamic relationship between top and bottom, between federal, state, and local; it fosters a creative partnership between the public sector and the civil society, including families and congregations, and even national and international bodies: "The principle behind the relationships between the different layers of this 'community of communities' should be that of subsidiarity.

7. Catholic Bishops' Conference of England and Wales, *The Common Good and the Catholic Church's Social Teaching*, http://www.osjspm.org/admin/document.doc?id=99.
8. Ibid.

In a centralized society, subsidiarity will mainly mean passing powers downward; but it can also mean passing appropriate powers upward, even to an international body, if that would better serve the common good and protect the rights of families and of individuals."[9]

The solutions to our common problems outlined in this book all fall within this framework and are most aligned with church teachings—certainly more than with the ideologies of the political left or right. Again, when it comes to the role of government, the NAE says:

> Evangelicals believe that government is a gift from God for the common good. Good governance creates the conditions in which human beings fulfill their responsibilities as God's image bearers and as stewards of God's creation. Government plays an important role in protecting life, preserving freedom, and creating an environment in which families, churches, businesses and other human institutions can thrive.[10]

When it comes to how we are to live together in our culture and society, I especially like the African idea of *ubuntu*. Leymah Gbowee, a Liberian peace activist, summarizes it well in his translation: "I am what I am because of who we all are."[11] As quoted at the outset of this chapter, Archbishop Desmond Tutu clarifies the meaning of the common good when he says, "You can't exist as a human being in isolation. . . . You can't be human all by yourself." He offered a definition of *ubuntu* in a 1999 book: "A person with *ubuntu* is open and available to others, affirming of others, does not feel threatened that others are able and good, for he or she has a proper self-assurance that comes from knowing that he or she belongs in a greater whole and is diminished when others are humiliated or diminished, when others are tortured or oppressed."[12]

The vision from these ringing statements, from church social teaching and the African ideal of *ubuntu*, is very compelling to a new generation. And it is that generation that will help us reclaim the common good. In

9. Ibid.
10. National Association of Evangelicals, "Government Relations: Bringing Biblical Values to the Political Sphere," http://www.nae.net/government-relations.
11. Leymah Gbowee, "Ubuntu Defined," Ubuntu Drum Circles, http://ucircles.org /ubuntu-defined.
12. Desmond Tutu, *No Future without Forgiveness* (New York: Doubleday, 1999), 33–34.

living a life for others, as many young people are now being drawn to, a person creates the opportunity, space, and atmosphere for the reality of community to emerge. Spiritual writer Henri Nouwen said it like this: "Community can make us think of a safe togetherness, shared meals, common goals, and joyful celebrations. . . . Community is first of all a quality of the heart. It grows from the spiritual knowledge that we are alive not for ourselves but for one another."[13] As a friend of mine, Burns Strider, said at his mother's funeral:

> A life lived for others is a life worthwhile. And a life lived for others creates community. Mamma didn't set out to create spaces where we could build communities. She simply lived a life full of care and love. She had fun. She had a blast. She didn't research or write about community. She just lived, lived well and lived for others. And we bask in the outcomes.

A Letter to an Insider

The presidential election of 2008 was historically significant, resulting in the first African American president of the United States. It also signaled a transition to the next generation, symbolized by the largest turnout of younger voters in American history. Barack Obama's presidential campaign and eloquent rhetoric invited people to project their hopes for political reform and a new American future onto his proposed presidency. And many did exactly that. His response on election night to a massive crowd at Grant Park in his hometown of Chicago signaled the new directions he had promised, and the historic turnout on his inauguration day, despite the frigid weather, turned a political event into a movement atmosphere.

I was there with Joy, Luke, and Jack. Joining us was their "uncle" Vincent Harding, a leading figure in the civil rights movement and part of the inner circle of Dr. Martin Luther King Jr.'s southern freedom movement. Vincent braved the cold with our family and told my boys

13. Henri Nouwen, "Community, a Quality of the Heart," in *Bread for the Journey: A Daybook of Wisdom and Faith* (New York: HarperCollins, 1996), meditation for January 23.

the stories of sacrifice from the civil rights movement and how this presidential inauguration day was so special in light of that history.

But from the first year of the Obama administration, some of those hopes began to fade, and before very long disappointment set in. Many made the mistake of putting their hopes in a political savior instead of remembering that change comes more through social movements than through electing the right person to the White House. It was the movement character of the 2008 election that gave it its deepest significance, rather than just the candidate running. Out of concern for that public disappointment and out of past friendship with the candidate, now president, I wrote this letter to Mr. Obama and handed it to him on March 5, 2010.

The letter has never been made public until now but is the word I would have to the "insiders." Those in power in this country need to know that many of us are committed to seeking and practicing a common good, and that we are willing to push and pull them to listen to and act with these movements that are changing our attitudes and practices for the better. And we have to constantly remind them of this—as I did a few years ago.

Dear Mr. President,

This year, no doubt, has been a difficult one for you, with challenges no one could have fully expected. I am sure there are times when you wonder why you decided to run for president in the first place, and put yourself under such harsh scrutiny and your family under all the strains. But it is a sacrifice that I know you did not commit to lightly.

I know the things that you have been up against—almost insurmountable odds. You and your team have repeatedly reminded us of all that you inherited—the most severe economic crisis since the Great Depression and two failed wars, and you now face a partisan intensity not seen in Washington for many years. . . .

But at an even deeper level, what is now lacking are vibrant and visible social movements. . . . The accomplishments of the FDR era and the JFK/Johnson period were due in no small measure to robust worker's movements and the civil rights movement. The robust activism of those independent progressive movements of the past created the space for major reforms and made those presidencies memorable. Social change

requires more than having a genuine "progressive" in the White House
. . . it requires a movement outside of the White House and Congress to
make fundamental reforms possible. We have to relearn the choreography
of the outside/inside "dance" that real change requires. . . .

I am very concerned about the deep disappointment I have felt everywhere among those who believed just over a year ago that swift and
sweeping political change was coming.

I am not speaking here of the ideological disappointment of the left,
who are not my main constituency. Rather it is the black voters who
overcame their cynicism to believe that another America might be possible, the Hispanic voters who dramatically shifted their allegiances,
evangelical and Catholic voters who decided to break with their recent
past (or their parents) because of what they heard from you, and, most
of all, the younger voters of every stripe who defied the conventional
wisdom of youthful political passivity and acted like citizens with a real
stake in the future—from Iowa on.

They all became the political movement that elected you—and it
clearly was a political movement, and not just a typical transfer of power.
It was real, it actually happened. But it is now disappearing rapidly and is
in danger of retreating into an even deeper cynicism than before, having
acted in faith for a hope that seems ever more dim.

I and many others understand the extraordinary challenges you have
faced, but I would respectfully suggest that such a crisis makes a bolder
style of leadership more necessary, and even more possible. . . .

You are aware, perhaps more than any other American president, of
the "call and response" tradition in the black church. You sat under it,
and in the midst of it, for many years at Trinity. It's why I most love to
preach in black churches. When the preacher "calls" and the congregation "responds," your sermon actually gets better, stronger, and deeper.
It can even change your sermon, taking you in directions you were not
planning to go. I have had the "amen corners" of black churches across
the country literally "pull" the sermon out of me.

My humble advice, Mr. President, is that you need to now find the
political equivalent of the black church's call and response. You need
to lead to the movement that elected you, over the heads of the special
interests and elites that now seem to run this country, and even over the
heads of the Congress and their leaders from both parties. When you
just start with where they are, you will never be able to lead the country

to a different place. The political movement that did indeed elect you now must become a social movement to galvanize the nation to achieve the things they voted for and you promised. If that kind of social movement does not emerge soon, I fear we will spiral even further downward.

Just after you were elected, you said that you would need "the wind of a movement at my back" to accomplish anything of real significance. I remember sending you an email that said something like, "Yes, and a movement at your front, to clear the path and pull you along when necessary." And I thought that you might understand the need for that more than most presidents have. You clearly need that wind at your back and your front right now. . . .

We need a leadership from you that can break through the 24-hour news cycle, the media punditry, and the failing incrementalism of cautious members and leaders of Congress. That would likely mean regular calls to action in your speeches directed at the country, and not just the Congress. It would require meeting with key constituency leaders and groups, not just to get their support for your agenda, but to actually help shape an agenda and strategy. And it will likely mean more events around the country to help mobilize a movement that could "change the wind" in the halls of Congress. Part of this requires a change in perspective—to see an independent movement on the outside as necessary and worth supporting (i.e., calling for it), rather than, at worst, as a threat or as a constituency that must be appeased.

You especially need to call to Main Street, be willing to finally take on Wall Street, and let the American people see that you are really on their side, and not the side of the banks who have shown such reckless and selfish disregard for the common good. The anger in the country about Wall Street—and Washington's relationship to Wall Street—is even deeper than is reported, and transcends political boundaries. . . .

What I am suggesting is, of course, a very risky strategy, which many or even most of your closest aides will likely tell you. But if your "calling" as president is to really lead the change we can believe in, it may be the best or even only way to accomplish your vision, or at least give it the best shot you possibly can. . . .

Just as Lincoln needed Frederick Douglass, Kennedy and Johnson needed King, and Roosevelt needed a robust labor movement, I believe that you now need the kind of social movement that is always necessary to make real change in Washington. Even you can't do this by yourself, as you must painfully realize every day now. . . . That is the kind of reciprocal relationship and complementary action I am proposing to you.

Mr. President, I have talked with other social movement leaders from various constituencies and we are ready to mobilize a movement to support you if you decide to lead this way. And we are preparing to do that, even if you decide on a more cautious direction. We feel a need to create a more independent and critical movement on the progressive side. Regardless of how you decide to lead, some of us will now begin to lead in more prophetic ways. We will, in particular, seek to use our relational and convening power in the faith community to chart a more prophetic course on behalf of the issues that are so central to us. And we will reach out directly to the people in our pews, our parishes, and our communities, empowering ordinary people to resist the cynicism and become real citizens again—like so many of them did when they elected you. . . .

God bless you, good brother. And know that I pray every day for you, for Michelle, and for the girls.

In hopeful expectation,

Jim Wallis

Two weeks later, at another meeting, the president told me he had read the letter. Today, it still expresses what is possible in the relationship between the insiders of politics and the outsiders of social movements.

A Letter to the Outsiders

Three years after the 2008 election, there rose up unexpectedly in the United States and quickly around the world a youth movement called "Occupy." It was a very diverse and decentralized movement, as described earlier in this chapter. It was not something to endorse so much as to engage, which I tried to do. After many conversations with the young people involved, whom I would often meet on the road, I decided to write them a letter too. The "outsiders" too need to be motivated and disciplined by a commitment to the common good, and young social movements sometimes need to be reminded of that. This was the purpose of my open letter to the Occupiers, which said in part:

You have awakened the sleeping giant, too long dormant but ever present, deep in the American democratic spirit. You have given voice to the unspoken feelings of countless others that something has gone terribly wrong in our society. And you have sparked a flame from the embers of both frustration and hope that have been building, steadily, in the hearts of so many of us for quite some time.

Throughout history, that task, which sometimes means saying and doing what others only think, has often fallen to young people. You have articulated, loudly and clearly, the internal monologue of a nation.

You are raising very basic questions about an economy that has become increasingly unfair and unsustainable for a growing number of people. . . . Keep pressing those values questions, because they will move people more than a set of demands or policy suggestions. Those can come later.

Try not to demonize those you view as opponents, as good people can get trapped in bad systems. Still, you are right for saying that we all must be held accountable, both systems and the individuals within them. The new safe spaces you have created to ask fundamental questions are helping to carve out fresh societal space to examine ourselves—who we are, what we value most, and where we want to go from here.

Keep asking what a "just economy" should look like and whom it should be for. But avoid utopian dreaming about things that will never happen. Look instead at how we could do things differently, more responsibly, more equitably, and yes, more democratically.

Keep driving both the moral and practical questions about the economics of our local and global households, for that is what the discipline was supposed to be about in the first place.

I know you believe that leaders on Wall Street and in Washington, DC, have failed you. Indeed, they have failed us all. But don't give up on leadership per se. We need innovative leadership now more than ever. And you are providing some of it.

And remember, nonviolence is not just a critical tactic but a necessary commitment to moral and civil discourse that can awaken the best in all of us. There is much to be angry about, but channeling that energy into creative, nonviolent action is the only way to prevent dangerous cynicism and nihilism. The anarchism of anger has never produced the change that the discipline and constructive program of nonviolent movements have done again and again.

Cultivate humility more than overconfidence or self-indulgence. This really is not about you. It's about the marginalized masses, the signs of the times, and the profound yearning for lasting change. Take that larger narrative more seriously than you take yourselves.

Finally, do not let go of your hope. Popular movements are the only forces that truly bring about change in society. The established order is never as secure and impervious to change as those who preside over it believe it to be.

And whatever you may think of organized religion, keep in mind that change requires spiritual as well as political resources, and that invariably any new economy will be accompanied by a new (or very old) spirituality.

May God be gracious to you and give you—and all of us—peace.

The letter traveled around the Occupy movement, creating conversations in my own travels when the young Occupiers come out to my speaking events. Whatever becomes of the Occupy movement, the lessons for those in social movements on the outside of politics remain important. Again, the discussions that ensue are always about the meaning of the common good.

Amazing Grace for the Here and Now

Finally, back to John Wesley, spiritual revival, and movements that change the world.

When I saw the powerful movie about William Wilberforce, *Amazing Grace*, I was deeply inspired by the story of this Wesleyan convert who made ending slavery the mission of his life. But the movie focused too much on the man and not enough on the movement that swept the United Kingdom and made the political victory possible. Likewise, it was more than the inspiring rhetoric of Dr. King that propelled the civil rights movement in the United States. It was the Birmingham campaign, the march to Montgomery, and the dramatic events in Selma that focused the nation's attention and led to important legislative actions.

Ultimately, it was millions of decisions made by ordinary people who wanted to see their country change.

And for many of us, this is a question of faith. Far too often, the religion of Christianity has been reduced to private faith or societal control. In this guise, it misses the very meaning of the Christ who entered the world to announce a whole new order of things, which he called the kingdom of God. This book has described how the private gospels of our time have missed the central message of the New Testament, which can help inspire a new vision for the common good that we desperately need—whether we are religious or not.

In times past, whenever people of faith have remembered the breadth and depth of Jesus's gospel of the kingdom, they have played a particular and necessary role in critical historical moments, and they have often been at the center of social movements that led to some of the biggest changes in the world. In fact, no social reform movement in modern times has succeeded *without* the central involvement of the faith community and the spiritual values they bring to political struggle.

When Christians get beyond their comfortable and privatized faith and the parochial claims of their religious institutions, they can again play that crucial role. Jesus calls us to *conversion* and to *community*, to personal salvation and to social justice, to individual transformation and to societal change. People come to Jesus Christ as persons, but then they join something called the body of Christ, which is the only community that exists to serve its nonmembers and has the vocation of demonstrating God's purposes in the world. The prophet Jeremiah described this role for the people of God as "seeking the welfare of the city" that you are in, even when you are in exile—as many of us often feel ourselves to be these days.

I have been excited about a new possibility for global Christianity for many years, ever since our core group met at Trinity Evangelical Divinity School in the northern suburbs of Chicago four decades ago. We were at a leading evangelical seminary, not a liberal one; some of us chose deliberately to go there to argue with our own evangelical tradition about what the Bible really says.

One of our first activities was finding every verse of Scripture about the poor, wealth and poverty, and social justice. We found more than

291

two thousand texts, which we then cut out of an old Bible. We were left with a "Bible full of holes," which I used to take out with me to preach. I remember saying, "This is the American Bible, full of holes, from all we have ignored and paid no attention to. We might as well all take our Bibles out and just start cutting out all these texts that we have abandoned."

We still have that old Bible full of holes in the Sojourners office today, and the now-famous story helped to inspire the publication of the *Poverty and Justice Bible* by the British Bible Society and the American Bible Society, in cooperation with groups like World Vision. This Bible takes all the Scriptures on poverty and justice, which the American churches had ignored and which we had cut out to make that point, and it puts them back in the Bible in World Vision orange! That Bible is a sign of hope to me, of a new generation wanting to put their Bibles back together again.

The Battle Ahead

We have fought two major battles over these last forty years, and a third fight now lies before us. This book has been about the next battle.

The first great battle was against the idea that faith was just a private thing. That was the way many of us had been raised—to be concerned only about "me and the Lord," remaining almost oblivious to the world around us, except in our continual efforts not to be "worldly." In this book I've told my story about how that battle played out in my own childhood and church.

When faith is merely private, then wealth, power, and violence remain unchallenged because religion isn't understood to be about such things. In fact, privatized faith is an asset to injustice, keeping the faithful complacent, complicit, or just quiet about it. It took a movement, but I believe that battle has now been won. Now, almost no one, even the most conservative Christians, would say that faith is merely a private affair with no implications for public life. Relating faith to public life and to society is now assumed to be both important and necessary, and the debate is only about *how* faith should publicly express itself.

The second great battle was against the claims of the then-new "religious right" that the only social issue about which Christians should be concerned was sexuality, one way or another. According to the media, abortion, homosexuality, and pornography were the only political issues that evangelicals cared about and would be voting on. We argued that Christians should be concerned about more than just two or three so-called moral issues, defined as "the social issues." In particular, we claimed that God's call to care for and defend the poor was absolutely central to biblical faith. We believed and preached that the God of the Bible was one of both compassion and justice. But we were also "pro-life" (meaning that abortion is a moral tragedy and we have to both prevent unwanted pregnancies and reduce the terrible number of abortions in America) and deeply committed to "family values" (meaning committed to the crucial integrity of marriage and the absolute key of parenting, without the scapegoating of gay and lesbian people).

Again, to restrict faith to only a few issues of mostly personal morality is to leave wealth, power, and violence unchallenged. Religion becomes a political support for injustice and for those who defend the status quo. After I was a guest on Jon Stewart's *The Daily Show* for the first time, many young people emailed me to say, "I didn't know that you could be a Christian and care about poverty, the environment, or the war in Iraq." Through my 2005 book, *God's Politics: Why the Right Gets It Wrong and the Left Doesn't Get It*, I encountered hundreds of thousands of people who didn't feel represented by a narrow religious right or a secular left and were seeking a biblical, theological, and spiritual foundation for social justice.

I think that battle too has now been won, with many now seeking a more holistic and biblical message. God's love for the most vulnerable—the children of the inner city, the hungry and the homeless, the global poor who are the victims of famines and pandemics, and the women and children caught up in the modern slavery of human trafficking—is being preached from many pulpits today, across the political spectrum. Caring for the poor is now seen as a sign of the kingdom of God, especially among a younger generation of believers. Conservative think tanks now speak of a Christian concern for the poor and invoke the term "social justice."

But the third great battle ahead of us will be about the *nature of the society* that God wants and, in particular, whether there is such a thing as *the common good*. It will be about the role of government; the role of the market; the role of the civil society; the role of churches, synagogues, and mosques, and their congregations and organizations; the role of families and local communities; and the role of the believer and the citizen.

Some say that caring for the poor is well and good but that government should have nothing to do with it, that private charity is the only answer to poverty. Capitalism should be left unregulated and unhindered to solve our problems with the "invisible hand of the market," and we should just trust that wealth will trickle down.

But others point to the rich tradition of the common good, in which we are all held accountable for how our behavior affects others. That ethos is deeply rooted in Catholic social teaching, in the historic evangelical revivals, in black and Latino churches, in the Protestant social gospel, in Judaism and Islam, and in the American Constitution itself, which says that government should provide for "the general welfare."

We have learned that the gospel does indeed say that *we are our brothers' and sisters' keeper*—called to love our neighbors and even our enemies. All the biblical prophets say that the test of any society's character is how it treats the poor, the vulnerable, and the stranger. That's what the Bible says, and to pass that test is what Jesus calls us to. The next battle is to understand and practice that vision by seeking the ethics of the common good in an age of selfishness. And to articulate the commonwealth of God in these matters will surely challenge the ideologies and idolatries of both the right and the left.

As we look ahead, I am greatly encouraged by the emergence of a new generation of Christians and believers from other faith traditions, a new cadre of leaders for such a mission. I trust both the personal faith and the social conscience of the young people I meet and work with every day. This is the demographic that will be the future of the church and other faith communities. They are men and women; white, black,

Latino, Asian American, and native peoples from across America; and, more recently, newly arrived internationals from around the world. They define themselves less by tribe and more by relationships and networks. They are people of deep faith, and at the same time respectful of inter-faith identities. They are activist and contemplative, people who connect their spirituality with social change. They greatly value their diversity of race, ethnicity, and culture; they are not encumbered by parochial or national identities; and they have a global worldview. They want to be in, but not of, the societies in which they live. They are pilgrims who seek countercultural community, and they also seek the welfare of the city they live in. They are sojourners in the midst of their societies.

The common good is never just about politics, though in recent elections some have made the mistake of thinking that it is. Putting one's hopes in candidates and parties has only led to disappointment, frustration, and dangerous cynicism. There are systems and structures that undergird and shape the limits of the political agenda, and challenging those limits to get to root causes and real solutions is always the prophetic task. Increasingly we will see a *post-candidate advocacy* around causes that define our politics. It is always movements that "change the wind," and only a change in the political wind can change the political policies in Washington, DC, and other capitals around the world. In more than four decades of engaging public issues, I have never seen the real changes we need come from inside politics. Instead, they come from outside social movements.

We people of faith, at our best, may be the ultimate independents, engaged in politics only because of people and issues that command our moral attention, and willing to challenge all political sides on behalf of them. Fighting for biblical justice and the common good, not partisan political goals, will be the core of that faithful politics. This book has examined the call to conversion, the call to the kingdom of God, the call to community, and the call to make the world into our parish—for the common good. Responding to the call for the common good is always a very personal decision. My hope and prayer is that we will all decide for the common good in our personal and public lives and that we will teach our children to do likewise.

295

Epilogue

Ten Personal Decisions for the Common Good

The common good and the quality of our life together will finally be determined by the *personal decisions* we all make. The "commons"—those places, as we noted earlier, where we come together as neighbors and citizens to share public space—will never be better than the quality of human life, or the *human flourishing*, in our own lives and households.

Here are ten personal decisions you can make to help foster the common good.

1. If you are a father or a mother, make your children the most important priority in your life and build your other commitments around them. If you are not a parent, look for children who could benefit from your investment in their lives.
2. If you are married, be faithful to your spouse. Demonstrate your commitment with both your fidelity and your love. If you are single, measure your relationships by their integrity, not their usefulness.
3. If you are a person of faith, focus not just on what you believe but on how you act on those beliefs. If you love God, ask God how to love your neighbor.
4. Take the place you live seriously. Make the context of your life and work the parish that you take responsibility for.
5. Seek to develop a vocation and not just a career. Discern your gifts as a child of God, not just your talents, and listen for your calling

rather than just looking for opportunities. Remember that your personal good always relates to the common good.

6. Make choices by distinguishing between wants and needs. Choose what is enough, rather than what is possible to get. Replace appetites with values; teach your children the same, and model those values for all who are in your life.

7. Look at the business, company, or organization where you work from an ethical perspective. Ask what its vocation is, too. Challenge whatever is dishonest or exploitative and help your place of work do well by doing good.

8. Ask yourself what in the world today most breaks your heart and offends your sense of justice. Decide to help change that and join with others who are committed to transforming that injustice.

9. Get to know who your political representatives are at both the local and national level. Study their policy decisions and examine their moral compass and public leadership. Make your public convictions and commitments known to them and choose to hold them accountable.

10. Since the difference between events and movements is sacrifice, which is also the true meaning of religion and what makes for social change, ask yourself what is important enough to give your life to and for.

Finding the integral relationship between your own personal good and the common good is your best contribution to our future. And it is the best hope we have for a better life together.

Index

299

sojourners

Faith in Action for Social Justice

Want to go deeper in connecting your faith to social justice? Visit Sojourners at **www.sojo.net**, where you can read commentary from Jim Wallis and guests on the **God's Politics** blog. Sign up for **SojoMail**, a weekly email newsletter featuring Jim Wallis' "Hearts and Minds" column. **Take Action** and advocate for the poor and marginalized through Sojourners' **Action Alerts** and **Mobilizing Campaigns**. Read award-winning *Sojourners Magazine* to learn more about faith-based advocacy. **Support** the work of Sojourners by becoming a monthly donor.

Visit **www.sojo.net** or follow us online at

Call us toll-free at **1-800-714-7474**